Rural Institutes Directory

VOLUME-1

Rural Institutes Directory

VOLUME-1

Editor
S. V. PRABHATH

SERIALS PUBLICATIONS
NEW DELHI (INDIA)

Edition: 2010

ISBN: 978-81-8387-442-7

Published by
SERIALS PUBLICATIONS
4830/24, Prahlad Street, Ansari Road
Darya Ganj, New Delhi-110002 (India)
Phone : 23245225. Fax : 91-11-23272135
E-mail: serials@sify.com

Contents

DELHI

GUJARAT

HIMACHAL PRADESH

JAMMU AND KASHMIR

JHARKHAND

KARNATAKA

KERALA

MADHYA PRADESH

Acknowledgement

We want to thank all those rural institutes who have furnished information for inclusion in the directory of rural institutes. The information furnished in the directory has been updated by supplementing information from other sources before it was sent for printing. The directory merely presents the information furnished by the rural institutes.

Therefore, the NCRI has no responsibility for the veracity of the information furnished. Nor is the NCRI responsible for any of the omissions and commissions in this regard. However, the NCRI has exercised due diligence in processing the information.

This is the first attempt to compile information on various rural institutions working in villages across India and the inclusion in the directory does not confer any particular right on the institutions as a recognition or conferment of some privilege and at the same time exclusion of an institute is not tantamount to any de-recognition or a value judgment on the institution concerned.

This is a routine/continuing exercise which will keep evolving and the Directory will be revised and updated periodically.

Introduction

Being the Council of Rural Institutes, NCRI's mandate requires identifying and working with such rural institutes whose contributions are well recognised by the population which these institutions serve. There are many institutions which have been in touch with the NCRI ever since its inception and they have been receiving support in some form or the other from the NCRI. To further strengthen such relationships and set in motion such processes leading to developing systems for identification of such rural institutes, this attempt to compile directories of hand picked institutions is being made.

The system of identification of rural institutions should be through a transparent and methodical process and this involves great deal of effort and development of suitable methodologies. In order to facilitate this process, the NCRI has decided to initiate compilation of directory of such institutions who are promoting development through education. The NCRI will bring out such directories which will help in the process of identifying institutes doing exemplary work in rural areas. The inclusion of an institution in the directory is not tantamount to recognition or conferring any membership on such institutions listed in the directory.

Before a policy is put into place we have to sift and churn such institutes by documenting the work they are doing. Slowly the process of recognising these institutions and positioning them as rural institutes will evolve. In the first phase we have consolidated the list of 125 institutions and more lists will follow. With a bevy of programmes on hand, it is very important to build partnerships with those institutions working with commitment having high integrity and such a directory will serve the developmental needs of not only the NCRI but also other organisations.

Dr. S. V. PRABHATH

ANDHRA PRADESH

Bhagavatula Charitable Trust

(1)	Contact person	:	B.V. Sreenivasa Rao Secretary Sri Rama murthy - 9441530994 08924253770
(2)	Designation	:	Joint Secretary
(3)	Contact No.	:	+91 (891) 255 0084 +91 (891) 250 8440
(4)	Mobile	:	+91 9346 33 11 81
(5)	E-mail	:	bctindia@yahoo.com
(6)	Website	:	www.bctindia.net
(7)	Address	:	47-9-37, Dwarakanagar Visakhapatnam, A.P., India, 530 016

About the organisation: The Bhagavatula Charitable Trust is bringing about a rural transformation which has been the vision of Mahatma Gandhi. In a dedicated way, the Trust has devoted itself to build the confidence of the people. The people themselves have become the instruments of the change with the Trust playing the role of an adviser. The Trust has involved itself in all aspects of rural life - education, agricultural development and growth of allied activities.

(a)	Year of establishment	:	1976
(b)	Registration No	:	412/76
(c)	Location	:	Visakhapatnam, Andhra Pradesh
(d)	Coverage area	:	100 villages in 3 mandals
(e)	Staff strength	:	89
(f)	Source of funding	:	BCT-KVK, MIBLOU
(g)	Approximate population served	:	whole district of Visakhapatnam
(h)	Target groups	:	farmers, artisans, women and youth

(i) Objectives:

- Create opportunities at the door steps of the villagers.
- Continuous self-improvement in the quality of their lives.
- Generating their leadership in solving their problems & utilizing their resources most effectively.

Details of Activities

Education: Innovative Experimental Primary Schools (IEP)- BCT currently runs 72 IEP schools in surrounding villages.

Model Residential High School - BCT has been running a residential model school from the 6th to 10th standard, and currently has 89 students drawn from over 50 villages in and around the school area.

Health Care- Early on BCT found that the twin evils that continue to plague the rural poor are ignorance and ill-health. The first was addressed by organising programmes that emphasised education and training. To tackle the latter, BCT established the Grama Arogyalayam Trust in 1985 to deal with health education as well as treatment of illness.

Community Health Training- Nine village women have been trained as multipurpose workers in 6 villages on the basis of one per thousand population. Every day they visit 6 houses each discussing health, hygiene, and public sanitation.

(j) Vocational training: Wasteland development, Women empowerment, Programmes designed for women empowerment are-

- Adda leaf stitching
- Nursery raising
- Papad making
- Screen printing
- Dairying and animal husbandry
- Tape weaving
- Poultry weaving
- Training of paravets, paramedics and village animators
- Screen printing
- Etikoppaka toy making

(k) Skill development: Community based rehabilitation programme— BCT linked the disabled persons by liaising with the governmental departments to get their regular assistance for bus concessions, medical certificates, renewal of railway passes, etc. BCT also identified and provided necessary skills and financial support for participants to earn some money on their own.

♦ ♦ ♦

Dangoria Charitable Trust

(1)	Contact person	:	Dr. Devyani Dangoria
(2)	Designation	:	Managing Trustee
(3)	Contact No.	:	040 – 27615148, 27661422
(4)	Mobile	:	9246886442
(5)	E-mail	:	dangoriatrust@yahoo.com dangoriatrust@sancharnet.in
(6)	Website	:	www.dangoriatrust.org.in
(7)	Address	:	Village Narsapur, Medak District, Andhra Pradesh, India.

About the organisation: In 1979, Dr. Devyani Dangoria with her personal resources, started the Dangoria Hospital for Women and Children in village Narsapur, Medak District, in the South Indian state of Andhra Pradesh. The Dangoria Charitable Trust was established two years later.

Health and Nutrition Outreach Programme was initiated by Dr Mahtab Bamji (Director grade scientist retd. National Institute of Nutrition, Hyderabad) in 1994, when she joined the Trust as Emeritus scientist. The three 'A' approach of creating 'Awareness', and improving 'Access' at an 'Affordable' cost is adopted, through community participation.

Women Health and Nutrition Entrepreneurs and Mobilisers: A successful model of health care delivery through trained Women Health and Nutrition Entrepreneurs and Mobilisers (HNEMS) has been developed. The results are encouraging. The health workers advise the community, particularly mothers, on health and nutrition and treat minor ailments. The community pays them for their services. They register all pregnant women and ensure anti-natal check-up, immunisation, and promote institutional deliveries, and family planning. HNEMs records deaths with age and cause and births with birth weight. Results in 5 villages covered by this programme are very encouraging.

(a)	Year of establishment	:	1981
(b)	Registration No	:	Trust - no number – registered trust
(c)	Location	:	Narsapur, Medak District, Andhra Pradesh
(d)	Coverage area	:	Narsapur Mandal in Medak district, AP
(e)	Staff strength	:	9-10 people in the Hospital; 6-7 volunteers in Home for the Aged age one doctor–full time, others-volunteers.
(f)	Source of funding	:	

- Govt. of A.P., NCRI, Ministry of New and Renewable Energy
- Department of Science and Technology
- Department of Biotechnology
- Government of India
- FAO regional Office for South East Asia
- Ministry of Food Processing Industries

- The Aurobindo Institute of Rural Development, Gaddepalli, Nalgonda District
- Central Research Institute in Dry land Agriculture (CRIDA), Hyderabad
- Fruit Research Station, Sangareddy
- Departments of horticulture, and education, Medak district
- The National Institute of Nutrition (NIN), Hyderabad
- The Central Building Research Institute (CBRI), Hyderabad Regional Centre.

(g) Approximate population served:

- Antenatal and post-natal obstetric care
- Gynaec surgeries
- Paediatric care and immunization. The bi-weekly antenatal clinics are attended by over 150 women. Yearly over 1000 deliveries are conducted and over 200 surgeries are done.
- Weekly paediatric clinics are also well attended. Immunisation is done free. An ambulance service takes care of transporting patients to Hyderabad in emergency.
- A friendly home shelter for over 30 elderly persons of both aged men and women.

(h) Target groups : Women

(i) Objectives: A continuous endeavor to serve the needy and empower the community through capacity building and social engineering.

1. To take quality health care to the doorsteps of rural community
2. To care for the elderly
3. To improve the health, nutrition, and educational status of the community, particularly women and children through awareness generation and participatory action.
4. To develop models of environmentally sustainable agriculture for food and nutrition security.
5. To improve rural sanitation
6. To develop on-farm and off-farm livelihood skills for women.

Details of Activities

(j) Vocational training : Out- reach programme in the surrounding villagers to evolve models for improving health, nutrition, environment and livelihood security. The last includes a Food processing and training centre, run by a society 'Mahila Udyog', which operates under the guidance of DCT.

(k) Skill development : Apart from on- farm skills, off-farm skills such as tailoring and embroidery, wicks making, food processing, and health -related training are imparted to women. Assistance is given in marketing.

(l) Organisations under establishment : Home for the Aged, Mahila Udyog Food Processing cum Training Centre.

♦ ♦ ♦

Deccan Development Society

(1) Contact person : A. Giridhar

(2) Designation : Joint Director

(3) Contact No. : +91-40-27764577, +91-40-27764744, +91-40-27764722, +91-40-27764722

(4) Mobile : +91 8451 282785

(5) E-mail : hyd1_ddshyd@sancharnet.in
hyd2_ddsppvr1@sancharnet.in
ddshyderabad@gmail.com

(6) Website : www.ddsindia.com

(7) Address : 101, Kishan Residency,
1-11-242/1, Street No. 5
Shyamlal Buildings Area,
Begumpet, Hyderabad,
Andhra Pradesh– 500 016.

About the organisation: The Deccan Development Society (DDS) is a two-decade old grassroots organisation working in about 75 villages with women's Sanghams (voluntary village level associations of the poor) in Medak District of Andhra Pradesh. The 5000 women members of the Society represent the poorest of the poor in their village communities. Most of them are dalits, the lowest group in the Indian social hierarchy.The Society has a vision of consolidating these village groups into vibrant organs of primary local governance and federate them into a strong pressure lobby for women, the poor and dalits. A host of continuing dialogues, debates, educational and other activities with the people, facilitated by the Society, try to translate this vision into a reality.

(a) Year of establishment : 1983

(b) Registration No : 1529/1983

(c) Location : Pastapur village, Zaheerabad Mandal, Medak District

(d) Coverage area : 75 villages

(e) Staff strength : 5000 women members

(f) Source of funding : State, National and international-Ministry of Human Resource Development, Indian Council of Agricultural Research, Central Social Welfare Board Ministry of Environment & Forests, Department of Science and Technology, New Delhi,National Bank for Agriculture and Rural Development (NABARD), Hyderabad.

(g) Approximate population served : 75 villages

(h) Target groups : Women, poor and Dalits

(i) Objectives:

The Deccan Development Society is formulating a working model for the people-oriented participative development in the areas of food security, ecological agriculture and alternate education. It is also trying to reverse the historical process of degradation of the environment and people's livelihood system in this region through a string of land related activities such as Permaculture, Community Grain Bank, Community Gene Fund, Community Green Fund and Collective Cultivation through land lease etc. These activities, along with taking care of the earth are also resulting in human care, by giving the women a newfound dignity and profile in their village communities. The society is trying to relocate the people's knowledge in the area of Health and Agriculture

Details of Activities

(j) Research : The Society has initiated a number of studies related to bio-diversity in agriculture. The major studies are:

- Economics of Ecological Agriculture in collaboration with the FAO.
- Uncultivated Foods in collaboration with the International Development Research Centre (IDRC) of Canada.
- CROPS OF TRUTH : Farmers Perception of Agro Bio-diversity
- Farmers Perception of the nutritional value of Traditional Foods
- Soil Fertility Management in semi arid India
- Seeds of Deccan : Science of Farmers
- Bt Cotton study in Warangal District of A.P
- Study on Alternative Public Distribution System.

(k) Vocational training : Permaculture, Community Grain Bank, Community Gene Fund.

(l) Skill development : Vermi-compost, On-farm Bio-diversity, Wasteland development.

♦ ♦ ♦

Haritha Association for Learning from Environment

(1)	Contact person	:	P. Usharani
(2)	Designation	:	Secretary
(3)	Contact No.	:	08744-255060
(4)	Mobile	:	9391059726
(5)	E- Mail	:	usha.puttagunta@gmail.com harithavaranam@gmail.com
(6)	Website	:	www.harithavillu.org
(7)	Address	:	Haritha Ecological Institute, P.B. No. 26; BCM Road, Palvancha; Khammam Dt., A.P., 507115.

About the organisation: "Evolve a holistic education that necessarily includes the cherished humanand national values, all the way from school through a close interaction with productive activities steeped in sustainability and innovation at the grass roots, not only for pure monetary economics, but also from the more comprehensive 'Ecology Energy Economics'". Inculcating sensitivity towards the trials and tribulations of the society in general and the rural areas and disadvantaged communities in particular, at the level of higher research institutions, would be a futile exercise as long as it does not commence with school education through productive activities. On the basis of the above conviction, Dr. Sudhakar, professor from IIT-Delhi started a school in 1988. Later, Sri Satyateertha joined their efforts at Haritha in 1994.

(a)	Year of establishment	:	1988
(b)	Registration No	:	The society was registered under AP (Telangana areas) public societies registration act 1350 Fasli (act 1 of 1350F): vide Regd.No.440 of 1992.
(c)	Location	:	Palvacha, Khammam District, Andhra Pradesh.
(d)	Coverage area	:	Nine mandals (mostly agency mandals) of Khammam district
(e)	Staff strength	:	25
(f)	Source of funding	:	NCRI, Asha, NGC and Our own earnings
(g)	Approximate population served	:	The area (nine mandals of Khammam district) covers a population of about 3 lakhs. The population includes day laborers from SC, ST and BC communities and a sizable Muslim community. The school itself caters to the needs of over 200 students and their parents. Further it is envisaged to cover over 500 rural women and 100 artisans most of whom belong to disadvantaged communities.
(h)	Target groups	:	Disadvantaged communities in our society

(i) Objectives:

(a) To establish, aid and administer educational and other institutions to impart education at all stages in all subjects for diffusion of knowledge;

(b) To develop and promote basic educational curricula with agricultural activities as foundation;

(c) To develop new teaching techniques based on experiences in daily life and natural surroundings;

(d) To protect and improve the natural environment including forests, rivers and wild life and develop awareness for the maintenance of ecological balance;

(e) To develop the scientific temper, humanism and the spirit of enquiry and reform among students and to strive towards excellence in all spheres of their individual and collective activity; and

(f) To engage in any other activity associated with the above objects.

Details of Activities

(j) Research: Promote Research & Development Activities with eco-friendly technology and renewable resources. For example, Bamboo-Building Technology", "Cycle Grinder", "Vethra" (container to keep warmth), 'Hold and Release Method" (prevents formation of dirty water from water usage), Teaching and Learning Material (TLM) with Bamboo.

(l) Skill development: Conducted training programmes in bamboo bow and bamcrete technology at places including the highest centres of excellence such as VNIT, Nagpur and IITD.Conducted teacher training programmes in using productive activities as experiments in main stream school education.

♦ ♦ ♦

Kasturba Gandhi National Memorial Trust

(1)	Contact person	:	G. Susila
(2)	Designation	:	Provincial prathinidhi
(3)	Contact No.	:	0883– 2458802, 2458415
(4)	E-Mail	:	kgnmt.seethanagaram@gmail.com
(5)	Website	:	N.A.
(6)	Address	:	P.O.Seethanagaram – 533287, Via Rajahmundry, East Godavari Dist. A.P.

About the organisation: KGNMT, Seetanagaram is one of the seniormost voluntary organizations formed and founded by Mahatma Gandhi in memory of Kusturba Gandhi. It has got centres nation wide in all states of India right from Kashmir to Kanyakumari. This Trust is engaging in Gram Seva and Arogaya Seva schemes and also extending its support to hospitals, crèche programme and training to Anganwadi workers.

(a)	Year of establishment	:	1945
(b)	Registration No	:	Q/R-1/64, 08 Jan 1964
(c)	Location	:	Rajahmundry, AP
(d)	Coverage area	:	All over A.P.
(e)	Staff strength	:	28
(f)	Source of funding	:	Kasturba Gandhi National Memorial Trust, Indore Madhya Pradesh, A.P. state welfare board, Hyderabad. Central social welfare board New Delhi. Women development and child welfare, A.P. Own agricultural resources and donations from volunteers.
(g)	Approximate population served	:	3,47,799
(h)	Target Groups	:	Women & Children of remote areas
(i)	Objectives	:	To give clear orientation on Gandhian Principles and Thought, to counsel on self reliance and self employment and to create awareness on environment protection and optimum utilization of available resources.

Details of Activities

(j)	Vocational training	:	Tailoring, machine/hand embroidering, preparation of phenyl, Zandu balm, coir yarn, doormats, etc.
(k)	Skill development	:	Session of youth on Gandhian approach and rural developments.

(l) Organisations under establishment :

1. KGNMT, Hydershacote, Via Langar house, Rangareddy district, Hyderabad – 500008.
2. Kasturba Grama Seva Centre,P.O Ankisettipally,Mandanapally Mandalam,Chittor District, A.P
3. Kasturba Grama Seva Centre, P.O. Seethanagaram, Seethanagaram Mandalam,Via Rajhamandry – 533287.
4. Kasturba Grama Seva Centre, P.O. Rajupalem, Chinakondepudi PanchayatVia Rajhamandry – 533287, E.G.DT.
5. Kasturba Maternity and child welfare centre and dispensary, P.O. Seethanagaram, Seethanagaram Mandalam,via Rajhamandry – 533287.
6. Coir Training Centre, KGNMT, P.O. Seethanagaram, Seethanagaram Mandalam,via Rajhamandry – 533287.
7. Short Stay Home, KGNMT, P.O.Seethanagaram, Seethanagaram Mandalam,Via Rajhamandry – 533287.
8. Crache Centre, KGNMT, P.O. Seethanagaram, Seethanagaram Mandalam,Via Rajhamandry – 533287.
9. Vocational Training Centre, KGNMT, P.O. Seethanagaram, Seethanagaram Mandalam,Via Rajhamandry – 533287.

♦ ♦ ♦

Medvan

(1)	Contact person	:	B. Manohar
(2)	Designation	:	President
(3)	Contact No.	:	9908523730 (Samson)
(4)	Mobile	:	+91 -98491-41433
(5)	E-mail	:	medvan@rediffmail.com medvan@gmail.com
(6)	Website	:	www.medvan.org
(7)	Address	:	H. No. 4-8-85/10/G Near Bharathiya Vidya Mandir Manjeera Pipeline Road, Manjeera Nagar, Sangareddy, Medak Dist.

About the organisation: Medak District Voluntary Agencies Network (MEDVAN) is a network of federation of voluntary agencies working on various issues viz. Child Labour, Women SHG's, Forest protection, Environment, Watersheds, improvement of Irrigation Tanks, Natural Resource Management, promotion of Literacy among children, Income Generation, Health Awareness etc. ... since most of these activities are interrelated, organisations have focused on more than activity.

(a)	Year of establishment	:	1994
(b)	Registration No	:	1760/1998
(c)	Location	:	Sangareddy, Medak District, Andhra Pradesh.
(d)	Coverage area	:	Telangana area / 44 mandals
(e)	Staff strength	:	45
(f)	Source of funding	:	UNICEF, MAMTHA, Chronic pair, DRDA
(g)	Approximate population served	:	20,00,000
(h)	Target groups	:	Child labour, women SHGs, forest protection, environment, Watersheds, improvement of irrigation tanks and natural resource management.

(i) Objectives:

- To provide a forum for like-minded voluntary organisations to share experience & strengthen collective action.
- To provide intellectual knowledge & capacity building to partner NGOs, staff and other stake holders.
- To do lobbying/advocacy at various levels to address the issues pertaining to health, education, environment, child labour, HIV/AIDS, human resources and land and agriculture.
- To mobilize linkages with various agencies for resources.

Details of Activities

Seven member organizations were involved in conducting IEC on health in seven mandals, with the assistance of A.P. Govt, through the District Medical and Health office (DM & HO).

Thirty two Organisations implemented the school sanitation programme in 38 mandals out of 46 mandals in the district, with the financial assistance from the UNICEF through the DRDA.

Six organisations are running child labour schools covering a total of 2,200 children in 10 mandals financed by the district labour department.

Five organisations are involved in implementing the watershed activities in about 30 villages with the financial assistance of the District Water Management Agency (DWMA)

Eight organisations have implemented the RIDF activities (similar to watersheds) in 40 villages through women SHGs assisted by NABARD through the DWMA.

Seven organisations are involved in community forest management (CFM), formerly known as Joint Forest Management (JFM), with the help of Divisional Forest Office (DFO), Medak.

(j) Organisations under establishment : A number of programmes like watersheds, RIDF (Rural infrastructure development fund) School sanitation, child labour schools, IEC on total health, Joint Forest Management, are being implemented successfully by the member organizations of MEDVAN, with the assistance of A. P. Government.

♦ ♦ ♦

Modern Architects for Rural India

(1)	Contact person	:	R. Murali, P Jayarama Rao (Finance Director)
(2)	Designation	:	Secretary
(3)	Contact No.	:	0870-2571208
(4)	Moble	:	9985644474
(5)	E-mail	:	marimail@rediffmail.com, mariwgl@gmail.com
(6)	Website	:	N.A.
(7)	Address	:	3-1-94 Kakatiya Colony, Opp Alankar Theatre, Hanamkonda, Warangal Andhra Pradesh - 506011

About the Organisation

MARI adopts a complete labour oriented approach from planning to execution and maintenance. The technology does not rely on machines and uses only local materials. Technical expertise is developed within the village, so money and labour are retained within the community. Strengthening the contribution of the community leads to jobs, understanding of the system and judicious internal circulation of the investment. Essentially, people learn the skills needed to sustain their land.

(a)	Year of establishment	:	1988
(b)	Registration No	:	123 21, January 1998
(c)	Location	:	Warangal, Andhra Pradesh
(d)	Coverage area	:	Warangal & Andhra Pradesh
(e)	Staff strength	:	350
(f)	Source of funding	:	N.A.
(g)	Approximate population served	:	N.A.
(h)	Target groups	:	Gibhabanda Thanda, Andhra Pradesh

(i) Objectives:

(a) Promotes natural resource management

(b) Land development

(c) Income generating programmes and joint forest management

(d) Conducting immunization and animal health campus

(e) Water and sanitation programmes

(f) Providing relief and rehabilitation to the affected people.

Details of Activities

(j) Research : MARI adopts a complete labour oriented approach from planning to execution and maintenance. The technology does not rely on machines and uses only local materials.

(k) Vocational training : Technical expertise is developed within the village, so money and labour are retained within the community.

(l) Skill development : Strengthening the contribution of the community leads to jobs, understanding of the system and money in people's pockets. Essentially, the people learn the skills needed to sustain their land.

♦ ♦ ♦

Rastriya Seva Samiti

(1)	Contact person	:	Ram Mohan Reddy
(2)	Designation	:	Project Director
(3)	Contact No.	:	91-08772242404/2244210 Fax: 91 – 0877 - 2244281
(4)	Mobile	:	9441079708
(5)	E-mail	:	N.A.
(6)	Website	:	N.A.
(7)	Address	:	Rashtriya Seva Samithi (RASS) Annamaiah Marg, AIR-Bye- Pass Road, Tirupati, Chittoor Dist, Andhra Pradesh, India – 517501.

About the Organisation

The Rashtriya Seva Samithi is undertaking research on social work and women related issues. It is also imparting vocational training to the target groups in tailoring, computer training, Arya work (Tamil nadu), and training of teachers to teach the mentally-retarded. The RSS is promoting the women Self Helf Groups (SHGs) on a large scale.

(a)	Year of establishment	:	1981
(b)	Registration No	:	31/1981
(c)	Location	:	Urban
(d)	Coverage area	:	3 States, Odisha, Tamil Nadu and AP
(e)	Staff strength	:	2000 workers and 500 AD Staff
(f)	Source of funding	:	Govt. of India, Govt. of Andhra Pradesh, Govt. of Tamil Nadu and several International Agencies, NABARD, Local Banks, SBI, Canara Bank, Andhra Bank.
(g)	Approximate population served	:	3.10 million population in 05 States (Andhra Pradesh, Karnataka, Odisha, Tamil Nadu and Delhi).
(h)	Target groups	:	0-6 years children, mentally handicapped, PH, deserted and old age people.

(i) Objectives

- Protecting the inalienable human rights
- Special protection for – women, children, the elderly, the sick, the challenged, the vulnerable sections
- Through peoples' initiative and ensuring – justice, peace, equality, fraternity

- Empowering people to assert their rights
- Enabling their fullest participation in development
- Full opportunities for –
  - o Education
  - o Capacity Building
  - o Human Resources Development
  - o Ensuring Better Living environments
  - o Strengthening
  - o Family bonds
  - o Community consciousness
  - o Democratic approaches

Details of activities: The RSS is promoting the women Self Helf Groups (SHGs) on a large scale.

(j)	Research	:	The Rashtriya Seva Samithi is understanding research on social work and women related issues.
(k)	Vocational training	:	Anganwadi workers training, teachers for mentally retired people, B.Ed. in distance mode.
(l)	Skill development	:	Helping Self-Help groups and income generating programmes.

♦ ♦ ♦

Swami Ramanada Tirtha Rural Institute

(1)	Contact person	:	Prof. M. Sudarshan Reddy
(2)	Designation	:	Chairman
(3)	Contact No.	:	08685 – 222880, 205076 / 77/ 80
(4)	Mobile	:	M.S.R-9989625228, Dr.H.R-9848591700
(5)	E-mail	:	srtri@rediffmail.com
(6)	Website	:	www.srtri.in
(7)	Address	:	SRTRI, Jalalpur (V), Boodhan, Pochampally (m), Nalgonda Dist., AP, 508284

About the organisation: SRTRI was established in 1995 at Jalalpur Village, Pochampally Mandal of Nalgonda District, Andhra Pradesh. The then Prime Minister of India Sri P.V.Narasimha Rao laid the foundation for the Institute with the noble objective of creating an appropriate platform for pro-active rural development initiatives in Andhra Pradesh. Within a short span of time, the Institute has emerged as one of the leading institutions in India working for cause of rural empowerment through suitable educational and vocational training initiatives. The philosophy of the Institute rests upon holistic approach wherein the rural people are provided with unhindered access to skills in latest sustainable technologies using improved tools and equipment for enhanced productivity and quality dimensions. Special emphasis is laid on capacity building and income generating of those who are underprivileged, downtrodden, women, unemployed youth, and other vulnerable sections of the rural community. The prime focus is on smaller technologies, which are sustainable and rural friendly so as to enable the rural poor earn sustainable incomes and lead quality of life, and thus bring in confidence among them to trigger off to a greater heights. Every initiative of the Institute represents a smaller step towards realizing Mahatma Gandhi's dream of making rural India the focal point of holistic development.

(a)	Year of establishment	:	1995
(b)	Registration No	:	3344/95/01/12/1995, registered under societies Act A.P.
(c)	Location	:	Pochampally mandal of Nalgonda District
(d)	Coverage area	:	All states in India.
(e)	Staff strength	:	50
(f)	Source of funding	:	Govt. of A.P., NCRI, Ministry of New and Renewable Energy
(g)	Approximate population served	:	Andhra Pradesh
(h)	Target groups	:	Rural areas
(i)	Objectives	:	

- To work for holistic rural development through training, education, extension, consultancy, research and development.

- To develop, assimilate, adopt and test, technologies including the indigenous and smaller technologies to ensure relevance to the rural requirements.
- To evolve and implement a package of education, training and gainful employment through flexible entry conditions.
- To maintain standards in the training component of the Training and Technology Development Center of each district.
- To provide training in the use of improved artisan tools and to innovate, modify smaller technologies to suit local requirements.
- To encourage self-employment and striving to create a strong base for the emergence of rural entrepreneurship.
- To develop and maintain a research and documentation center with a view to act as a resource center for studies on rural development.
- To develop an up-to date audiovisual center for producing the necessary software and audio visual aids for its educational training and extension work.
- To establish and maintain information technology network to enable easy access to information and to create an interface between the rural producers and users.

Details of activities: The institute offers vocational training in producing food and agro products, forestry, chemical engineering, electrical, textile, leather, rubber, live stock and metal products. It also offers training in Information Technology, textile related trades, entrepreneurship development programme and in surface ornamentation. The institute works in association with NCRI.

(j) Vocational training : Information Technology, Surface Ornamentation, Food Processing, Entreprenuership, Automobile & Diesel Mechanisms, Seed-Quality testing-DNA fingerprinting, Renewable Energy Applications for Rural Livelihood promotion.

(k) Skill development : Engineering Trades, Textile related trades, Textile Printing & Dyeing, Zardozi.

♦ ♦ ♦

Youth for Action

(1)	Contact person	:	Venkataramanayaa
(2)	Designation	:	President
(3)	Contact No.	:	040 – 27791830 , fax 27791829
(4)	Mobile	:	9866706131
(5)	E- Mail	:	vedvon@yahoo.co.in
(6)	Website	:	www.youthforaction.in
(7)	Address	:	Plot No. 20-21, Sree Nivas Banjara Nagar, Tirumalagiri, Secunderabad – 500 015

About the organization: Youth for Action (YFA) is an organization based in Hyderabad, which started in a humble way, and in its period of existence of a little over a decade, established itself in the realms of natural resources management, as well as effective organization of human resources and collective problem addressal. YFA as an organisation, was inspired by the selfless work of Baba Amte, the first Indian to get the Gandhi Peace Award. During his visit to the state of Andhra Pradesh and the district of Mahaboobnagar in connection with the "Bharat Jodo" or "Knit India" movement, he showed overwhelming concern for the degrading eco-system and its impact on the eroding livelihood patterns in the villages. In a series of sharing sessions with a group of young men, who had already started organising the people in an informal way to meet their food security needs, he first mooted the idea of an organised team to put in efforts at the grassroots level searching for sustainable solutions to the problems.

(a)	Year of establishment	:	1986
(b)	Registration No	:	1528/F, dt 13th July 1986
(c)	Location	:	Tirumalgiri, Secunderabad
(d)	Coverage area	:	Gulbarga district, Karnataka; Mahbubnagar in Andhra Pradesh.
(e)	Staff strength	:	30
(f)	Source of funding	:	Krishi Vignan Kendra, NCRI, Hyderabad, Dept. of Science & Technology, New Delhi.
(g)	Approximate population served	:	90,000
(h)	Target groups	:	Rural, youth, women, farmers
(i)	Objectives	:	

- To promote social development of people's particularly through women.
- Institutional development/promotion of SHGs.
- Awareness about social rights, gender education, skill education and training.
- To generate natural resources such as land, water and vegetation through water shed management activities.

Details of Activities

Promotion of need based higher education for livelihoods and skill empowerment of young men and women. Conceptualizing and implementing locally driven educational initiatives and services for economic empowerment and employment of young men and women in Mahaboobnagar District of Andhra Pradesh.

(j) Research : Research particularly in the area of dry land agriculture, alternative farming option through research effort of bio-technology.

(k) Vocational training : Seed production, Watershed management, Drip irrigation, Mango grafting, Orange budding,Organic composting, Vermi compost making, Soil Testing, Tissue Culture Lab contributing in producing qualitative plants of Neem, Teak and Gerbera flowers.

(l) Skill development : Leather goods, tailoring, embroidery, computer, electrical wiring, house wiring, nursery management, seed production and leaf plates.

♦ ♦ ♦

ARUNACHAL PRADESH

Arunachal Pradesh Seva Sangh

(1)	Contact person	:	Vishal Nath Rai
(2)	Designation	:	Secretary
(3)	Contact No.	:	03602277218, Fax 2277218
(4)	Mobile	:	9402275630
(5)	E- Mail	:	apss_mdtc@rediffmail.com
(6)	Website	:	N.A.
(7)	Address	:	Doimukh, Pampupare District, Arunachal Pradesh, PIN- 791112

About the organisation: Arunachal Pradesh Seva Sangh (APSS) is a Gandhian organization promoting economic activities through Khadi village industries. It has the distinction of being the 1st registered non-government organization in the State of Arunachal Pradesh. Though officially registered in 1979, the genesis of APSS could be seen way back in 1962 during Chinese aggression on Indian soil when the Sarvodaya world with Gandhian ideology decided to create a non-violent force organizing SHANTI SENA activities on national borders to fight aggression. In 1963 the work was initiated with establishment of 12 peace centres by Akhil Bhartia Shanti Sena Mandal in the then NEFA, the present Arunachal Pradesh. It has trained hundreds of trainees and continuously working for rural development and self-employment of the youth and bringing in new programmes to meet such needs.

(a)	Year of establishment	:	1979
(b)	Registration No	:	SR/ETA/1 dt: 19th June 1979
(c)	Location	:	Doimukh, Pampupare District,Arunachal Pradesh
(d)	Coverage area	:	Arunachal Pradesh
(e)	Staff strength	:	17
(f)	Source of funding	:	Khadi and village industries commission, NCRI
(g)	Approximate population served	:	60,000
(h)	Target groups	:	Local, tribal, women and children

(i) Objectives:

The main objective is to develop the skills of tribals of Arunachal Pradesh for income generation in the artisan sector and to promote a continuous design development process for development of tribal skills.

Details of Activities

(j)	Research	:	Agriculture, technology
(k)	Vocational training	:	Scooter/Bike repairing, spinning, tailoring, weaving, preparation of candles, incense sticks, computer Hardware & software and mobile repairing

(l) Skill development : Entrepreneurship development program, spinning, cotton weaving, candle making, mustered oil, cane furniture and also hundred of children are benefited every year through child welfare programs. It is continuously working for rural development and self-employment of youths and bringing new programmes to meet such needs.

♦ ♦ ♦

National Youth Project

(1)	Contact person	:	Sri Hari Pado Biswas
(2)	Designation	:	President
(3)	Contact No.	:	0360-2292810,
(4)	Mobile	:	98625 63890
(5)	E-Mail address	:	nyparunachal@gmail.com haribiswas@sify.com
(6)	Website	:	N.A.
(7)	Address	:	National Youth Project – AP, 1st Floor, Taba Building, Opp. Civil Secretariat, E-Sector, Papum Pare, Itanagar, Arunachal Pradesh.

About the organisation: The movement "National Youth Project" took birth, with its office in the Mahatma Ghandi Sewa Ashram in the year 1970 under the directorship of Dr. S.N.Subba Rao, who has devoted his whole life for nation building activities, especially by mobilizing youth power. The National Youth Project known for its social relevant work which is doing many developmental programmes in association with various departments and ministries like State Council for Science and Technology, Khadi & Village Industries Commission, NABARD, Ministry of Youth Affairs, HRD and other reputed NGOs like Ekta Parishad, ICYO, AYC, WAY etc. National Youth Project is known for its social relevant work which is doing many developmental programmes.

(a)	Year of establishment	:	1970
(b)	Registration No	:	292, Dated, the 28th April 1992 (New Delhi)
(c)	Location	:	Rural, Urban & Backward areas
(d)	Coverage area	:	Villages - 656 Mandals - 65 District - 16
(e)	Staff strength	:	Teaching / Technical: 32 Non teaching / Non Technical: 46
(f)	Source of funding	:	Project basis under various Govt. ministries
(g)	Approximate population served	:	1.5 Lakhs
(h)	Target groups	:	Youth, women, children

(i) Objectives

- To promote the interest and all round welfare of the YOUTHS in the country.
- To enable welfare organizations to formulate and carry out common programmes, including YOUTH projects.
- Organised various camps for all round development of the youth.

- To provide a common programme for the voluntary agencies concerned with growth and development to share their cherished ideas and through which to enable them to speed up the process of concerted for action.
- Field based partnership projects with government and NGOs to conserve bio-diversity/ ecology for sustainable development.
- Development of educational materials for formulation of environmental education in order to create environmental awareness to general mass.
- Policy support to the government to safe guard the bio-diversity as well as the cultural & heritage of the region for the benefit of the indigenous.

Details of Activities

(j)	Research	: Eco Tourism a money spinner for Arunachal Pradesh, Role of NGO's for Development of Arunachal Pradesh.
(k)	Vocational training	: Handloom & Handicrafts, Screen Printing & Internet, DTP, Handloom and handicrafts, Spinning & Weaving, Mushroom Growing & Vermi compost.

• • •

ASSAM

Gramya Vikash Mancha

(1)	Contact person	:	Prithibhusan Deka
(2)	Designation	:	President
(3)	Contact No.	:	(03624)-283888/283740
(4)	Mobile	:	+919864292294
(5)	E- Mail	:	gvm_ngo@sify.com
(6)	Website	:	N.A.
(7)	Address	:	At: No. 1 Bardhanara P.O: Dakshingaon District: Nalbari, Assam India, PIN: 781350.

About the organisation: Gramya Vikash Mancha is a non profit organization working with the excluded section of society since 1999. The organization has been registered under Society Registration Act XXI of 1860 as well as under Foreign Contribution Regulation Act, 1976. Besides, the organisation is registered under Income Tax Act and donation to the organization is exempted under section 80 G. The organization has about 3000 active volunteers in different parts of Lower Assam. The organisation is managed by an Executive Committee, formed for a period of three years.

(a)	Year of establishment	:	1999
(b)	Registration No	:	RS/ NAL/ B/ 246/ 39 of 2000-2001
(c)	Location	:	At: No. 1 Bardhanara, District: Nalbari, Assam, India
(d)	Coverage area	:	347 villages under Nalbari, Kamrup (Rural), Baska and Barpeta district of Assam.
(e)	Staff strength	:	83 full time
(f)	Source of funding	:	a) NCRI, b) NABARD, c) UNICEF, d) Actionaid India, e) Indo Global Social Service Society (IGSSS), f) Sir Dorabji Tata Trust, g) Sir Jamsetji Tata Trust, h) North Eastern Development Financial Corporation (NEDFi), i) DFID, j) European Commission Humanitarian Aid (ECHO), k) Association for India Development.
(g)	Approximate population served	:	10,000 farmers, 2000 artisans associated with bamboo craft, pottery, handloom and weaving etc.,
(h)	Target Groups	:	Marginalized section particularly from Scheduled Tribe, Schedule Cast, minority, Physically challenged person, displaced persons due to natural calamity and conflict situation.

(i) Objectives

The organization is working with a vision to create a peaceful, prosperous, egalitarian and exploitation free society in every village.

Details of Activities

(j) Research	:	Social Action research on a) conflict resolution, b) Disaster Risk Reduction through schools, c) Promoting accessibility to different entitlements, d) livelihood Security
(k) Vocational training		a) Training on Basic Computer operation, b) Training on Participatory planning, c) Training on Management of rural development programs, d) Training on Disaster Risk Reduction strategies and mechanisms, e) Peace and conflict management
(l) Community mobilization	:	Mobilized approx. 30 thousand farmers in a common platform, 200 SHGs formed and promoted, 100 farmers club, promoted a network among grass root organization namely Social Initiative for Transforming Action (SINTA), Village level women committee in 300 villages, village level development committee among marginalized section.
(m) Skill development	:	a) Bamboo Craft production , b) Pottery wares , c) Handloom and weaving, d) Water hyacinth products, e) Vermi composting, f) Homestead farming

♦ ♦ ♦

Institute of Integrated Resource Management

(1)	Contact person	:	Dr. H. Dhattatreya
(2)	Designation	:	Chief Executive officer
(3)	Contact No.	:	03712236230
(4)	Mobile	:	09435744444
(5)	E- Mail	:	iirm2000@gmail.com, dattarayae@gmail.com
(6)	Website	:	N.A.
(7)	Address	:	B.S.Road, PO. Dekargaon, Tezpur, Sointpur – 784501, Assam.

About the organisation: IIRM was started in 2000.Towards the last part of 2005, IIRM started micro-finance operation as counter veiling power for the needy masses by providing minimum financial assistance in the form of loan. Because IIRM believes micro-finance is one of the viable interventions to support livelihood in a sustainable manner. In 2010, because of the restriction on NGOs' involvement in micro-finance operation by Government of Assam, IIRM created a new entity for its Microfinance activity and established the Integrated Management of Microfinance and Networking Services (IMMAN) as a section 25 company registered under the companies Act 1956. Now IIRM, in collaboration with IMMAN, provides financial assistance to farmers as and when required. Recently IIRM started its networking with BAIF development Research Foundation., Pune and BARC , Mumbai.

(a)	Year of establishment	:	2000
(b)	Registration No	:	RS/SPR/242/A/09 of 2000-2001
(c)	Location	:	Tezpur, Dist-Sonitpur, Assam
(d)	Coverage area	:	Assam and Arunachal Pradesh
(e)	Staff strength	:	20
(f)	Source of funding	:	State Institute of Rural Development, Ghy. Dept. of Science and Technology, Govt of India. Dept of Bio-Technology, Govt of India. G. B. Pant Institute of Himalayan Environment and Development, Almora. Central Social Welfare board, New Delhi. Assam State AIDS Control Society, Govt. of Assam. Development of North Eastern Region, New Delhi. Development Commissioner (Handicraft), Govt of India. Caritus India.
(g)	Approximate population served	:	Almost 10000

(h) Target groups : Rural Folk

(i) Objectives

1. To promote livelihood practices among needy mass in order to provide an alternative source of credit mechanism for those whose accessibility to formal lending institutions are very poor.
2. Conservation and popularization of bio resource through research and studies.
3. Transfer of Technologies/ recent issues/up gradation to farmers' field through training, demonstration etc.
4. To empower, secure and enhance living conditions of rural people by efficient use of resources, skill-upgradation and employment opportunities.
5. To organize capacity building training programmes for strengthening farmer's capacity in terms of sustainable development and create self employment opportunities.
6. To support the weaker sections in a community – disabled, disadvantageously placed i.e. women, children etc by initiate, promote and support crisis management services.

Details of Activities

(j) Research : Action research in agriculture and Livestock sector Development : Community development programme in respect of sustainable livelihood and socio- economic upliftment of community people.

Community Mobilisation : Group formation and implementation of any project through group.

(k) Vocational training : Vocational training on agriculture and livestock, computer, welding, weaving, handicraft and carpentry

(l) Skill development : Skill development training on Agriculture, Livestock and Fishery.

(m) Organisations under establishment : Integrated Management of Microfinance and Networking Services (IMMAN).

♦ ♦ ♦

Rashtriya Gramin Vikas Nidhi

(1) Contact person : Dr. Amiya Kr. Sharma

(2) Designation : Executive Director

(3) Contact No. : 0361-2452320

(4) Mobile : 9435118871

(5) E-Mail : rgvnho@gmail.com

(6) Website : www.rgvnindia.org

(7) Address : Aruna Complex, 2nd FloorOpp. Bye Lane No. 8, Rajgarh Road, Guwahati – 781 003

About the organisation: Rashtriya Gramin Vikas Nidhi (RGVN) was founded in April 1990 as a development support organization in response to the need for an organization to fund those working with the poor on livelihoods in remote areas where mainstream financial institutions do not reach. RGVN was mainly initiated to fill the credit gap between FIs/commercial banks and poor people in rural areas. RGVN's mission is to improve the quality of life of the poor and otherwise underprivileged rural and urban people through social action. RGVN began its operations in the North East and later on expanded to other parts of Eastern India. RGVN now operates in 14 states of the country. RGVN's founder sponsor was Industrial Financial Corporation of India (IFCI). The other sponsors of RGVN are Industrial Development Bank of India (IDBI), National Bank for Agriculture and Rural Development (NABARD), and Tata Social Welfare Trust (TSWT).RGVN was founded by Shri S.M. Palia, former Executive Director, IDBI. Shri S.M. Palia was also the founder Chairperson of RGVN. Dr L.C. Jain, an eminent Gandhian and former member of Planning Commission was also one of the Governing Board members of RGVN during the initial years. Shri Deep Joshi, a Magsaysay award winner, was also the former Chairperson of RGVN.

(a) Year of establishment : 20.4.1990

(b) Registration No : 230 (S)90-91/212

(c) Location : Guwahati

(d) Coverage area : 8 North Eastern States, Odisha, Bihar, Jharkhand, Chhattisgarh, eastern U.P. and coastal A.P.

(e) Staff strength : 52

(f) Source of funding : Sponsored by IDBI, NABARD, IFCI and TSWT;

(g) Approximate population served : 2 lakhs approx.

(h) Target groups : Social and economically backward groups

(i) Objectives

- Promote, support and develop voluntary organizations engaged in the social and economic uplift of rural and urban poor, physically and socio-economically handicapped people;
- Improve the pace and quality of economic development, especially relating to the village

and decentralized sector;

- Focus attention on groups which are disadvantageously placed in society, but have the potential for pursuing socially and economically productive activities;
- Assist the urban and rural poor especially tribals, scheduled caste, women and children for their economic self sustenance.

Details of Activities

(j) Research

- Gender Budget Analysis Centre
- Social Impact Assessment for Calcom Cements
- International Watershed Management Institute (IWMI) – Tata Project
- Baseline Study, Third Party Inspection and Social Audit of Border Areas of Assam
- Assignment with Oxfam India
- Need Assessment Study for Hindustan Cocoa Cola Beverages Pvt. Ltd.
- Impact Study of Microfinance on the Economic and Social Development
- Impact Assessment of Women Oriented Schemes

(k) Vocational training : Weaving, Poultry, Fishery, System of Rice Intensification (SRI)

(l) Skill development : Capacity building of NGOs, CBOs & SHGs; Volunteers, Training on Accounting, Computer, Communication skills & Personality Development, NGO development, Community Mobilization etc.

♦ ♦ ♦

Shanti Sandhana Ashram

(1) Contact person : Mrs Hembhai

(2) Designation : Secretary

(3) Contact No. : 0361 2307138

(4) Mobile : 09435014428

(5) E- Mail : santisadhan@yahoo.com, inandayal@yahoo.com

(6) Website : www.shantisadhanaashram.com

(7) Address : Shantivan Basistha, P. O. Basistha, Guwahati, Assam - 781029

About the organisation: This organization is one of the pioneering in championing the cause of literacy in the backward district of Assam, which it started as a literacy as a movement of the people (LAMP) in 1989.

(a) Year of establishment : 1986

(b) Registration No : 147 of 1986-87

(c) Location : Shantivan Basistha, PO. Basistha.

(d) Coverage area : Rural areas in Assam

(e) Staff strength : 20

(f) Source of funding : Government aided, private funding.

(g) Approximate population served : 411 students per year

(h) Target groups : Illiterates in backward areas

(i) Objectives

To make all the children in the villages in and around the city of Guwahati, in Assam, to go to the Govt. schools after attending the pre-primary or primary level of study through formal education.

Details of Activities

(j) Vocational training : Games, Yoga and computer

(k) Skill development : Youth orientation and awareness program

(l) Organisations under establishment : 8 centres in different districts of Assam.

♦ ♦ ♦

BIHAR

Bihar Educational Development Society

(1)	Contact person	: Mr. Jai Kumar Palit
(2)	Designation	: Chairman
(3)	Contact No.	: 0631 – 2227505, fax 0631 - 2222871
(4)	Mobile	: 9431225252
(5)	E-Mail	: jkp_beds@indiatimes.com Jss_palit @yahoo.com
(6)	Website	: N.A.
(7)	Address	: 56, Gautam Budha Road, Gaya – 823 001, Bihar.

About the organisation: The BEDS, Gaya was established in the year 1993. The Society is also registered under foreign contribution act vide reg no 031090030 dated 17.8.1998 under the Ministry of Home Affairs, Govt of India.The organisation has been working for the development of education, art and culture. The institute has been organising vocational education programmes for economic enhancement for the rural youth also been providing necessary support for establishing production centres of handicrafts, garments agro based products and other local demands at village level for the self-employment of rural youths, both men and women.

(a)	Year of establishment	: 1993–94
(b)	Registration No	: 23/93-94
(c)	Location	: Gaya district, Bihar
(d)	Coverage area	: Bihar
(e)	Staff strength	: 25
(f)	Source of funding	: Government of India, ministry of education, United states- Seattle peoples for progress in India.
(g)	Approximate population served	: 60, 000
(h)	Target groups	: Non-literate, semi-literate, unemployed youth, men and women from urban and rural areas.

(i) Objectives :

- To undertake, aid, promote and co-ordinate teaching, research, training and consultancy in technical, social, fundamental sciences, vocational training, health and medicale care, management training and other development works and to undertake related activites.
- To undertake, organise and facilitate study courses, conference, lectures, seminar and the like to promote the objects of orgns.
- To undertake, organise and implement different programmes for the welfare of SC, SC, BC and other weaker sections of the society.
- To work for the welfare of the physically handicapped persons and to undertake all related acivities that is necessary for their educational, economic social and psychological development.

- To co-operate with other institution in India and abroad having objects wholly or patly similar to those of our orgn by exchange of teachers or experts and by undertaking such other activities as may be considerd conducive to closer co-operation with such other orgns.

Details of Activities

(j)	Research	:	Conditions of the women's prisoner in central jail of Bihar and their rehabilitation sponsored by national commission for women, Govt. of India, New Delhi. Removal of illiteracy among women, a case study of Bihar sponsored by ministry of HRD, New Delhi.
(k)	Vocational training	:	Typing, shorthand, painting, computer education, radio and TV mechanism.
(l)	Skill development	:	Tailoring, embroidery, handicrafts, food preservation methods and marketing to rural women. This training is being supplemented by providing interest-free microcredit loans to these women through self-help groups (SHGs), with each SHG consisting of 5 to 10 women.
(m)	Organisations under establishment	:	B.R. Ambedkar coaching institute, Gaya.

♦ ♦ ♦

Bihar Institute of Economic Studies

(1) Contact person : Dr. Pyare lal

(2) Designation : Director

(3) Contact No. : 91-612-2520721, Fax: 2520409

(4) Mobile : 9431015209

(5) E- Mail : bies@sify.com

(6) Website : www.bies.in

(7) Address : 1, IAS Colony, Kidawipuri, Patna – 800 001.

About the organisation: BIES is a non-profit organisation established in the year 1990 by a group of experience in their respective fields and conducted activities like self employment programme, agriculture, capacity building etc.

(a) Year of establishment : 1990

(b) Registration No : 407/89-90, dt: 25/1/1995

(c) Location : Patna.

(d) Coverage area : Bihar, Jharkhand, Assam, Sikkim, U.P., M.P.

(e) Staff strength : 30

(f) Source of funding : Planning Commission, Ministry of Rural Development, Ministry of Social Justice & Empowerment, Ministry of Agriculture, Ministry of Home Affairs, Ministry of Health and Family Welfare, CAPART, Rural Development (U.S.A.) for social action (CASA).

(g) Approximate population served : 1 crore

(h) Target groups : Rural people of disadvantaged group

(i) Objectives

BIES conducts Social Science Research and Evaluation, provides Consultancy on Developmental Issues, Design and Implement Action Programmes and Organises Seminars/Workshops on Socio-economic development.

Details of Activities

(j) Research : Over the past seventeen years, BIES has successfully completed several projects on Health, Population, Human Rights, Education, Rural Development, Watershed, Tribal Development and has carried Emergency Flood Relief. BIES has also conducted Workshop on Social Defence, Panchayati Raj, Land Reforms and Economic Development.

- A Study on Response, Attitude and Adoption of Family Planning Measures in Bihar
- A Study of Record of Rights in Land in Bihar
- A Study of the Impact of Welfare and Measures under Tribal Sub-Plan in Bihar
- Census Data Based Study on Mal Paharia Tribes in Bihar
- A Study on Dynamics of Marketing of Selected Fruits in Bihar
- A Study on Demand and Supply of Medicinal Plants in Bihar, Jharkhand, and Sikkim
- Impact Assessment Study of various Rural Development programmes in the Dibrugarh district, Assam and in Balia district, Uttar Pradesh
- Emergency Flood Relief to 1551 families in the Jhanjharpur and Andhratharhi blocks of the Madhubani district in Bihar
- A Study of Perception of Programme Beneficiaries and Non-Beneficiaries of the Need for and Utility of Family Welfare Programme in Bihar.

(k) Organisations under establishment: BIES, Madhuvani, North Bihar.

♦ ♦ ♦

Bihar Vidyapeeth

(1)	Contact person	:	Sri. JN Sahai
(2)	Designation	:	Chairman
(3)	Contact No.	:	0612-2262819
(4)	Mobile	:	09835073076
(5)	E- Mail	:	N.A.
(6)	Website	:	N.A.
(7)	Address	:	Sadaqat Ashram, Patna -10, Bihar.

About the organization: Bihar Vidyapeeth was established by Dr. Rajendra Prasad, the first President of India in 1921 along with Mahatma Gandhi and Maulana Majharul Haq. Rajendra Prasad worked as Vice-chancellor in Bihar Vidyapeeth from 1923 to 1927. The institute provides education to the children, computer training and, runs a library free of cost. Sadaqat Ashram is the headquarters of the Bihar Vidyapeeth, a National University. This place is more famous for the fact that Dr. Rajendra Prasad, the first President of India spent the last few days of his life at this place, in retirement. There is a small museum in the Sadaqat Ashram that displays his personal belongings.The beautiful bungalow of Sadaqat Ashram in Patna is situated at the bank of the river Ganga. This fantastic location of the Sadaqat Ashram attracts many tourists every year. Here people visit the museum to learn more about the last days of Dr. Rajendra Prasad's life. Being the headquarters of the Bihar Vidyapeeth the Sadaqat Ashram of Patna is also an important place with respect to the educational system of Bihar. Some of major decisions regarding the functioning of this National University are taken in this Ashram.

In 2008, the Government of India made a grant of Rs. Three crore for a Institute of Rural Development on Gandhian lines. Bihar Vidyapeeth is in the process of establishing the envisaged institute which it has named Rajendra Gram Sanjeewan Sansthan. The idea is to integrate projects of rural development with an educational centre on the lines of Nai Talim.

(a)	Year of establishment	:	1921
(b)	Registration No	:	705 J (dated 17-sept-1928) under society registration act.
(c)	Location	:	Patna.
(d)	Coverage area	:	Bihar
(e)	Staff strength	:	16
(f)	Source of funding	:	Self funding
(g)	Approximate population served	:	In thousands
(h)	Target groups	:	Youth under the age of 18 to 30 yrs.
(i)	Objectives	:	To provide education and computer training to maximum number of people in and around this Bihar Vidyapith.

Details of activities:

j) Skill development : Computer training and carpentry.

k) Organisations under establishment : Rajendra Smriti Sanghrahalaya.

♦ ♦ ♦

Kasturba Centre for Social Regeneration

(1)	Contact person	:	Sri. Jiweshwar
(2)	Designation	:	Co-Ordinatior
(3)	Contact No.	:	N.A
(4)	Mobile	:	09431049194
(5)	E- Mail	:	jiweshwar @hotmail.com/ Kasturba centre@in.com
(6)	Website	:	N.A
(7)	Address	:	"Shailchit", Gokul path (Nala paar), Patel Nagar, Patna, Bihar-800024.

About the organization: Set up on 22 February, 2002, the Kasturba Centre for Social Regeneration (KCSR) is a NGO whish is named after Kasturba Gandhi who Gandhiji described as his main source of inspiration and a valuable co-worker.When Gandhiji launched the Satyagraha movement in Champaran in 1917, he realized that India lived in villages and hence rural regeneration was a must for the success of his campaign. He therefore combined revolution with reconstruction. He prepared the first blueprint of the Constructive Programme in Champaran; Kasturba was in the forefront of Satyagraha movement as well as the Constructive Programme. She was instrumental in bringing women in the movement. Incidentally, it is women who benefited more from the constructive programme.

Kasturba passed away on 22 February 1944 while in detention in Aga Khan Palace, Poona. Kasturba Centre for Social Regeneration is our tribute to that great soul.

The institute works on Basic education (Nai Talim), Khadi and other household industries, Training of the youth and Dissemination of Gandhian literature through Libraries including mobile libraries, Publication of relevant books in Hindi and Imparting media literacy.

(a)	Year of establishment	:	2002
(b)	Registration No	:	1014 dated 03 September 2008
(c)	Location	:	Bihar
(d)	Coverage area	:	Bihar
(e)	Staff strength	:	Regular – 5, Field -25
(f)	Source of funding	:	NCRI, Gandhi Smriti, Handicraft, Govt. of India, State Govt, IGNOU.
(g)	Approximate population served	:	At West Champaran-800, at Bihar- 300, at Uttar Pradesh-150
(h)	Target Groups	:	Children and women
(i)	Objectives	:	Nai Talim education to children and women

Details of Activities

(j)	Research	:	Sishu panchayat, bal sansad in more then 100 schools.
(k)	Vocational Training	:	Carpentry, charkha spinning, weaving of Baswan Buti sarees, Mithila painting, Sikki grass weaving.
(l)	Skill Development	:	Spinning regulary for women
(m)	Organisations under establishment	:	(1) Kalian (2) Prajapathi Shaishnik Sansthan (3) Grameen Rachnatmak

♦ ♦ ♦

Samanvaya Ashram

(1)	Contact person	:	Dr. Dwarko Sundarani
(2)	Designation	:	Director
(3)	Contact No.	:	0631-2200506
(4)	Mobile	:	09939602508
(5)	E- Mail	:	samanvayashram@hotmail.com
(6)	Website	:	N.A.
(7)	Address	:	Samanvay Ashram Bodhgaya - Bihar, India-824231.

About the organisation: Samanvay Ashram situated at Bodh Gaya, Bihar, was inaugurated by Acharya Vinobha Bhave on April 18, 1954. He handed the management of the ashram over to Shri Dwarko Sundrani, a trusted aide, on September 29, 1954. Samanvay Ashram literally means a living centre dedicated to understanding and reconciliation, concord and harmony, adjustment and assimilation, and synthesis and integration. Land for this ashram was donated to Vinobha Bhave during the Bhoodan movement. Since 1954, the Samanvay Ashram has worked towards the betterment of the downtrodden in the Bodhgaya community.

(a)	Year of establishment	:	1954
(b)	Registration No	:	N.A.
(c)	Location	:	Bodh gaya, Bihar.
(d)	Coverage area	:	Bihar
(e)	Staff strength	:	20
(f)	Source of funding	:	Private organizations like Asha Stanford and Asha Berkeley.
(g)	Approximate population served	:	20 lakhs
(h)	Target groups	:	Children from the lowest section of society.
(i)	Objectives	:	To educate children of the age group 5 to 10 who belong to the lowest section of society.

Details of Activities

The project at Samanvay involves sponsoring the education of 25 children, of the age group 5-10 years. These children are from the lowest section of society, and belong to the Mushar and Bhogta community. The members of this community are extremely poor and have little or no food or land, much less education.

(j)	Research	:	Based on Gandhian values, the ashram is a center for research & training in education and development, and aims to fulfill Gandhiji's vision of "Building from Below unto the Last.. ".
(k)	Vocational training	:	Dairy, irrigation, agricultural techniques, animal husbandry, etc.

♦ ♦ ♦

Society for Rural Industrialisation

(1)	Contact person	:	Deepankarsen Gupta
(2)	Designation	:	Chief Functionary
(3)	Contact No.	:	0651-2540668
(4)	Mobile	:	9431170906
(5)	E- Mail	:	rupcon@inranchi.com; sri.ranchi@gmail.com
(6)	Website	:	www.sriranchi.org
(7)	Address	:	Bariatu, Ranchi, Bihar-804009.

About the organization: Society for Rural Industrialisation (SRI) is a national level voluntary organization. SRI is committed to render scientific and technological support for rural development, based on present and emerging global knowledge. The relevant knowledge bank is identified and the most potential one adopted. It is then converted into technology which villagers can adopt, own and manage. Through a scientifically planned training and post training support, the technology is transferred to become a part of rural life. Thus SRI endeavors to change the role of the marginalized community, from that of a mere recipient of welfare measures, to that of a responsible partner in the development process.

(a)	Year of establishment	:	1979 (Regd. 1984)
(b)	Registration No	:	1/84 Patna under society registration act FCRA No: 337800015
(c)	Location	:	Ranchi
(d)	Coverage area	:	Bihar state
(e)	Staff strength	:	82
(f)	Source of funding	:	Ranchi Regional Development Authority, World Bank, Dept. of Agriculture, Jharkhand, DRDA, Koderma dist., UNDP.
(g)	Approximate population served	:	40,000 mostly Tribal, (110 per batch)
(h)	Target groups	:	Tribals
(i)	Objectives	:	They work to bridge the technology gap between urban and rural areas. By research & development, technology transfer & mobilization.

Details of Activities

Social Animators were first introduced in all 91 villages of Angara Block and the system was transferred to more than 60 NGOs.

- Connected 18 villages in Jharkhand and Bihar through satellite to share knowledge.
- Scientific analysis and operational principles shared with 90 NGOs and built up strong Social Monitoring groups in two blocks.

1. Techno-scientific activities of SRI is conducted through three thematic groups,
   - Technology for Marginal farmers.
   - Technology for Village women
   - Technology for Rural professionals
2. SRI being a Science & Technology based organization, innovation has always been its focus. Innovations of SRI can be classified into three groups
   - Innovative Concepts & Institutions
   - Product Innovation
   - System & Process Innovation

(j) Research

a. Product Innovations:

- Enveloping Arch Foundation for Small Dams
- Random Rubble-filled Blocks for Superstructure
- Rubble-sand Compacted Foundation for Village houses
- Roofing with Concrete Rafter and Planks
- Polylined Rain Water Harvester
- Flexi dam: Post Monsoon Rivulet Water Diverter
- Washer Pump
- Manual Lac Processing Station
- LED Reading Lamp with Solar PV Charging
- Mahua Kismis

b. System & Process Innovations:

- Participatory Perspective Plan Preparation (P4 Exercise)
- Commercial Mushroom Spawn Production at Village level
- Hydraulic Control of Eco-hatchery for Fish Breeding
- Large Reservoir Fishery
- Flow-net Analysis for Ground Water
- Teaching Aid for Credit Management

(k) Vocational training : Bamboo Craft, Carpentry, Cycle Repairing, Electrical and Electronics,Fabrication, Food Processing, Home Lighting, Mason, Pump and farm equipments two wheeler maintenance.

(l) Skill development : Language (in training) specially trained for job as trainers with the help of institutes, local NGOs.

♦ ♦ ♦

CHATTISGARH

Agrocrats Society for Rural Development

(1) Contact person : Dr. Rajnish Gupta

(2) Designation : Secretary

(3) Contact No. : 0771-3291936, 4066808

(4) Mobile : 99930 99490

(5) E-Mail address : agrocrats_society@rediffmail.com

(6) Website : www.agrocrats.org

(7) Address : Agrocrats Society for Rural Development, B-8, Raj Nagar, Sai Vatika, Deopuri, Raipur, Chhattisgarh - 492 015

About the organisation:ASORD is NGO based in Chhattisgarh India is created by like minded people who are up to making a huge difference in the world.This institute was formed to educate ,development of the society .It has a well equipped office building of 1000 ft2 located at Shailendra Nagar, Raipur and a Research & Development Centre at VIP Road, Raipur with complete facilities of testing equipments, Residential Training cum Processing Centre – "Krishi Rishi Ashram" in 8 acres of area 130 kms. from Raipur at Village – Kergaon, Block – Gariyaband.

(a) Year of establishment : 1995

(b) Registration No : 2833

(c) Location : Rural, Backward Area, Tribal Area

(d) Coverage area : Villages – 167 Mandals-6

(e) Staff strength : Teaching / Technical: 15 Non teaching/Non Technical: 20

(f) Source of funding : Agriculture, Tribal & Rural Development Department of Government of Chhattisgarh & India.

(g) Approximate population served : 4335

(h) Target groups : Youth, women, Farmers

(i) Objectives

- To create self-employment in the rural population by multi-dimensional approaches.
- Collection, preservation, documentation and registration of bio-diversity.
- Development of co-operative and participatory psychology among rural community.
- Research on natural co-existence for sustainable development.
- Development of alternative sustainable path through compatibility of indigenous and modern technologies.
- Promotion of women and child development programmes.
- Promotion of education, literacy, health and family planning awareness.

Details of Activities

(j) Research : Socio - Economic, Adoption of technology, Indigenous Technology, Cropping Pattern, pest Control Methods.

(k) Vocational training : Market led extension management, Concept, formation & Mobilization of SHG's, FIG's & Farmers Club, Concepts of Micro Finance, Collection, Procurement, storage and Processing methods Of MFP, Production technology of Lac Cultivation.

(l) Skill development : Production technology of medicinal plants, Impotance of bil- Compost & methods of preparation, environment management Framework, management of common property, resources in Schedule frame, PRA & Micro Plan preparation.

♦ ♦ ♦

Dharohar Vikas Sansthan

(1)	Contact Person	:	Mr. Surendra Tiwari
(2)	Designation	:	Secretary
(3)	Contact No.	:	07774- 231423
(4)	Mobile No.	:	098261 37248
(5)	Email	:	dharohar.t@rediffmail.com, dharoharvikassanshant@gmail.com
(6)	Website	:	On Process
(7)	Address	:	Vivekanand Nagar,Near Kisan Rice Mill, Ambikapur, Dist.- Surguja (Chhattisgarh) Pin- 497001

About the Organization: Dharohar envisions a world where everyone is a Change maker: a world that responds quickly and effectively to social challenges, and where each individual has the freedom, confidence and societal support to address any social problem and drive change. The institute strives to contribute to the sustained well-being of people, particularly in the tropics, through collaborative strategic and applied research and related activities, and by promoting the transfer of appropriate new technologies and the adoption of new methods of social organisation, for national development.

Dharohar believes in working together for Economic and social justice; Respect for human rights and democracy; Gender equality; Peace and non-violence; Sustainable use of natural resources; Respect for cultural diversity; and Development with equity.

(a)	Year of Establishment	:	Year 2004
(b)	Registration No.	:	CG State-798
(c)	Location	:	Chhattisgarh
(d)	Coverage Area	:	All Chhattisgarh
(e)	Staff Strength	:	14
(f)	Source of funding	:	Donation & Central &State Govt.
(g)	Approximate population served	:	20000 aprx.
(h)	Target Group	:	Womens, Farmers, Youth, unemployed workers, SHG Group, PRI Members

(i) Objectives

- Research, Study, Trainings, Conservation of environment, Traditional art & culture and Social issues.
- Work in health and education developments.
- Capacity building of women, unemployed youth, people below poverty line.
- Stable the research and technical resource center in villages.

- Establishment of Yoga Training Center, Sports & Library for physical and mental development of society.
- Agriculture development and promotion of income generation programme.

Details of Activities

(j)	Research	:	Socio Economic study of PTG- Pahari korwa, Impact assessment of MNREGS at Distt Surguja, CG.
(k)	Vocational Trainings	:	Honey production, Lakh Cultivation, Vermi compost, Mushroom production etc
(l)	Skill Development	:	SRI paddy cultivation, fruit and vegetable farming.

♦ ♦ ♦

Gandhi Seva Ashram

(1)	Contact person	:	Rajendra .K. Singh
(2)	Designation	:	Secretary
(3)	Contact No.	:	07774-323328
(4)	Mobile	:	09425254403
(5)	E- Mail	:	rksgsa@yahoo.com sqssambikapur@rediffmail.com
(6)	Website	:	N.A.
(7)	Address	:	Devganj Road, Ambikapur, Surguja dist, Chattisgarh (India) -497001

About the organisation: Sri Gandhi Seva Ashram (SGSA) is a non profit grass roots development organization, committed to reduce hunger and poverty from tribal areas of north Chattisgarh, India. SGSA works towards advocating for ensuring food through democratizing the resource distribution and development process. SGSA railed the ideas on to the track of reforming the institutions and internalizing democratization.

(a)	Year of establishment	:	1986
(b)	Registration No	:	18151(dated. 22/04/1987) Regd under M.P. Registration act 1973(44)
(c)	Location	:	Surguja Dist of Chattisgarh
(d)	Coverage area	:	180 villages of 12 blocks of sarguja, Koria, Jashpur, Bilashpur districts.
(e)	Staff strength	:	19
(f)	Source of funding	:	UNDP, Khadi and village industries commission, Canadian High commission, Ministry of Rural development, Gol,Central social welfare board, State government.
(g)	Approximate population served	:	50,000 approx.
(h)	Target groups	:	Tribals in north Chattisgarh area
(i)	Objectives	:	Upliftment of tribals in Chattisgarh, livelihood promotion, gram swaraj, awareness and education.

Details of Activities

(j)	Research	:	On Public distribution system- change of ration cards, developed new shops for the people underbelow poverty line.
(k)	Vocational training	:	Folk dances, folk songs, plays, etc

(l)	Skill development	: Training on hand pump maintainance to the youth and women, Technical guidance to the potters, training in electric fitting, motor winding, preparation of bangles from lac for 150 members, training in black smith work ie., in preparing tools, & building materials.
(m)	Organisations under establishment	: Peoples organizations, 1) women's group called Sawangin Mandal 2) chhaua Panchayat for children and adolescents.

♦ ♦ ♦

Saathi Samaj Sevi Sanstha

(1)	Contact person	:	Sri. Bhupesh Tiwari
(2)	Designation	:	President
(3)	Contact No.	:	07786-242852
(4)	Mobile	:	09301529334/ 09425259152
(5)	E- Mail	:	saathibastar@yahoo.co.in; bhupeshtiwari @rediffmail.com
(6)	Website	:	N.A.
(7)	Address	:	Village Kumharpara, Post Girola Tehsil-Kondagaon, Dist Bastar, Kondagaon, Chhattisgarh– 494226.

About the organisation: SAATHI was founded in 1988 in a village called KUMHARPARA, Kondagaon, District Bastar. Its history is linked to the creative skills of the three people who founded SAATHI – Bhupesh Tiwari, Late Bhupendra Banchhore and Harilal Bharadwaj. They are ceramic professionals trained at the Gramoday Sangh in Bhadrawati, Maharashtra. It was during their tenure at the Gramodaya Sangh, that they were inspired by the ideology of Mahatma Gandhi and Kumarappaji and social work ideals of their teacher late Shri S. K. Mirmira.

(a)	Year of establishment	:	1989
(b)	Registration No	:	25941
(c)	Location	:	Kumharpara, Tehsil-Kondagaon, Dist Bastar, Chhattisgarh
(d)	Coverage area	:	Chattisgarh
(e)	Staff strength	:	7
(f)	Source of funding	:	NCRI
(g)	Approximate population served	:	5000
(h)	Target groups	:	Women, disabled, harijans, adivasis and other backward classes

(i) Objectives

The main objective of the organisation is to propagate and develop art and crafts of the region; and to propagate various government schemes aimed for the integrated development of the rural sector through workshops and camps. Other objectives include; conducting adult education programs, mainly working towards the progress and upliftment of women, disabled, harijans, adivasis and other backward classes. SAATHI has also been working towards the conservation of the environment spreading the awareness and disseminating information about best practices in agriculture like using natural manure, bio-fertilizers etc.

Details of Activities

- Establishing sixteen Common Facility Centers (CFCs) equipped with machinery, tools, furnaces, curing tanks and buildings for supporting various crafts such as wrought iron work, pottery, bamboo and bell metal work all over the Bastar District.

- Propagating low cost housing technology and construction of houses using such technology for rural communities.
- Working with artisans for development of their personal tool kits which help them enhance their productivity.
- Working closely with government agencies at the district, state and central levels to implement various programs for artisans and rural communities.
- Organising and participating in approximately 500 exhibitions for handicrafts at the national and international levels.
- Establishing and running an alternative school for children of rural artisans and other communities.
- Establishing and running a rural training institute for artisans – Vishwakarma Gurukul – with financial assistance of the National Council of Rural Institutes (NCRI).

(j) Vocational training : In handicrafts, establishment of Self Help Groups (SHGs) of women, artisans and rural communities.

(k) Skill development : Conducting design development workshops for training craftsmen in different skills and crafts covering approximately 5000 people.

♦ ♦ ♦

DELHI

Association of Voluntary Agencies for Rural Development

(1)	Contact person	:	PM Tripathi
(2)	Designation	:	Director
(3)	Contact No.	:	011-23234690/ 23236782 Fax: 011-23232501
(4)	E-mail	:	avard@bol.net.in; avard@vsnl.com
(5)	Website	:	N.A.
(6)	Address	:	5(FF) Institutional Area, 1st Floor DeenDayal, Upadhyaya Marg New Delhi 110 002

About the organisation: Established in 1958, a network of over 500 autonomous voluntary organisations spread across the country. Membership is open to all voluntary agencies involved in rural development. A member of Asian NGO Coalition, ICVA and Commonwealth Foundation. Registration: Society. The institute builds awareness and gives training and action on Panchayat Raj; community development programme in villages and settlements of Bikaner Tehsil includes awareness generation, community organisation, sensitisation through workshops and village-wise follow-up campaigns; involved in micro-level planning and women's political empowerment through gram panchayats. Provides consultancies for USAID, Plan International; North-East India (Majuli Island in Jorhat district of Assam).

(a)	Year of establishment	:	1958
(b)	Registration No	:	N.A.
(c)	Location	:	New Delhi.
(d)	Coverage area	:	All over India
(e)	Staff strength	:	20
(f)	Source of funding	:	Ford Foundation, IGSSS, ActionAid, CAPART.
(g)	Approximate population served	:	1crore
(h)	Target groups	:	Women, tribal, SC/ST in rural areas.
(i)	Objectives	:	Promotes cooperation and understanding among voluntary agencies working for rural communities; serves as a link between national and international NGOs.

Details of Activities

(j)	Research	:	Women empowerment in 4 states i.e.,W.B, Maharashtra, Chattisgrah, and M.P
(k)	Organisations under establishment	:	AVARD Odisha, AVARD Naugarh, U.P, Koksara, dist Kalahandi.

• • •

Pradan

(1)	Contact Person	:	Mr. Soumen Biswas
(2)	Designation	:	Executive Director
(3)	Contact No.	:	011-26518619, 26514682, 26528534
(4)	Mobile	:	N.A.
(5)	E-Mail	:	Headoffice@pradan.net
(6)	Website	:	www.pradan.net
(7)	Address	:	Post Box No.3827 3 Community Shopping Centre Niti Bagh, New Delhi-110049

About the Organisation: PRADAN is a voluntary organisation registered under the Societies Registration Act of India. Established in Delhi in 1983, PRADAN was pioneered by a group of young professionals, all of whom were inspired by the conviction that individuals with knowledge resources and empathy for the marginalised must work with communities at the grassroots in order to help them overcome poverty.PRADAN believes that the path towards conquering economic poverty is through enhancing the livelihood capabilities of the poor and giving them access to sustainable income earning opportunities. In the process, the poor must be enabled to break free from their past, develop an alternative vision of their future and set achievable goals. They must be equipped with the technical, organisational, negotiating, and networking skills that will facilitate the fulfillment of their goals.

(a)	Year of establishment	:	1983
(b)	Registration No	:	201
(c)	Location	:	New Delhi
(d)	Coverage area	:	Backward Regions Of India
(e)	Staff strength	:	268
(f)	Source of funding	:	National And International
(g)	Approximate population served	:	N. A.
(h)	Target Groups	:	Rural India, Women, Child Development

(i) Objectives

- Promoting and nurturing self-help groups (SHGs) of poor women and strengthening them as organisations to leverage institutional finances for members' livelihoods.
- Developing and introducing locally suitable economic activities to increase productivity and incomes among SHG members; building synergic collaboration with a wide variety of stakeholders.
- Mobilising finances for livelihood assets and infrastructure from government bodies, donors, banks, and other financial institutions.

- Setting up mechanisms to sustain the livelihood gains made by the poor communities. Challenged by the abysmal poverty of millions of people across India, Pradan has resolved to reach out to 1.5 million poor people in the next 10 years as a part of its vision, pradan 2017.

Details of Activities

- Nurturing Self-Help Groups: Promotion of Self-Help Groups (SHG), provide guidance and assistance to women; identifying and promoting home-based Enterprises, financial intermediation, livelihood planning, and social Empowerment.
- Forest-based livelihood: Dwindling forests and the implementation of protection-oriented public policies, tasar cocoon production, lac cultivation and production, and trading of siali leaf plates, farm forestry.
- Natural Resource Management: Programmes comprise of enhancing productivity in agriculture; diversifying into new crops; setting up irrigation systems; and instituting entirely new ways of managing the natural resource base.
- Livestock development: Promotion of dairy and goat rearing activities in the project areas of Jharkhand, Odisha, and Rajasthan.

♦ ♦ ♦

GUJARAT

Buniyadi Shikshan Rachnatmak Sangh

(1)	Contact person	:	Arvindbhai C. Desai
(2)	Designation	:	President
(3)	Contact No.	:	02622 220134 (o)
(4)	Mobile	:	098251 33534
(5)	E-Mail	:	hss1961@gmail.com
(6)	Website	:	www.halpatisevasangh.org
(7)	Address	:	Halpati Seva Sangh Kamgar Ghar, Station Road, Bardoli Dist: Surat, Gujarat -394602.

About the organisation: Buniyadi Shiksan Rachnatmak Sangh is a union of nearly 500 educational institutions from entire South Gujarat which have been running schools and hostels (from 1 to 12) in remote tribal villages and contributing social reform and human welfare. Even B.Ed., P.T.C. colleges are serving the society on the lines of Gandhian principles of non violence and creative activities which can build and develop the overall personality of students.The members of Buniyadi Shiksan Rachnatmak Sangh have been working for the society so as to carry on the Gandhian work of practical learning for the students with respect to farming, craft, clean liners, and routine work by themselves.

(a)	Year of establishment	:	10-07-2003
(b)	Registration No	:	Society Registration Act 1860 Regi No: Guj/1102/surat
(c)	Location	:	Bardoli Dist: Surat (Guj)
(d)	Coverage area	:	South Gujarat (Surat, Narmada, Tapi, Navsari, Bharuch, Valsad, Dang, Vadodara, Panchmahal , etc)
(e)	Staff strength	:	7500 (Including Hostel & Ashram School)
(f)	Source of funding	:	Membership fees and Donations
(g)	Approximate population served	:	5 Lakhs
(h)	Target groups	:	Tribal population and welfare activities in rural areas.
(i)	Objectives	:	To spread Gandhian philosophy in learning education and developmental activities.

Details of Activities

(j)	Research	:	Study of rural areas of South Gujarat with respect to population education, health, hygiene and as well as basic welfare work, environmental imbalance.

(k)	Vocational training	:	Black smiths, Carpenters, Driving, Welders, Wireman, Computer, Growing Nursery, Carpets weaving, Tailoring, etc.,
(l)	Skill development	:	Development of Rural skills like, Black smithy, Carpentery, driving, Welding, Wiring, Computer, Growing Nursery, Carpets weaving etc.
(m)	Organisations under establishment	:	Have the network of all activities with nearly 500 institution from South Gujarat.

♦ ♦ ♦

Gujarat Vidyapeeth

(1)	Contact person	:	Dr. Rajendra Khimani
(2)	Designation	:	Secretary
(3)	Contact No.	:	079-27541392, 40016204 (R) 27541288, (vc) 079-27546767(secretary)
(4)	Mobile	:	09825957967
(5)	E- Mail	:	registrar@gujarat vidyapith.org
(6)	Website	:	www.gujaratvidyapith.org
(7)	Address	:	AshramamRoad, Ahmedabad, Pin-380 014.

About the organisation: Gujarat Vidyapith was founded by Mahatma Gandhi on October 18, 1920 to liberate the Indian youths from the shackles of British colonial rule. As against the British colonial education system, propounded by Lord Macaulay, that produced human resources for the oppressive British Empire, Gandhi wanted his Vidyapith to prepare the youths for the task of national reconstruction and usher in 'Hind Swaraj', the India of his dream.

Gujarat Vidyapith was established as a national university without a government charter. Gandhiji was its life-long chancellor. Professor A T Gidwani was its founder vice-chancellor. Later, many more institutions, colleges and schools were affiliated to the Vidyapith. In 1923, the total number of students in these institutions stood at 30,000. After Gandhiji, Sardar Vallabhbhai Patel, Dr. Rajendra Prasad and Morarji Desai adorned the post of chancellor of the Vidyapith.

The institute imparts higher education with an integrated system of education teaching from the nursery to the doctorate level.

(a)	Year of establishment	:	1920 ,it is a deemed university since 1963
(b)	Registration No	:	Ahmedabad E-591
(c)	Location	:	Ahmedabad
(d)	Coverage area	:	All over the country
(e)	Staff strength	:	26
(f)	Source of funding	:	U.G.C. (University Grants Commission)
(g)	Approximate population served	:	30,000 students per year.
(h)	Target groups	:	Students
(i)	Objectives	:	

To prepare workers of character, ability, culture, and dedication for the conduct of the movements connected with the regeneration of the country in accordance with the ideals given by Mahatma Gandhi.

Details of Activities

(j) Research : Education, Gujarati, Hindi, Rural Economics, History, Sociology, Social work, Gandhian Philosophy, Jainism, Buddhism, Science and Non-violence, Journalism and Mass Communication, Library and Information Science, Archival Science, Computer Science, Micro biology, Physical education, Home Science, Rural Management, Population and Adult Education, Peace Studies and Conflict Resolution.

(k) Vocational training : Light music, Computer hardware, Chhanda Shastra, Art and Craft.

(l) Skill development : Instrumentation, Yoga, Audio-video.

(m) Organisations under establishment :

- Mahadev Desai Samajseva Mahavidyalaya (Mahadev Desai College Of Social Work), Ahmedabad
- Mahadev Desai Gramseva Mahavidyalaya (Mahadev Desai College Of Social Work), Sadra
- Mahadev Desai Shareerik Shkshan Mahavidyalaya (Mahadev Desai College of Education), Sadra
- Mahadev Desai Gramseva Mahavidyalaya (Mahadev Desai College Of Social Work), Randheja
- College of Education (Shikshan Mahavidyalaya)
- Hindi Teachers Training College {Hindi Shikshak Mahavidyalaya)
- Praudh Shikshan (State Resource Centre for Adult Education)
- Nirantar Shikshan (Continuous Education)
- Gramvyavasthapan Kendra (Rural Managment Centre)
- Biogas Research & Microbiology Centre
- Tribal Research & Training Institute
- Bhartiy Bhasa Sanskriti Sansthan
- I. T, I., Shahibaug, Ahmedabad
- Krushi Vigyan Kendra (K.V.K.), Dethali
- Krushi Vigyan Kendra (K.V.K.), Randheja
- Krushi Vigyan Kendra (K.V.K.), Ambheti
- Kocharab Ashram, Ahmedabad
- Gujarat Kumar Vinay Mandir, Ahmedabad
- Gramseva Kendra, Dethali
- Gramseva Kendra, Bhalada
- Gramseva Kendra, Bochasan
- Gramseva Kendra, Bharel
- Gramseva Kendra, Ambheti

♦ ♦ ♦

Jagruti Trust

(1)	Contact person	:	Ashwin Kumar D. Parmar
(2)	Designation	:	Director
(3)	Contact No.	:	02744-224870/ 220297
(4)	Mobile	:	09426392871
(5)	E- Mail	:	ad-kabir@yahoo.co.in
(6)	Website	:	N.A.
(7)	Address	:	115, jagruthi complex, near fountain, PO Deesa, Banaskantha dist, Gujarat – 385535.

About the organisation: The trust is working for the education of pre-primary through Balwadis. The trust is working for upliftment of poor people in social aspect, awareness of human rights, removal of untouchability, child labour and problems of women by contacting personally, health problems of SC, ST, OBC and other weaker sections. Works for environment by eco-club, plantation, seminars and rallies on awareness of environment, plants, animals, birds, forests, rivers, land, water and pollution.

(a)	Year of establishment	:	1976
(b)	Registration No	:	E 191 Banaskantha (28-12-1976)
(c)	Location	:	Banaskantha district, Gujarat.
(d)	Coverage area	:	Entire Gujarat
(e)	Staff strength	:	150
(f)	Source of funding	:	Self funding
(g)	Approximate population served	:	3000 approximately.
(h)	Target groups	:	Children, women, SC, ST, OBC and other weaker sections
(i)	Objectives	:	Upliftment of SC, ST and OBC and other weaker section of the society by educational social and economic activities.

Details of Activities

(j)	Research	:	Medical checkups by mobile van and works to eradicate diseases like Polio, AIDS, TB, Hepatitis, etc.
(l)	Skill development	:	Working for health problems of SC, ST, OBC and other poor people of weaker section. Running a dispensary to solve health problems.
(m)	Organisations under establishment	:	Two ashram shalas, with hostels, three high schools, three uttar buniyadi vidyamandirs. The trust is running 16 units for educational purpose.

♦ ♦ ♦

Lokbharti Gram Vidyapeeth

(1)	Contact person	:	Dr. H.B. Suthar
(2)	Designation	:	Principal
(3)	Contact No.	:	+91 2846 - 283322
(4)	Mobile	:	09427247429
(5)	E- Mail	:	lokseva_mahavidyalaya@rediffmail.com
(6)	Website	:	www.lokbharti.org
(7)	Address	:	Lok Bharti, Sanosara, Taluka – Sihor District: Bhavnagar, Gujarat, INDIA.

About the organisation: Inaugurated on 28th May, 1953 by Shri Kaka Saheb Kalelkar, the Great Gandhian, and based on the Sarvodaya principles of truth and non-violence, the Lok Bharti Gramvidhyapith is an ideal example that shows how basic and higher education can contribute towards solving rural problems practically.Basic education has to spread to even the lowest rungs of society, and this alone can still instill a sense of humility in people. With this as the foundation, Lok Bharti imparts knowledge to its students which is suitable to the Indian psyche and culture, as well as useful to society at large, Not only is this basic education given free without any fee, the needy students are also given scholarships.The Lok Bharti campus is situated on the river bank of Sindari, amidst seven ponds and expanses of greenery, 450 students stay in hostel and 250 members stay in staff quarters- like one big family. They provide a suitable environment for the experiment of community life.

(a)	Year of establishment	:	1953
(b)	Registration No	:	Recognised under 2F and 12 B of UGC act.
(c)	Location	:	Bhavnagar
(d)	Coverage area	:	Gujarat
(e)	Staff strength	:	33
(f)	Source of funding	:	UGC grant in aid - Rs. 44.3 lakhs
(g)	Approximate population served	:	300 students every year, and 2000 villagers
(h)	Target groups	:	Rural poor children, tribals and differently abled students.
(i)	Objectives	:	The aims and objectives of Lok Bharti are represented by the motto, Vidya or introspective knowledge of self, and Avidya or knowledge and skills that one learns in life, must be taught together in correlated manner based on practical, productive labor and social living together.

Details of Activities

- Kinder Garten Camp : Such camps were held at Lok Bharti P.T.C. Centre. The P.T.C. students of first and second years and F. Y. B.R.S. students are imparted such training which is now very systematic. Tribal Area Camp: Through direct practical work, lectures, surveys, health activities and children's education a study of the tribal life-style, their economic condition, their exploitation, their beliefs, marriage songs and their relation with the forest is undertaken.
- Gram Shibir (the village camp) : There is an intensive study camp for the T.Y.B.R.S. students. The institution has adopted 30 villages around Lok Bharti and in any village a ten-day camp is organized to enable the students to know and understand an Indian village, its problems and its strengths and weaknesses so that they can feel the pulse of real India.
- Educational Tours : Educational tours have been made an integral part of the syllabus of Lok Bharti which enables the students to see and experience what they have read or imagined.

(j) Research :

Lok Bharti has been keenly aware since its establishment about the significance of research work in education. But in the early years we could undertake only surveys related to economics conditions, social plight of Harijans and the status of women.

Then we adopted the approach of trying out the various varities of crops such as Sankar-4 cotton, Tuwer Pigeon Pea, ground-nuts, Millet and then propagate the results. When chemical fertilizer was first introduced, we worked on its various uses and then followed the promotion and propaganda of farming methods, how to make Gur - Jaggery brighter, horticulture and compost were made popular among the farmer through extension and research work. Thus Lok Bharti played a very significant role in the field of research from its very establishment.

Lok Bharti also prepared people mentally to understand and accept the findings of research work. This work was done very intensively and well. Thus first we confined our activity to spread information about information about applied research carried by other institution of All India Standing.

(k) Vocational training : Many occasions such as celebration of national festivals in villages, rural camps, week-end programmes, placement with farmer-families, accident or natural calamities and relief-works undertaken during such disasters are used as means to carry out extension work as a part of useful educational activity

(l) Skill development : Agriculture, goshala, watershed programmes, nursery plantations etc.

(m) Organisations under establishment : (1) The Post Graduate Centre for Higher Rural Studies (M.R.S. - Master of Rural Studies) (2) Graduate Basic Training Centre.

• • •

Maitri Vidyapith

(1)	Contact person	:	Dr. Jayshreeben Desai
(2)	Designation	:	Chief Functionary
(3)	Contact No.	:	02752-220988
(4)	Mobile	:	09825994474
(5)	E- Mail	:	maitrividyapith@gmail.com
(6)	Website	:	www.maithrividyapith.org
(7)	Address	:	Surendranagar, Gujarat.

About the organization: Maitri (friendship) is to inculcate the qualities of compassion, love and dedication for the entire living world by means of non-expectant behaviour. The educational structure created to develop the above qualities and virtues is the 'Vidyapith'. This institute aspires to produce such teachers, sanyasins of education in the society and create such atmosphere that would inculcate in them the sense of dedication and martyrdom for the society and the country. To run educational institutions, chhatralayas and right schools to impart education from pre-primary to graduation.

(a)	Year of establishment	:	1974
(b)	Registration No	:	E210 under Public Charitable Trust.
(c)	Location	:	Surendranagar,
(d)	Coverage area	:	Gujarat
(e)	Staff strength	:	16 including hostel staff
(f)	Source of Funding	:	From Gujarat Government for schools and staff salaries.
(g)	Approximate population served	:	15,000
(h)	Target Groups	:	Children, handicapped, aged, diseased, and the destitutes.
(i)	Objectives	:	To prepare dedicated and intelligent teachers and social workers who are prepared to work in the rural areas.

- To establish and manage medical treatment centres for the diseased, the suffering, the destitute, the handicapped and the aged people.
- To develop the 'Bal-Bharti' activity for the development of the children.
- Social and economic development for economically backward classes.
- To organize cultural programmes keeping in view our folk culture

Details of Activities

(j)	Vocational training	: Vocational training courses, celebrates festivals training camps, youth camps, yogasan camps.
(k)	Organisations under establishment	: 1)M.D. Doshi Lok vidyalay – surendranagar,only for boys. Present strength is 300. 2) Manav mandir Manjula Kanya Vidyalaya only for girls– present strength 150. (Regd.No.E-308)

♦ ♦ ♦

Nootan Gram Vidyapeth

(1)	Contact person	:	Dr.Sudheer Bhai H.Jani
(2)	Designation	:	Principal and Dean
(3)	Contact No.	:	02643- 281085
(4)	Mobile	:	9426878550
(5)	E- Mail	:	sudheerbhaijani@ yahoomail.com
(6)	Website	:	N.A.
(7)	Address	:	Thava, Valiya, Bharuch Gujarat-393130.

About the organisation: This is a Degree College established in 1989 and after ten years this college is affiliated to Veer Narmad University. Nootan Gram Vidyapeth, is located in Tribal pocket of Gujarat State. The course offered is Bachelor of rural studies (BRS).

(a)	Year of establishment	:	1989
(b)	Registration No	:	F 157 Surat (dt.2/11/1966), Established under Gandhi vidyapith.
(c)	Location	:	Bharauch, Gujarat
(d)	Coverage area	:	Gujarat
(e)	Staff strength	:	22
(f)	Source of funding	:	Grants from the state Government
(g)	Approximate population served	:	5000
(h)	Target groups	:	Tribal people
(i)	Objectives	:	To educate the tribal youth in the area of rural studies

Details of Activities

(j)	Research	:	Social auditing for rural employment
(k)	Skill development	:	Electric connections in the village, Need assessment survey, Sanitation, Gobar gas, drop out education.

• • •

Samaj Seva Mahavidyalay

(1)	Contact person	:	Jayatibhai N Patel
(2)	Designation	:	Chief Functionary
(3)	Contact No.	:	02625-222038
(4)	Mobile	:	09925328808
(5)	E-Mail	:	N.A.
(6)	Website	:	N.A.
(7)	Address	:	Gandhi Vidyapeeth, Vedchhi,Valod, Tapi-384641.

About the organisation: This institute is located in a small village named Vedchhi, situated in the backward area of Surat district in Gujarat. Shri Jagatram Dave, along with Shri Chunibhai Mehta started teaching young children of the village and finally Vedchhi Swaraj Ashrama (residential community centre) was found places for attaining higher education. In 1967, Gandhi Vidyapith was founded. Since 1980 it functions in the name of Samaj Seva Mahavidyalaya (the college of social services). Now a 4 year degree course in Samaj Shastra and 3 year degree course in Agriculture is being conducted. Gandhi Vidyapith holds about 113 acres of land, of which 80 acres are under plough, producing sugarcane, paddy, vegetables, mangoes and other mined crops. While the rest of the land is covered by approach roads, buildings, water works etc.

(a)	Year of establishment	:	1980
(b)	Registration No	:	F157 Surat(dt.2/11/1966), Established under Gandhi vidyapith, college code : 53.
(c)	Location	:	valod, Gujarat
(d)	Coverage area	:	Gujarat
(e)	Staff strength	:	50
(f)	Source of funding	:	Main source is from the profits of agriculture produce and by donations & grants from Govt.
(g)	Approximate population served	:	7,500 students
(h)	Target groups	:	Students
(i)	Objectives	:	To provide higher education to the children in the village Vedchhi.

Details of Activities

(j)	Research	:	Tours, camps, group discussions etc.,
(k)	Vocational training	:	Cleaning, functions & prayers
(l)	Skill development	:	Runs Balwadis, social services, encourage village industries, propagate against alcoholism, adult education.

♦ ♦ ♦

Suruchi Shikshan Vasahat Trust

(1)	Contact person	:	Ram Kumar Singh
(2)	Designation	:	Managing Trustee & Director
(3)	Contact No.	:	02622-220095/220258
(4)	Mobile	:	09377774764
(5)	E- Mail	:	atrcbardoli@gmail.com
(6)	Website	:	N.A.
(7)	Address	:	Suruchi Vasahat, PO Box No 4, At- Bardoli, Dist- Surat, Gujarat-394601.

About the organisation: This trust was established in 1988 and is based on Nai talim education and undertakes works on 'Sarvodaya Samaj. Shri Mohanbhai Parikh, a Gandhian and a technician with deep knowledge of agriculture, was identified to lead and give shape to this holistic approach. Suruchi Technical Center came into being in 1960 with this holistic approach in mind for serving the landless poor by not only improving their functioning by improved and user-friendly tools but also provisioning Vocational training that can lead them to newer and skilled occupation that fetches more income. During this era Land Gift Movement of Acharya Vinoba Bhave was impressing many landowners and one such generous person donated the land in the outskirts of Bardoli, a historical town famous for its Bardoli Satyagraha by Sardar Vallabhbhai Patel during independence struggle. This set the point of departure for Suruchi.

(a)	Year of establishment	:	1988
(b)	Registration No	:	E2624/surat regd.no. Societies act, 1950
(c)	Location	:	Bardoli
(d)	Coverage area	:	6 districts of south Gujarat
(e)	Staff strength	:	Full Time: 24, Part Time:18
(f)	Source of funding	:	60% from own production, 40% through project funding from NABARD, KVIC, DST, NCRI etc.
(g)	Approximate population served	:	40 villages around 20 talukas.
(h)	Target groups	:	All needy and poor people of Surat, Tapi, Dangas, Nvasari and Bharuch

(i) Objectives

- Develop technologies that help poor farmers embrace scientific agriculture.
- Help them understand science in their daily life.
- Teach them intelligent and user-friendly craftsmanship. So they can express themselves and achieve progress.

Details of Activities

- Design and development of more than hundred agri-tools.

- Development of replicable village model of vermi compost production unit. Development of ergonomically suitable workstation layout of smithy.

(j) Research

- To undertake all sorts of research activities related to rural and tribal development and collaborate with likeminded R &D and Design Institutions for fulfillment of our objectives.

(k) Vocational training

- Providing technical and management training to the poor and tribal rural youth. Both boys and girls to create a young professional cadre in the villages.

(l) Skill development

- Developments of appropriate design of box type solar cooker, Damru Chulha, solar distill water unit and Garbage gas manure plant.

(m) Organisations under establishment : In a quest to better organize the efforts an institute was registered on 07 September 1963 under trust act with a name of Suruchi Chhapshala Trust (Printing Press). Three centers commence in one after the other keeping these objectives in mind, simultaneously:

(i) Agricultural Tools Research Center

(ii) Yantra Vidyalaya

(iii) Suruchi Chhapshala

♦ ♦ ♦

Vishwamangalam

(1)	Contact person	:	Manubhai Patel
(2)	Designation	:	The Secretary
(3)	Contact No.	:	02772-239522 02772-239283
(4)	Mobile	:	9427853583
(5)	E-mail	:	anera 123@gmail.com
(6)	Website	:	N.A.
(7)	Address	:	Viswamangalam, ANERA, Vishvamangalam, (Post), Himmatnagar, SabarKanta (Dist), Gujarat–383 001

About the organisation: Vishwamangalam was established at Anera village in Himmatnagar Taluka of Sabarkantha district in North Gujarat, situated at a distance of about 10 kms from Himmatnagar town, in the year 1959 to conduct experiments and exercises in rural development. In the beginning the institution has only one campus at Anera village but later another campus was developed which is known as Vrindavan campus. Vishwamanglam is a exclusive organization in Himatnagar taluka meant to catalyse self-reliant development among the backward rural people of the Sabarkantha district. Vishwamanglam is a pioneering voluntary organization in Sabarkantha district and is a symbol of well knit rural development complex. All the multifarious rural development activities of this complex are under the management of a trust which had been established on 8 Jun 1959 by a band of committed social activists. The basic structure of Vishwamangalam is to awaken the people, to make them identify their own problems and to prepare them to devise their own solutions and plan of action. The activists in Vishwamangalam believe that, today, the fight has to be fought against wide-spread illiteracy, ignorance, inequity, injustice and misery.

(a)	Year of establishment	:	23-07-1960
(b)	Registration No	:	It was registered a trust under the Bombay Public Trust Act 1950 (Registration No.F-21 dated 23.7.1960).
(c)	Location	:	Vishvamangalam, Himmatnagar, SabarKanta, Gujarat
(d)	Coverage area	:	Sabar Kantha, Gujarat
(e)	Staff strength	:	72
(f)	Source of funding	:	NCRI, Ministry of Social Welfare Board.
(g)	Approximate population served	:	5,000
(h)	Target groups	:	General

(i) Objectives

The aim of Vishwamangalam is to create a new society – Sarvoday Society. So, it performs various activities of peoples education along with its school education programme.

The speciality of the work of people's education conducted by Vishwamangalam is that volunteers are not engaged on jobs for this work, but teachers of various Vidyalayas perform this task as an integral part of education of their own students.

Details of Activities

Vishwamanglam's involvement in community education began with its establishment in the year 1959. Services which this organization provides are mainly education-centred. Educational development work of Vishwamangalam has been fairly successful and what is remarkable is that it is effectively integrated with social, economic and psychological development of the rural people. Vishwamangalam's target population was fortunate in the farsighted leadership of Vishwamangalam that came into help them to mobilize themselves for their own progress in development. In order to induce a psychology of goodwill among the villagers, an affectionate and loving treatment was extended to them. A massive programme of social education was undertaken to wean them away from the evils of such intoxicants as drinking liquor, smoking 'bidi' and consuming opium which were responsible for ruining their health and damaging their economic condition.

The following activities of people's education are performed with the objective that the students may understand social problems and help in their solutions and may perform their duty with compassion for poor of the country.

- Village services: Teachers and students go to village and perform the following activities on occasions like Gandhi Jayanti Week and Sarvoday Parva.
- Exhibitions: Day-by-day new areas of knowledge and science are explored.
- Social Welfare Scheme: Vishwamangalam conducts 30 Balwadis with the help of 57 Bal-Sevikas in 30 villages of the region and every year, they impart basic education to 1000 children.
- Khadi Gramodyog: At Vishwamangalam Khadi is used for clothes. The staff members of the institute wear khadi clothes. Students' uniform is also of khadi.

(j) Vocational training : Education, women development, animal husbandry, plantation, Khadi Gram Udhyog, Creche management and Sarvodaya work.

♦ ♦ ♦

HIMACHAL PRADESH

Society for Soicial Upliftment Through Rural Action

(1)	Contact person	:	Mr. Subhash Mendhapurkar
(2)	Designation	:	Founder and Director
(3)	Contact No.	:	+ 91 1792 283725 + 91 1792 283772 + 91 1792 283716
(4)	Mobile	:	N. A.
(5)	E-mail	:	sutrahp@gmail.com
(6)	Website	:	www.sutra.org.in
(7)	Address	:	P.O. Jagjit Nagar, Via: Jubbar, District Solan, Himachal Pradesh, India, 173 225

About the organisation: "SUTRA was founded to act as a 'conscious keeper' of society. In order to achieve that, we needed to establish our credibility first which was done through service provision model, and then we started acting as Conscious Keepers by raising number of issues that affect Gender Equity". Subhash Mendharpurkar grew up in the slums of Pune in an asset-less family. He later studied at university where he obtained a Postgraduate certificate in Community Development. After working as a free-lance journalist and lecturer in undergraduate colleges, he founded SUTRA with the support of other NGOs in 1977. SUTRA is active in Himachal Pradesh, a small and hilly state near the Himalayas in North-West India. Being one of India's richer states, the net per capita income equals about 2000 (US $ 45) Rs., but this number is difficult to measure as it is mainly a subsistence economy that prevails.

(a)	Year of establishment	:	1977
(b)	Registration No	:	3690/85; Shimla
(c)	Location	:	Solan, Himachal Pradesh
(d)	Coverage area	:	Himachal Pradesh
(e)	Staff strength	:	30-600 voluntary, most of them women
(f)	Source of funding	:	Health Water resources
(g)	Approximate population served	:	.....
(h)	Target groups	:	women, child, Dalit, single women, children
(i)	Objectives	:	SUTRA believes that all the democratic institutions created under the Constitution of India shall fulfil their constitutional obligations towards citizens only when people are collectively empowered and the state evolves all its policies based on the principle of micro-credit.

Details of Activities: Through building local women groups in order to participate in local governance. Local self-help groups in which the violence women encounter is discussed and appropriate solutions are sought. It is also a basis for encouragement in their daily struggle.

(j) Research

- Reproductive health
- Declining male:female ratio/female foeticide
- Sustainable micro-credits
- Transparency of local governance

(k) Vocational training

- Micro-credits are organized. All the women of a community save a small amount per month and then decide who most in need of it is. They are mostly used to buy income generators such as cattle.
- Education and sensitization of teenage boys and girls about gender and equity issues.
- Other projects such as watershed development and crèches are developed in function of the current needs. Such flexible projects allow an all-round support to women in their daily lives.

(l) Skill development : One-day and one-week-long camps are organized where women are taught the basics about nutrition and other most important aspects of their daily lives are addressed.Gender and Equity & Life Free From Violence. Micro-Credit, Local self-governance, Awareness programme for teenagers

(m) Organisations under establishment : SUTRA shares its knowledge with other NGOs. Members of other organisations are given training and resources are produced and readily available to other NGOs, government and UN bodies.

♦ ♦ ♦

JAMMU AND KASHMIR

Jk Developmental Action Group

(1)	Contact person	:	Sri. Mushtaq Ahmad
(2)	Designation	:	Chairman
(3)	Contact No.	:	0194-2476243
(4)	Mobile	:	09906684250, 09906962414
(5)	E- Mail	:	mushtaq@jkdag.org, info@jkdag.org
(6)	Website	:	www.jkdag.org
(7)	Address	:	PB No. 1158, Shivpora, Batwara, Srinagar- Jammu & Kashmir, 190001

About the organisation: JK Developmental Action Group (JK DAG) is a voluntary organization established in the year 2000. JK DAG tackles underlying causes of underdevelopment so that people can become self-sufficient. Recognizing that general masses both men and women especially the weaker sections of the society suffer from menaces like poverty,illiteracy,hatred and backwarness,JK DAG places special emphasis on working with these sections to create permanent social change and transformation of society. Discarded and needy are at the heart of JK DAG's community-based efforts to improve basic education, prevent the spread of HIV, increase access to clean water and sanitation, expand economic opportunity and protect natural resources. JK DAG also delivers emergency aid to survivors of war and natural disasters, and helps people rebuild their lives.

(a)	Year of establishment	:	2000-2001
(b)	Registration No	:	Registration No.5150-S under the J&K State Societies Registration Act-1V of 1998
(c)	Location	:	Srinagar
(d)	Coverage area	:	Jammu and Kashmir state
(e)	Staff strength	:	12
(f)	Source of funding	:	Central, state government and private foreign institutions.
(g)	Approximate population served	:	2000
(h)	Target groups	:	Discarded and needy
(i)	Objectives	:	To make Gandhian thought an integral part of the modern educational curriculum in the rural institutions. Strengthen teacher training facilities for Gandhian basic education.

Details of Activities

Agriculture and Natural Resources, Education, emergency relief, health, HIV/AIDS, Nutrition, Water, Sanitation and Environmental Health, and economic development.

(j) Skill development : CARE works with farmers to increase their crop and livestock yields through activities such as planting new seed varieties, animal husbandry, home gardening and irrigation.

• • •

Self Employed Womens Association

(1)	Contact person	:	Imtiyaz Hussain
(2)	Designation	:	Patron-in-Chief
(3)	Contact No.	:	09419018453
(4)	Mobile	:	09797070185
(5)	E-Mail	:	sewajk@yahoo.com, sewaorganisationjk@gmail.com
(6)	Website	:	N.A
(7)	Address	:	58-Govt. Housing, Colony, Chanapora Srinagar, Kashmir, India-190015.

About the Organisation

(a)	Year of establishment	:	1994
(b)	Registration No.	:	2162-S of 1994
(c)	Location	:	Srinagar
(d)	Coverage area	:	All Districts of Kashmir Division of Jammu and Kashmir State.
(e)	Staff strength	:	Technical 15, Non Technical 10
(f)	Source of funding	:	Government funding, Donations
(g)	Approximate population served	:	5000
(h)	Target groups	:	Youth, Women, Rural Community

(i) Objectives

- To provide and extend social welfare services to people in general and for women in particular and work for their socio economic and livelihood development and empowerment.
- To establish vocational education and training centers in every block of the state.
- To open new avenues of employment for un-employed youth and women by establishing different income and employment generation units whether in farm or non-farm sectors.
- To establish Employment and Technology Resource Centers for Transfer of Technologies (TOT) up to commercialization stage.
- To organize workshops, seminars, capacity building programmes, trainings and demonstrations etc for popularization of science and technology etc.
- To rehabilitate the destitute affected by natural climates or otherwise and create facilities for all-round rehabilitation etc.

Details of Activities

1. Agriculture Extension & Management.
2. Socio Economic & Livelihood Development.

3. Vocational Education & Trainings
4. Transfer of Technologies (TOT) and capacity buildings.
5. Entrepreneurship Development.
6. Rehabilitation and development of Artisans.
7. Information ,Education and Communication (IEC)
   - Popularization of Science & Technology, demonstration and dissemination
   - Transfer of Technology through agriculture extension.
   - Vocational Education & Trainings.
   - Trainings and Capacity Building
   - Entrepreneurship Development.

(j) Vocational training

1. Computer Hardware
2. Poultry Farming
3. Vegetable Cultivation
4. Computer Aided Designing in Handicraft Industry
5. Hybrid Seed Formation.
6. Live-Stock Development

(k) Skill development

Handi crafts.
Computer Hardware
Diary Development & Milk Processing
Medicinal Plants Cultivation

(l) Organisations under establishment

♦ ♦ ♦

JHARKHAND

Badlao Foundation

(1)	Contact person	:	Ms. Rashmi Anand
(2)	Designation	:	President
(3)	Contact No.	:	06433 -228592
(4)	Mobile	:	N.A
(5)	E- Mail	:	badlaofoundation@rediffmail.com
(6)	Website	:	N.A
(7)	Address	:	At: Mihijam, P.O. : Mihijam, Dist. - Jamtara, State : Jharkhand Pin : 815 354

About the organization: "Badlao" means Change. The formation, functioning and development of Badlao Foundation confirms it is committed to strive to bring change in society that stands for socially transformed qualitative state of self-reliance, based on equity and justice.

Badlao Foundation stands for equality and equity-based gender-just, socially self- reliant transformed society.

(a)	Year of establishment	:	1982
(b)	Registration No	:	Under Indian Trust Act 1882 Vide No.131/1982-83 dated 14.9.1982
(c)	Location	:	Jharkhand
(d)	Coverage area	:	Now it covers 534 villages of 21 blocks in six districts viz. Deoghar, Dumka, Jamtara, Godda, Sahebganj and Pakur of Santhal Parganas division of Jharkhand state, India.
(e)	Staff strength	:	9
(f)	Source of funding	:	Foreigndonors ICCO, Netherlands KKS (Karl Kubel Stiftung), German Agency supported by European Commission CCF (Christian Children's Fund), USA Indiandonors District Rural Development Authority, Jamtara, Pakur and Dumka Khadi Village Industry Commission (KVIC), Mumbai National Bank of Agriculture and Rural Development (NABARD), Dumka and Jamtara
(g)	Approximate population served	:	In lakhs

(h) Target groups : Badlao Foundation works amongst the rural population. Its primary constituencies include Santhal and Paharia communities, Scheduled Castes and other families living "Below Poverty Line".

(i) Objectives : Badlao Foundation endeavors to empower people for social transformation to achieve self-reliance and gender justice through participatory efforts and to ensure ecological balance. People in Badlao are committed and competent to creatively initiate and persevere on their tasks, to uphold human dignity, to strive for an equitable social structure and to enable women and socially disadvantaged to claim their rights.

Details of Activities

(j) Research : On Micro Finance

(k) Vocational training : Workshop on Right to Information, Legal Awareness of Women through Women Advocates,Workshop on "Rural Reconstruction and Voluntary Organizations", Workshop on "Adivasi Daughters and Property Right" (In collaboration with Voluntary Action Network).

(l) Skill development : Livelihood Promotion, Environment & NRM, Child Development, Community Health & Sanitation, Lobby and Advocacy, Education.

(m) Organisations under establishment : Jharkhand Swechhik Sanstha Manch

VHAJ (Voluntary Health Association of Jharkhand)

Voluntary Action Network

♦ ♦ ♦

Gramin Samaj Kalyan Vikas Manch

(1)	Contact person	:	Md.Hashmat Rabbani
(2)	Designation	:	Secretary
(3)	Contact No.	:	06562-222867
(4)	Mobile	:	09431159447
(5)	E-Mail	:	gskvm@yahoo.com
(6)	Website	:	www.gskvm.org
(7)	Address	:	Jailhata, Daltonganj, Palamu Jharkhand- 822101.

About the organisation: Dreaming together for a better world for all; to establish just society based on the value of equality, Justice, democracy and brother hood, where no one remains hungry, illiterate, exploited, homeless and deprived of fundamental right.

The Gramin Samaj Kalyan Vikas Manch (GSKVM) is charitable, secular, Indian, non-profit, non-government voluntary organization (NGVO) of Palamu, Jharkhand. It serves all the deprived humanity without distinction of race, caste & religion. The organization empowers a society based on the value of equality, justice, democracy and brotherhood by the valued dedicated volunteer and ideologists of Maulana Azad, Bapu, J.P. and Mother Teresa.

(a)	Year of Estalishment	:	1990
(b)	Registration No	:	339
(c)	Location	:	Jharkhand
(d)	Coverage area	:	Palamu, Garhwa, Latehar, Deoghar & Dumka Distrits in Jharkhand.
(e)	Staff strength	:	Full Time 10 Part Time 15
(f)	Source of funding	:	Government, Dist. Administration & Foreign Funding
(g)	Approximate population served	:	50,000
(h)	Target groups	:	Women, children disable, youth, mentally ill people, tribals & farmers.

(i) Objectives

- To eradicate poverty and promote self reliance by improving the quality of life of the poor, deprived community through meaningful socio-economic growth in all phases of life.
- To educate, organize, advocate and empower the rural poor for promoting development as a liberting force aimed at gender equity, social justice ,self empowerment and entitlement realization.
- To promote support and develop a civil society by providing opportunity and securing rights of the underprivileged section of the society.

- Through effective presence with the poor and marginalized accompanying them as they empower themselves and affirm their dignity leading to fullness of life.

Details of Activities

(j)	Research	: Tribal Education.
(k)	Vocational training	: Youth & Women.
(l)	Skill development	: PMEGP Beneficiaries, Unemployed people.

♦ ♦ ♦

Kasturba Khadi Gramodyog Sansthan

(1) Contact person : Shankar Singh

(2) Designation : Manager

(3) Contact No. : 06522 290500; 0651 2482655

(4) Mobile : N.A.

(5) E-Mail : N.A.

(6) Website : N.A.

(7) Address : Khadi Bhawan, Muri, P.O – Chota Muri, Randhi District, Jharkhand, 835101.

About the organisation: Kasturba Khadi Gramodyog Sansthan has established production of khadi and sale counters in Muri, Silli, Gola, Kujar, Chaihasa, Ranchi, under RPDS programme training in silk production and manufacturing in Sudur Gram under Chaihasa district to generate income and occupation to 1000 people of that area in the year 1995-96 and was very successful. The organization is providing occupation to 100 people every year in different ways. Apart from the manufacturing of khadi other creative work like folk education, importance of health and good agricultural practices are imparted in the Sudur Gram.

KKGS is direct listed with Khadi and Village Industries Commission, Mumbai. Under the KVIC programmes this Sansthan started functioning for Khadi as many other village industries training programmes to create employment in the rural area. The Sansthan provides training as well as production in Khadi. Previously also thousands of artisans were trained and engaged in Tasar silk spinning, weaving, tailoring and designing, by the Sansthan.

(a) Year of establishment : 07/03/2006

(b) Registration No : Society Registration Act of 21/1860

(c) Location : Chota Muri, Jharkhand

(d) Coverage area : Tribal areas of Jharkhand

(e) Staff strength : ....

(f) Source of funding : Khadi and Village Industries Commission, District Rural Development agencies of state Govt.

(g) Approximate population served : 10000

(h) Target groups : women, artisans.

(i) Objectives : It mainly works on Silk Weaving, Designing, Training and production of silk. Its area of operation is Tribal areas of Jharkhand.

(1) The social objective of providing employment.

(2) The economic objective of providing saleable articles.

(3) The wider objective of creating self-reliance among the people and building up of a strong rural community spirit.

Details of Activities: Manufacturing and training of Khadi Cloth & Sale of Ghani oil, Training of Carpentary Black Smithy, Educaiton, Health etc.

Since last two years KKGS, Muri is imparting training in Tasar Silk spinning, weaving, tailoring and designing under NCRI programmes successfully.

♦ ♦ ♦

People Institute for Development & Training

(1)	Contact person	:	Indira Das Gupta
(2)	Designation	:	Chair person
(3)	Contact No.	:	+91-11- 29532408, 29531282, 29531296 +91-11-2953299529531296
(4)	Mobile	:	09810816150
(5)	E- Mail	:	info@peoplesinstitute.com pidt2007@gmail.com, pidt@del6.vsnl.net.in
(6)	Website	:	www.peoplesinstitute.com; www.anandalaya.org; www.volunteerindia.org
(7)	Address	:	The People's Institute for Development and Training (PIDT) "People's House" A-12 Paryavaran Complex Saket-Maidangarhi Road Saidullajab, New Delhi-110030

About the Organisation: People's Institute for Development and Training is an action research and teaching–learning institute. It's acronym PIDT means "oppressed" in most North Indian languages. PIDT seeks to catalyze development of humane, sustainable and egalitarian societies. PIDT works to ameliorate social conditions of oppression and deprivation by increasing the capacities of people and the opportunities available to them so that they may design different futures for themselves. PIDT uses participatory planning and full engagement strategies, triggering mechanisms of resistance inherent in people's struggle for freedom, ensuring that they retain ownership of the development process, and kindling a desire for continuous growth and transformation.

(a)	Year of Establishment	:	1980
(b)	Registration No.	:	....
(c)	Location	:	New delhi
(d)	Coverage Area	:	Jharkhand, Chattisgarh
(e)	Staff Strength	:	100 full time professional and field staff, 350 part time cadre members, and about 1500 site-based community volunteers.
(f)	Source of Funding	:	NABARD, GIST, BASHY ETC.,
(g)	Approximate population Served	:	500,000
(h)	Target Groups	:	ST, SC, OBC,women and children.
(i)	Objectives	:	

PIDT operates on integrated organising principles in it's programmes rather than departmental management structures and thus maximises on the potential capacities of all it's members who have a common resolve.

Details of Activities

- Awareness Generation and Training for Transformation
- Sustainable Agriculture, Heath, Nutrition & Environment
- Self Reliant Non Farm Employment Generation
- Sanghati Vipani - Collective Marketing
- Value Based Education
- Cultural Regeneration
- Research & Advocacy

(j) Research : Research and Advocacy for Peace, Femininity and Sustainability

(k) Vocational Training : Computer e- learning, radio, handloom, pottery.

(l) Skill Development : Sustainable Ecology through Environment Regeneration.

The areas they work in had been depleted of natural resources through commercial logging, single cash-crop plantation and heavy use of chemical fertilizers. PIDT has sought to reintroduce local seed varieties, organic farming methods, watershed development and plantation to re-green the land and harvest its bounty for sustenance of the people themselves rather than the greed of a few.

♦ ♦ ♦

Shramajivi Unnayan

(1)	Contact person	:	Amiyo Choudary
(2)	Designation	:	Executive Director
(3)	Contact No.	:	0657-2755350
(4)	Mobile	:	09430746960
(5)	E- Mail	:	su.jharkhand@gmail.com, succf-shr@sify.com
(6)	Website	:	www.shramjiviunnayan.org
(7)	Address	:	Village post office: Goborghusi, Via: Patamda, East Singbhum, Jharkhand-832105.

About the organisation: Shramajivi Unnayan is registered in 1983 as a voluntary development organization and started working in Patamda block. At present it is functioning in 12 blocks under 4 districts of Jharkhand state. Gobarghusi, Patamda is situated 20 kms. away from Jamshedpur, Dist.-East Singhbhum. The Communication office is located at Jamshedpur, the industrial city of Jharkhand, which is functioning as advance planning cell, state level project monitoring, and planning and co-ordination purpose.

In 1982, to start with, various problems had been observed in the areas like – major occupation of the local people was agriculture which was dependent on erratic rainfall and selling of forest produce. Rest of the year they were forced to migrate. The health status of the community was very poor. Basic infrastructures were not exists. 90% of the villages in this block were devoid of electric connection. Education percentage, rate of daily wages were very low. Women atrocities and exploitation was very high. Shramajivi Unnayan had initiated its venture against this background.

(a)	Year of establishment	:	1983
(b)	Registration No	:	142 (83-84)-Patna, under societies act, Jharkhand 1313(Dt. 11/03/2008).
(c)	Location	:	Jharkhand
(d)	Coverage area	:	At present it is functioning in 12 blocks under 8 districts of Jharkhand state.
(e)	Staff strength	:	Full time 18 and other 42
(f)	Source of funding	:	From Government, foreign source and own source
(g)	Approximate population served	:	2 lakhs.
(h)	Target groups	:	Rural poor in Jharkhand
(i)	Objectives	:	Upliftment of rural Jharkhand, 'Prakriti', 'Parivartan' and 'Swabalambi Vikas'.

Details of Activities

S. U. started its activities with the objective of self-reliance of the farmers and to check migration through promotion of agriculture, land-water management, creation of irrigation facilities, cultivation of medicinal plants, conservation & regeneration of forest, promotion of bio-fertilizer, bio-pesticides and so on tapping resources from different donor agencies and Government departments. Training on Agriculture, dry-land farming, animal rearing, and bio-compost preparation and on different vocations has also been started for knowledge building & Skill development. To promote equity and justice in the rural areas was another one focus.

Now by adopting proper technologies which have been transferred to the villagers, agricultural income has been increased through vegetable growing, extension of animal husbandry, micro enterprises and also they now earn from Govt. employment guarantee scheme on daily basis. The scenario of the area changed a lot and quality of life of the people has been improved a lot due to various interventions by S.U. The development process can be divided in many phases through its entire journey of ever two & half decades.

The following are the educational activities taken up by the organisation.

- R I P (reading improvement program)
- S Q I P (School quality improvement program)
- Bridge Course
- S H G (self help group) Literacy program
- Balwadi
- VEC.PTA (Village education committee, Parents teacher association)
- AQIP (Anganwadi quality improvement program)
- CFV (Child friendly village)
- Child well being committee

(j)	Research	:	Herbal health with nutrition & environment protection, Naturalresource management.
(k)	Vocational training	:	Workshops, yoga, cultivation of medicinal plants, healthcamps.
(l)	Skill development	:	Local self governance

♦ ♦ ♦

KARNATAKA

Bijapur Integrated Rural Development Society

(1)	Contact person	:	Shri. Mahantesh Adappa Agsimundin
(2)	Designation	:	Managing Director
(3)	Contact No.	:	08351 - 260260
(4)	Mobile	:	94481 17058
(5)	E-Mail	:	birdshungund1990@rediffmail.com
(6)	Website	:	N.A.
(7)	Address	:	Atmasakshi building, Near Nagalinganagar, Hungund, Dist: Bagalkot, Karnataka– 587118

About the Organisation

BIRDS has 16 years of experience in rural development sector. Its main aim is to improve socio-economic condition of rural poor women without bias towards caste or creed.

(a)	Year of establishment	:	02-10-1989
(b)	Registration No	:	172/89-90, FCRA No: 094470012 Dt. 15-10-1990
(c)	Location	:	Hungund, Karnataka
(d)	Coverage area	:	117 villages, 6 Tandas, 5 Blocks and 3 districts
(e)	Staff strength	:	55
(f)	Source of funding	:	OXFAM – U.K. Ministry of Rural Development,
(g)	Approximate population served	:	NABARD Karnataka State Women's Development Corporation, CAPART.
(h)	Target groups	:	Women, rural poor, children & weaker sections
(i)	Objectives	:	

1. Community Organisation
2. Information, Education and Awareness, Health Awareness and Sanitation Activities
3. Rehabilitation and Resettlement
4. Health and Family Welfare Activities
5. Watershed Development Activities

Details of activities:

(j) Vocational training activities in the following areas:

- Lambani dresses
- Baskets and mats
- Glass frame work
- Embroidery (hand and machine)
- Screen-printing, book binding, sweet stall and garment packing boxes.
- Hand made paper, paper covers, greeting cards, paper bags
- Catering and bakery products
- Agarbathi/inscence sticks
- Readymade garments
- Candles
- Liquid and powder soap
- Liquid and powder soap
- Plain, egg, oil and herbal shampoo
- White Phenyl
- Poshak powder

♦ ♦ ♦

Sathya Education & Rural Development Society

(1) Contact person : M Jaishankar

(2) Designation : Chairman

(3) Contact No. : 08150-314111

(4) Mobile : 9972111336

(5) E- Mail : satya_bgp2007@rediffmail.com

(6) Website : N.A.

(7) Address : Kaderennagaripalli (V), Mallasandra Po, Bagepalli, (Talik) Chikballpur Dist., Karnataka, 561207

About the organisation: The organization taken a shape at the versatile efforts of a core group of social activists who are highly sensitive to the prime needs of under privileged and neglected sections of the society. Eversince its inception the society is striving hard to uplift the poor through various need based intervention. This society was formerly known as "Reddy Friends Sports and Cultural Association" – Kadirennagaripalli. This society is working on charitable lines and 'not for profit'. This society is operating its activites from Bagepalli Tq, Chikballapur District, and Karnataka State.

(a) Year of establishment : 1955

(b) Registration No : 224/2000-2001

(c) Location : Chikballpur Dist, Karnataka,

(d) Coverage area : Karnataka, Kerala

(e) Staff strength : ...

(f) Source of funding : NABARD, Nehru Yuva Kendra Sangathan

(g) Approximate population served : ....

(h) Target groups : Rural poor, tribals.

(i) Objectives :

- The society is following participatory approaches right from planning to implementing people based action is promoted in all endeavours.
- A society where opportunities go equally to all walks of life without discrimination and bias move with better brotherhood, intimacy, mutual co-operatiion and affectionate care.
- People based action design for people of the people and implemented by the people.
- The society plays a catalystic role in the development action as well as in people's emposwerment.
- To promote sustainable occupation through Dairy Science & Technology.
- To propogate the significance of Gandhi an Philosophy among rural folk more particularly among project participants.

- To promote value addition activites related to Dairy such to Bio-Gas, Vermi Compost, animal waste Bye-Products.
- To float as 'a development fund' to entail the project participants to continue the occupational as well as Gandhian Philosophical initiation even after the completion of the project period.

Details of Activities

(j)	Vocational training	:	The Society gives training on various vocational subjects as a means to Income Generating for groups and individuals.
(k)	Skill development	:	The Society is promoting self help groups of neighbours (SHGs), members of a family (Family Clubs), and farmers (Farmers' Clubs) for easy access of micro credit to uplift their economic condition.
(l)	Organisations under establishment	:	(1) A Sub Centre of Government Polytechnic, Neyyattinkara (2) The Society runs the centre at Mangalakkal in Thiruvananthapuram district to the betterment of youth.

♦ ♦ ♦

Swami Vivekananda Youth Movement

(1)	Contact person	:	Dr. M. A. Balasubranyam
(2)	Designation	:	C.E.O.
(3)	Contact No.	:	(08228) 265412, 265877
(4)	Mobile	:	+ 91 9686666312
(5)	E-mail	:	svym@svym.org.in
(6)	Website	:	http://blog.svym.net
(7)	Address	:	Hanchipura Road, Saragur, Heggada Devana Kote Taluk, Mysore District Karnataka, Pin – 571 121

About the Organisation

A group of young medical students led by Dr.R.Balasubramaniam at the Mysore Medical College (in Karnataka State , India) were starting to feel that the career in medicine they dreamt of pursuing was very different from the practice of medicine around them. They believed they had in them to make a difference and make a positive impact on the lives of the poor & the marginalized. And so, they started the Swami Vivekananda Youth

Movement (SVYM, for short), with initial assets of high ideals and all the positive benefits of inexperience.SVYM's principle area of operation is the Heggadadevanakote Taluk in Mysore District of Karnataka, India. Here, it has various institution-based and community based Health and Education projects and also undertakes several Community Development Initiatives, catering to a populace of about 300,000 comprising both tribals and non-tribals. The reach of these activities also extend to the neighbouring Taluks, namely Hunsur, Nanjangud and Gundlupet.

(a)	Year of establishment	:	1984
(b)	Registration No	:	122/84-85
(c)	Location	:	Rural/Urban
(d)	Coverage area	:	Mysore, Bijapur, Rayachure, Kodagu and Dakshina Kannada districts of Karnataka
(e)	Staff strength	:	600 Professional (150 technical staff)
(f)	Source of funding	:	State/Centre and International
(g)	Approximate population served	:	3 lakhs
(h)	Target groups	:	Tribals, urban and rural poor
(i)	Objectives	:	To facilitate and develop processes that improves the quality of life of people.

Details of Activities

(j)	Research	:	A study of spending patterns on health and exploring options for healthcare financing in H.D. Kote Taluk.

- Assessment of training needs of medical professionals and social workers for dealing with cases of domestic violence and sexual harassment against women
- Evaluation of oral health status of people with HIV/AIDS
- Screening and Early Evaluation of Kidney Disease among the rural population of H.D. Kote Taluk
- Screening for factors that predispose to Chronic Renal Failure, among people in and around Saragur in H.D. Kote Taluk.
- Assessment of knowledge related to the functioning of School Development & Monitoring Committees (SDMCs) and Gram Panchayaths among SDMC members in H.D. Kote Taluk.
- Eyecare infrastructure mapping and assessment of blindness in Periyapatna Taluk of Mysore District.

(k) Vocational training : Development of youth leaders and human development initiatives through forms of art and culture.

(l) Skill development : Master programme in management of non-profit organization. Tribal centre for learning in basic education, yoga and computers, music and Skill development activities

(m) Organisations under establishment : Tribal Joint Action (Federation of NGOs of Karnataka, working for tribes) credibility alliance from Delhi, Federation of Voluntary organisations of Karnataka working for rural development, Voluntary health action association of Karnataka, Bangalore. Two foreign offices are located in North America and the UK.

- Vivekananda Memorial Hospital, Saragur

Vivekananda Memorial Hospital, Kenchanahalli

Anti Retroviral Treatment Center, Mysore

Viveka – Tribal Center for Learning, Hosahalli-The school is recognized by

the Department of Education, Government of Karnataka and also the National

Institute of Open Schooling.

Viveka – School of Excellence, Saragur

Vivekananda Institute of Indian Studies (VIIS)

♦ ♦ ♦

Vivekananda Girijana Kalyana Kendra

(1)	Contact person	:	Sharma Ranganath
(2)	Designation	:	Chief Coordinator
(3)	Contact No.	:	91 8226 244025
(4)	Mobile	:	9449599380
(5)	E-Mail	:	vgkkbrh@sancharnet.in
(6)	Website	:	www.vgkk.org
(7)	Address	:	Vivekananda Girijana, Kalyana Kendra BR Hills – 571 441. Phone: 91 8226 244025

About the Organisation

VGKK is an organization with a mission of "Sustainable development of tribal people through rights-based approaches to health, education, livelihood security and biodiversity conservation". Founded in October 1981 by Dr. Sudarshan, a social worker and tribal rights activist belonging to the state of Karnataka. He is a doctor by profession and is well known for his contributions to the upliftment of the forest dwelling tribes (mainly Soligas) in the Chamarajanagar district of Karnataka. He is also a recipient of the Right Livelihood Award and the Padma Shri . VGKK has also worked with tribals in the states of Tamil Nadu, Arunachal Pradesh and the Andaman and Nicobar Islands and has interacted with about 20000 people. The organization has always had a tribal youth as its

President. Presently, Jadeya Gowda one of the first few children who was taught by Dr. Sudarshan is the President. He went on to do a graduation and post-graduation in agriculture and is presently doing his PhD at the University of Agricultural Sciences, Bangalore.

(a)	Year of establishment	:	1981
(b)	Registration No	:	1960 93/81/82
(c)	Location	:	BR Hills
(d)	Coverage area	:	Whole of India
(e)	Staff strength	:	More than 100
(f)	Source of funding	:	NABARD Govt. of Karnataka, Mc Arthur
(g)	Approximate population served	:	Foundation DFI State trust
(h)	Target groups	:	Students and hostels

(i) Objectives

- To implement a comprehensive, holistic, need-based, gender & culture-sensitive, community-centered, system of health care integrating indigenous health traditions.
- To establish an education system that is specific to the tribal language, culture and environment.

- To promote biodiversity conservation and sustainable harvesting of Non-Timber Forest produce.
- To ensure livelihood security through sustainable agriculture, Vocational training and value addition of forest produce.
- To empower tribal communities through Sanghas (People's organisations) and Women's Self-Help Groups.

Details of Activities

Health

Health care, specifically curative medical care, has been chief entry point of VGKK into the Soliga community, into the community.

- 20 bedded Tribal Hospital with laboratory, X-ray and Operation Theatre providing free Medical care.
- Telemedicine and screening for Rheumatic heart disease.
- Mobile Medical Unit.
- Community based preventive, promotive and rehabilitative programmes for Dalits, health workers and house surgeons.
- Control/eradication of leprosy, tuberculosis, epilepsy, blindness, cancer; mental health, dental health and community based rehabilitation programme.
- Nutrition, safe drinking water & sanitation.
- Traditional medicines & revitalization of local health traditions
- Tribal Auxiliary Nurse Midwife (ANM) programme.

Education

Speciality of our school is emphasis on tribal culture, language and environment specific education with vocational education.

- School (Pre-school to Class X) for more than 500 tribal girls and boys with hostel facilities for 200 students with a sports school
- Four Non-formal schools in remote forest areas
- Pre-university college
- Industrial Training Institute & Job Oriented Course in Forestry
- Drama school
- Science college & ANM Training school

Vocational Training & Production

The project imparts training to women, men and school drop-outs in the various cottage industries like weaving, incense-stick making, coir-rope making, bakery, tailoring and knitting, handicraft, beekeeping, carpentry and printing.

Networking & Advocacy

- Participation in "Tribal joint Action", a federation of voluntary organisations working for tribal people.
- Promotion of tribal federations

Conservation & Livelihood Security

- Sustainable harvesting of NTFP and processing - Honey, Amla and herbal medicines.
- People's action against forest fire, poaching and quarrying.
- Capacity building of tribal co-operatives
- Environmental education in the school.
- Conservation, education and eco-tourism

Sustainable agriculture – organic farming and seed bank promotion.

♦ ♦ ♦

KERALA

Kerala Educational Development and Employment Society

(1)	Contact person	:	Shri. N. Balagopal
(2)	Designation	:	Secretary
(3)	Contact No.	:	0471-2328560
(4)	Mobile	:	09447064944
(5)	E- Mail	:	kedesindia@yahoo.com
(6)	Website	:	www.kedes.org.in
(7)	Address	:	509, Sangeeth Nagar, Thycaud P.O Trivandrum-695014.

About the organisation: Kerala Educational Development and Employment Society (KEDES) came to the fore in 1983, initiated by a committed team of enlightened social workers of Kerala, under the leadership of the world famous social activist and reformer P.N. Panicker. He was the father of many non-formal education movements like KANFED, literacy campaigns such as 'Total Literacy 1986 ', and novel institutions like Kerala Grandhasala Sanghom (Kerala State Library Council). In fact, the Kerala Grandhasala Sanghom is currently running over 7,000 libraries. Though this eminent personality passed away in 1995, Panicker has been the moving spirit behind Kerala's socio-cultural during the later half of the century and KEDES was founded to act as a torch bearer for all round development.

(a)	Year of establishment	:	04-04-1983
(b)	Registration No	:	189/83 Travancore-Cochin Literary Scientific and Charitable Societies Act 1956.
(c)	Location	:	Trivandrum
(d)	Coverage area	:	Kerala
(e)	Staff strength	:	87 (includes contract staffs)
(f)	Source of funding	:	Self Generation, Donations and Govt. Grants
(g)	Approximate population served	:	100 lakhs
(h)	Target groups	:	Rural Population with focus on youth and women
(i)	Objectives		

The main objective of KEDES is to reduce poverty by investing in the development of human capital with the aim of building skills and making knowledge available to all members of civil society for long-term sustainable development. KEDES encourages, assists villagers to set up rural and small industries under the Khadi and Village Industries / Micro & Small Industries Programme of the Govt. of India so as to give relief to the poor by providing full time or part time employment afterimparting necessary training and ensure fair and reasonable wages. The emphasis of KEDES is in organizing vocational, skill based training, ICT controlled education/online education that are employment oriented apart from providing general awareness for inclusive growth. The institution works with the principles and philosophy of Gandhian School of Economics as well as practices the 'Nai Talim' education system.

Details of Activities

In order to make the rural populace self-sufficient, it is always better to organise awareness programmes in the villages, instead of providing them access to the resources. KEDES is also of the view that: 'Attaining self-sufficiency is the key to Sustainable Development'.

KEDES has taken up a number of projects to educate the rural masses through awa reness and training programmes. The Institution has earned appreciat ion and support from the Government bodies and local agencies for conducting training programmes on income generating activities and skill-training to create sustainable livelihoods through locally available resources.

(j)	Research	: Encourages Research Activities to eradicate illiteracy and poverty with scientific inputs and people's participation.
(k)	Vocational training	: Organises regularly vocational training programmes to educate the youngsters for self employment-wage employment and co-employment.
(l)	Skill development	: Skill development for employability enhancement is the core objective of the institution so as to develop marketable skills which is an important impediment in getting decent employment and improving the economic conditions of the youth.
(m)	Organisations under establishment	: PN Panicker foundation.

• • •

Mitraniketan

(1)	Contact person	:	Dr. Raghu Ram das
(2)	Designation	:	Principal and Project Coordinator.
(3)	Contact No.	:	Ph: 0472-2882045, Fax: 0472-2882045
(4)	Mobile	:	09446701529
(5)	E- Mail	:	kvmitra@satyam.net.in
(6)	Website	:	www.mitraniketan.org, http://www.mitrakvk.org/
(7)	Address	:	Mitraniketan, Mitraniketan Post Vellanad, Trivandrum, Kerala – 695 543.

About the Organisation: Mitraniketan is an experimental non-profit social and educational project, founded by K.Viswanathan near Vellanad, his native village, 30 km from Trivandrum, the capital of Kerala in south India. The project was begun with a view to offering education and training in a holistic spirit to primarily socially underprivileged children and youngsters. The organization focuses on alternative education mode for development.

(a)	Year of establishment	:	1956
(b)	Registration No	:	11/1967
(c)	Location	:	Rural area
(d)	Coverage area	:	100 Villages and backward areas Schools
(e)	Staff strength	:	Total - 110 (Teaching and Non Teaching), 15 Adminstrative People.
(f)	Source of funding	:	Foreign projects, NCRI, Dept of Science and Tech., New Delhi.
(g)	Approximate population served	:	1000 Served
(h)	Target groups	:	Rural Wome, Youth and Back ward Clases

(i) Objectives

- To promote need based education for sustainable rural development and agriculture.
- To promote Gandhian principles of basic education for strengthening rural education programs.
- To undertake research in social and rural development.
- To build the capacity of NGOs and educational institutions on Gandhian philosophy of education and development.
- To provide extension service to village community for self reliance.

Details of Activities

(j)	Research	:	Paddy Cultivation, Home farming
(k)	Vocational training	:	Pottery, Plumbing, Carpentry, Printing and book Binding, Automobile, Computer Training, Welding, Coer Mat.
(l)	Skill development	:	Tissue Culture, from micro-credit to soap-making; carry bag making, health and nutrition training, basic reading and writing skills to rural women.
(m)	Organisations under establishment	:	Nursery and Kindergarten called Sisu Bhavan, primary and secondary schools called Vikas Bhavan, Mitraniketan People's College (MPC) , Open University (IGNOU) Study Center, Study Center for NIOS (National Institute of Open Schooling) certification, women's empowerment / extension programmes, Education Extension Center at Wayanad, Center for Education, Research, Innovation and Development (CERID).

♦ ♦ ♦

Vinobaniketan

(1)	Contact person	:	Parivrajika A.K. Rajamma
(2)	Designation	:	Founder member
(3)	Contact No.	:	91-472-2892263
(4)	Mobile	:	9544082080
(5)	E-Mail	:	contact@vinobaniketan.org
(6)	Website	:	http://vinobaniketan.org
(7)	Address	:	Vinobaniketan post, Aryanadu (via), Tiruvananthapuram Dist, Kerala-695 542.

About the Organisation: Vinoba Niketan is a charitable women's institution rendering services to the weaker sections of society for the past 52 years on Gandhian lines. It is situated in a tribal belt in Thiruvananthapuram District, Kerala, surrounded by forests, hills and streams. Vinoba Niketan was founded in 1954 by the spiritual daughter of Vinoba Bhave and Sanyasin, Parivrajika Rajamma. It is housed on 10.50 acres of land and has buildings for upper primary school, tribal hostel, Vocational training, library, museum, khadi and village industries, guest house and prayer hall. Vinoba Niketan runs a nodal literary centre for literacy programmes for the villages near the Ashram.

(a)	Year of establishment	:	1954
(b)	Registration No	:	78-1956
(c)	Location	:	Aryanadu, Tiruvananthapuram
(d)	Coverage area	:	Nationwide
(e)	Staff strength	:	35
(f)	Source of funding	:	Ministry of Textiles, Tribal welfare, Rural Development,NCRI ,State Govt. aided schools.
(g)	Approximate population served	:	one lakh
(h)	Target groups	:	S.C/S.T, Below Proverty Line.

(i) Objectives

- To foster Equality, Universal Brotherhood and World Peace according to Sarvodaya principles, through dedicated selfless service in the social, educational and cultural fields.
- To generate 'organised women's power' for achieving the above objective.
- To provide basic and higher formal education to girls in an atmosphere of mutual care, service to humanity, and compassion for all.
- To instill moral values and impart spiritual education to young minds amidst the sylvan surroundings in which the institution is located.

- To promote the welfare of the Scheduled Tribes and marginalised groups through Vocational training, besides formal education, and conduct training courses for women for self-employment and rural development.
- To translate the Gandhi-Vinoba vision of Gram Swarajya in practice through programmes aimed at self-employment, rural development and self-governance.
- To keep alive the spirit of Gandhi-Vinoba through imparting education on their philosophy and ideals of Sarvodaya Samaj.

Details of Activities

The purpose of the Rural Institute is to develop the whole personality of a child, as against provision of mere theoretical knowledge as in the conventional system of formal education. This purpose is achieved through training in vocational and cultural activities, honing their skills and talents, and helping them identify professions appropriate to their preference and aptitude. The Upper Primary School at the Ashram is linked to this Rural Institute.

(j) Vocational training : The vocations which are available for learning at the institute are: music training, painting, welding, plumbing, animal husbandry, agriculture, electronics repair, electrical works, book-binding, soap-making, tailoring and dress making.

(k) Skill development

- Grama Sevika Training Programme: The training programme for Grama Sevikas is supported by CAPART.(Council for Advancement of People's Action and Rural Technology) on a continuous basia. Each course runs for a duration of one year, during which the trainees are orientated to rural socio-economic development services.
- Ambedkar Hasta Shilpa Vikas Yojana-This project, supported by the Ministry of Textiles, Government of India, is being implemented in Puruthipara village of Aryanadu Bamboo Crafts Cluster in Thiruvananthapuram District. The 5-year project started in the year 2007 with the aim of developing the cluster into a "Bamboo Crafts Center of Excellence" through effective establishment and management of a community enterprise, which makes use of common infrastructure to create value-added products for employment and revenue generation. At the same time, it is aimed for and preservation of the rich crafts heritage of the area and community, with a spirit of competitiveness among indigenous micro enterprises.

(l) Organisations under establishment : Nursery School/ Creche for Children-We currently have one creche for 25 children aged 3-6 years - all the children are from the Kanikkar community (Scheduled Tribes). The creche is supported by the Ashram by way of one Teacher and one Helper. The children are provided nutritious food, vitamin supplements, toys, etc., and medical aid when required.

♦ ♦ ♦

Wayanad Girijana Seva Trust

(1) Contact person : Baburaj, O. M.

(2) Designation : Chairman

(3) Contact No. : 04935 236346

(4) Mobile : 09947421050

(5) E-Mail : wgstrust2002@gmail.cojm

(6) Website : wgstrust.org.in

(7) Address : Mattilayam Post, Vellamunda (Via) Wayanad Dist., Kerala-Pin. 670731

About the Organisation: Wayanad Girijana Seva Trust a charitable Institution registered in 2002 with the prime and ultimate objective of contributing the process of education with focus on Re-schooling the School Drop-Outs among the children from the impoverished Tribal (aboriginal) communities in Waynad District, Kerala State. As the first steps towards achieving the objectives the trust started Vivekananda Residential Tribal Vidyalaya in 2002 (Accredited by National Institute of Open Schooling, HRD Ministry, Govt. of India).

(a) Year of establishment : 2002

(b) Registration No : 46/2002

(c) Location : Mattilayam

(d) Coverage area : Across Wayanad Dist.

(e) Staff strength : 20 (Twenty)

(f) Source of funding : Through public donation

(g) Approximate population served : 205 tribal children resides & study in the school run by this Trust.

(h) Target groups : 205 children belong to impoverished tribal community

(i) Objectives : To provide education to the drop out tribal children arranging basic amenities for them to live and study.

Details of Activities

(j) Vocational training : Computer, Tailoring & Embroidery and Bamboo crafting.

(k) Skill Development : Bamboo crafting training helps to develop their skills also.

♦ ♦ ♦

MADHYA PRADESH

Bal Mahila Vikas Samithy

(1)	Contact person	:	Indra Bhushan
(2)	Designation	:	Dy. Secretary
(3)	Contact No.	:	0751-2457438
(4)	Mobile	:	98262-99566
(5)	E-Mail	:	bama1988@rediffmail.com bama1988@yahoo.co.in
(6)	Website	:	N.A.
(7)	Address	:	VAMA-Bal-Mahila Vikas Samiti (VAMA), H.O: C-9 Maharana Pratap Nagar, Near Jiwaji Club, Gwalior-474 009.

About the Organisation: VAMA is a non-profit voluntary organization, aims at establishing an egalitarian society based on the rights so that the poor, marginalised and deprived have equal participation in all spheres. VAMA has been working in the various blocks of Gwalior, Chambal and Bundelkhand region of MP which is mainly characterised by remote geographical outreach and core backwardeness. It is also registered under the foreign contribution regulation act (FCRA) and 12 A & 80 G of income tax act, 1961. It is working for the empowerment of dalits, poor and marginalised communities to address their immediate needs and better access to entitlements and rights. VAMA has been preparing the deprived and backward communities in itts work area to help them understand the importance of issued like the gender equity/adverse sex ratio, reproductive and child health, sanitation etc., VAMA is bringing them together through the formation on SHGs. It is carrying out the capacity building of the villagers through community based training programs and information dissemination. VAMA is also laying greater stress on the immediate fuflfillment of livelihood necessities of the community through participation.Being constantly engaged in raising awareness about land and women rights (the Hindi word VAMA means an empowered woman).VAMA is also helping emancipate deprived women from exploitation.VAMA made its foray into microfinance in July 2006 with a strong background of two decades of social work.

(a)	Year of establishment	:	1988
(b)	Registration No	:	218087
(c)	Location	:	Gwalior, M. P.
(d)	Coverage area	:	M.P. 3, 4 Gwalior Datia Sagar, Vidisha
(e)	Staff strength	:	47
(f)	Source of funding	:	Nabard, Kasa (missionary) , RCF pro NRHM (GOI)
(g)	Approximate population served	:	More tan 12000
(h)	Target groups	:	Health, weaker sections, Dalits

(i) Objectives : To promote activities focused on the development of the downtrodden, backward, Dalits and the tribal communities.

- To work for the communities in such a way that they develop spirit for mutual co-operation, participation, gender equity, integrity and justice.
- To promote education and awareness on health and nutrition, the use of science and technology based on traditional pattern.

Details of Activities

- Attention of the district & local administration has been developed.
- The organisation Vama has experience on various trainings like the issues of women empowerment, training of Asha's Panchayat Raj issue.
- Special focus on sensitive issues like violence against women, female foeticide and sex determination.
- Efforts for sustainable environmental and ecological management.

(j) Vocational Training : Community based natural resource management program benefiting 469 families of Dalit communities. The organisation is successfully running ANM Nursing School in Datia District.

(k) Skill Development : To motivate women for regular meetings and to inculcate the banking habits, the organisation extended credit facilities largely for self-employment and productive purposes like farming, horticulture, animal husbandry, diary, poultry, goatery and small shops and small scale enterprises.

♦ ♦ ♦

Deen Dayal Research Institute

(1)	Contact person	:	Sri Bharat Pathak
(2)	Designation	:	General Secretary
(3)	Contact No.	:	Tel.: 91-7670-265 353 91-5198-224 427 Fax: - 91-7670-265 510
(4)	Mobile	:	09329125074/9425812598
(5)	E- Mail	:	drichitrakoot@chitrakoot.org
(6)	Website	:	www.chitrakoot.org
(7)	Address	:	Siyaram Kutir, Chitrakoot, Dist-Satna (M. P.) 485331

About the Organisation: Deendayal Research Institute (DRI) was founded in 1972 by Nanaji Deshmukh to validate the philosophy of Integral Humanism propounded by Pandit Deendayal Upadhyaya (1916-1968). Integral Humanism gives us a vision for India that, with an approach to man and his relationship to society that is integral and complementary, could transform India into a self-reliant and compassionate example for the world to follow.The project, called the Chitrakoot Project or the 'Campaign for Self-Reliance', was launched on 26th January 2005 in 80 villages around the Chitrakoot area in Uttar Pradesh and Madhya Pradesh.

(a)	Year of establishment	:	1972
(b)	Registration No	:	3636, under society Registration act 1860
(c)	Location	:	Dist-Satna , Madhya Pradesh
(d)	Coverage area	:	500 villages surrounding 50 KM radius of Chitrakoot, Madhya Pradesh.
(e)	Staff strength	:	540
(f)	Source of Funding	:	The Wadia group, ICAR,KVIC,IDRF,Sir Dorbji Tata Trust, M.Pcouncil of science and technology.
(g)	Approximate population served	:	Three lakhs
(h)	Target groups	:	People in the villages.
(i)	Objectives	:	The aim is to achieve self reliance for these villages by 2005. When complete in 2010, the project hopes to make the 500 villages surrounding self-reliant and serve as a sustainable and replicable model for the India and the world.

Details of Activities

Spreading of Reawakening: The workers of the Institute conducted a village by village survey to achieve the objective.

Chitrakoot Project: Started on 26th January 2002 under Chitrakoot's self-reliance project, 500 Villages in 500 kms radius with Chitrakoot as Centre, will change their destiny by their own hands. One hundred self reliance centres have been chosen to give this project a concrete shape which aims at building a prosperous society. In the first phase of the project, 80 villages have become self reliant and the remaining are all set to achieve self reliance within the remaining time period.

No life with out water: The highlights the importance of water –Don't Let the Pitcher Break – Husband may Die. This shows that the water was more precious than the life of a person. Where there is scarcity of drinking water, one cannot think of enough water for agriculture. DRI understood the difficulty of the villages and gave priority to arrangement of water.

Education and Health: After making farmers self reliant financially, Deen Dayal Institute focused on other issues of self reliance. Quality education and grooming facilities were provided to ensure the next generation of the country becomes valuable citizens.

(j) Research : Established an "Educational Research Centre" (ERC) at Chitrakoot for doing field based research to reshape the whole educational system according to the need of time.

ERC comprises departments like "Mobile Scientific Laboratories" to demonstrate such experiments that have direct bearing on rural life, "Computer Software Development" to develop the educational software for Rural Children.

(l) Skill Development : Bamboo crafting, fruits and vegetable processing, bakery production, garment manufacturing, screen printings etc.so that they may become "Self -Reliant" since their childhood.

(m) Organisations under establishment :

Krishna Devi Vanvashi Balika Awasiya Vidyalaya, Majhgawan: A residential school of the same nature is situated at Majhgawan. It is for 100 tribal girls.

Parmand Ashram Padhati Vidyalaya, Ganiwan: In the direction of Uttar Pradesh in a village called Ganivan, located 35 Km from Chitrakoot, one more residential school has been started for the village children.

Deendayal Research Institute has established Gurukuls on the ancient Gurukul educational pattern. Children of all social strata will live and learn in the Gurukul.10 Gurukuls, each with a capacity to house 20 students have been constructed.

Kasturbagram Rural Institute

(1)	Contact person	:	Sri Jayshree Kavimandan
(2)	Designation	:	Principal
(3)	Contact No.	:	0731-2874065, 2874442
(4)	Mobile	:	94253 13404
(4)	E-Mail	:	contact@kgri.org Jayshree_kavimandan@rediffmail.com
(5)	Website	:	www.kgri.org
(6)	Address	:	Kasturbagram Rural Institute, Khandwa Road, Indore, Madhya Pradesh - 452 020

About the Organisation: Kastubagram Rural Institute, an autonomous college affiliated to Devi Ahilaya University,was established in 1963 by National council for rural higher education government of India,New Delhi in co-operation with Madhya Pradesh government and Kasturba Gandhi National Memorial Trust established by Mahatma Gandhi in the memory of Kasturba Gandhi. The Institute was affiliated to Devi Ahilaya University in 1969 and earned autonomous status in 1988. Modern higher education instead of ameliorating the rural problems has lured the educated and talented youth towards urban areas, consequently the base for overall development, that is Rural Development has suffered a lot and the very foundation of our civilization and culture has been shaken. With this in mind, the University Education Committee headed by Dr.Sarvepalli Radhakrishnan proposed to the Government of India the establishment of 14 Rural Institutes all over the country from 1956 to 1963. In this spirit a Special Rural Institute for Women was established under the patronage of Kasturba Gandhi National Memorial Trust at Kasturbagram with the joint efforts of Central and State Government on 8th. July 1963 for the development and empowering of Rural women through higher education.

(a)	Year of establishment	:	1963
(b)	Registration No	:	Functioning under 'Kasturba Gandhi National Memorial Trust, Indore, MP, a Registered society
(c)	Location	:	Indore, Madhya Pradesh
(d)	Coverage area	:	Villages – 10 Mandals-1 Districts-1
(e)	Staff strength	:	Teaching/Technical – 8Permanent Teaching, 9 /4 Non-teaching/Non Technical – 9.
(f)	Source of funding	:	State Government
(g)	Approximate population Served	:	Madhya Pradesh
(h)	Target groups	:	Children, Youth, Women
(i)	Objectives	:	To serve for the development rural women and children.

Details of Activities

(j) Research	:	Educational of Rural Children. , Rural problems, Rural Health
(k) Vocational training	:	Computer Course, Dairy Science, Journalism, Food preservation, Garment Technology, physical education & Yoga
(l) Skill development	:	Tailoring, working with rural people, preparation of Audio Visual aids, Physical Education & yoga, Toy making.

♦ ♦ ♦

Mahatma Gandhi Chitrakoot Gramodaya Vishwavidyalaya

(1)	Contact person	:	Dr. Thapak
(2)	Designation	:	Registrar
(3)	Contact No.	:	07670265411
(4)	Mobile	:	09450225061
(5)	E-Mail	:	vcmgcgv@rediffmail.com drgsingh@rediffmail.com,
(6)	Website	:	www.ruraluniversity-chitrakoot.org
(7)	Address	:	Satna District, Madhya Pradesh – 485 780.

About the Organisation: MGCGV was established on 12th Feb. 1991 on the banks of the holy river Mandakini through a separate MP Govt. Act (9, 1991) on the auspicious day of Mahashivaratri at Chitrakoot, Distt. Satna (M.P.). The main objectives of the University are to provide education and dissemination of appropriate technology. Gramodaya University's activities veer round rural development. For more than a decade, its constructive indelible impression is felt in all the dimensions of rural development through its education, research and extension activities. The University creates human resource, develops appropriate technology, conducts research and extension in sustainable agricultural techniques for rural livelihood and proper management of rural resources, and it also imparts mass education for the empowerment and awareness of the rural population including women. The University has taken keen interest in exploring alternative sources of energy, developing skills in rural artisans. The MGCGV has jurisdiction in the entire state of Madhya Pradesh. The University is making efforts to establish its centre at various places. The MGCGV has jurisdiction in the entire state of Madhya Pradesh. The University is making efforts to establish its centre at various places.

(a)	Year of establishment	:	1991
(b)	Registration No	:	This is a rural university by the Govt. of Madhya Pradesh through legislature by an Act on February 12,1991
(c)	Location	:	The rural university was established in rural area
(d)	Coverage area	:	Rural university
(e)	Staff strength	:	More than 200
(f)	Source of funding	:	State/UGC and self finance
(g)	Approximate population served	:	Madhya Pradesh
(h)	Target groups	:	Disadvantages Groups like SC/ST/BC/TRIBAL
(i)	Objectives	:	The Mahatma Gandhi Chitrakoot Gramodaya Vishwavidyalaya, Chitrakoot is established to promote the cherished mission of Mahatma Gandhi for rural development. With this broad mission in the mind, the Gramodaya University

has introduced various mini mission and submissions, since its inception in the year 1991.

Details of Activities

(j)	Research	: Sustainable Agricultural techniques for rural lively hood. Proper management of rural resources.
(k)	Vocational training	: Mass education for empowerment and awareness of rural people.
(l)	Skill Development	: The University offers multidisciplinary higher education courses up to doctoral level in the disciplines of agriculture and animal sciences, applied sciences, environment, GIS and remote sensing, agricultural engineering, food technology, information technology, management, education, languages, communication, fine arts, humanities, social sciences etc.

♦ ♦ ♦

Mahatma Gandhi Seva Ashram

(1)	Contact person	:	Ran Singh Parmar
(2)	Designation	:	Secretary
(3)	Contact No.	:	0751-2491653, 0755-5223821
(4)	Mobile	:	09425126467
(5)	E- Mail	:	gandhiashram_joura@rediffmail.com
(6)	Website	:	N.A.
(7)	Address	:	At Alapur, Post Joura, Dist. Morena, Madhya Pradesh.

About the Organisation: Mahatma Gandhi Seva Ashram (MGSA) is a Gandhian organisation believing in action through non-violence in the district of Morena (Chambal Valley). It was set up by veteran Gandhian Subba Rao with an initial fund of Rs 16,000 left over from the Gandhi Centenary year celebrations. The organisation works with youth and primitive tribal groups, and helps set up khadi spinning/weaving, and oil crushing units. It also manages schools for tribal children and undertakes advocacy and awareness programmes related to land rights. It conducts activities related to soil and water conservation, farmers' training programmes, managing of Krishi Seva Kendra, maintaining grain banks, etc.

(a)	Year of establishment	:	1970
(b)	Registration No.	:	1904
(c)	Location	:	Joura
(d)	Coverage area	:	12 districts in Madhya Pradesh.
(e)	Staff strength	:	MGSA has 62 field activists. It has training/ conference facilities for 500 people at Joura, its headquarters, and a training centre for 200 persons in Gwalior.
(f)	Source of funding	:	N.A.
(g)	Approximate population served	:	Its major achievements include forming a task force in 29 districts in Madhya Pradesh to resolve the land related problems of SC/STs, distribution of 3.5 million pattas (land entitlements) to poor families, and withdrawal of 5,80,000 cases of encroachment against the tribal community. It helped start the administrative process to convert 925 forest villages into revenue villages and helped regain forest land and revenue land in certain districts.
(h)	Target groups	:	Marginalised community
(i)	Objectives	:	

- To consolidate and strengthen grass root mobilisation for re-establishing people's rights and ownership over land and livelihood resources.
- To develop the Mutual Help Group (MHGs) with the long-term perspective of socio-economic and political empowerment of women and the community.
- To develop land and livelihood resources for ensuring food security and livelihood of marginalised communities.

Details of Activities

- Organising cadre training for both men and women to sustain the mass mobilisation
- Organising people's forums, public hearings, partners meets, and state level committee
- Initiating political advocacy at local and state level
- Organising training on land rights issue for both field activists and villagers
- Organising the women's representative conference at state level
- Formation of mutual help groups (MHG) in villages, and providing training, establishment of credit linkage, and financing
- Organising training, exposure visit, refreshment course on livestock management for both model and focus villages
- Organising training on allied agricultural activities such as honey collection, cocoon collection, etc

(j) Vocational training : MGSA is engaged in a two-year programme to develop land-based economy for life sustenance of the marginalised community in twelve districts in Madhya Pradesh. The main theme of the programme is policy advocacy.

◆ ◆ ◆

Manav Jeevan Vikas Samiti

(1)	Contact person	:	Nirbhay Singh
(2)	Designation	:	Secretary
(3)	Contact No.	:	07626-275223, 275232
(4)	Mobile	:	09755408866/ 09425157561
(5)	E-Mail	:	mjvskatni@yahoo.in
(6)	Website	:	www.mjvs.org
(7)	Address	:	Village: Bijaori, Post-Majhagawan, Distt.- Katni (M.P), India, Pin-48501.

About the Organisation: MJVS was founded to focus on the issues of the Natural Resource Management and livelihood. Since agriculture is the livelihood for nearly 85% of the region's population, the center began to experiment with sustainable agriculture. Earlier it fuctioned as Grameen Vikas Pratishthan, which were one of the organizations within the Ekta Parishad network. Between 1992 and 1999, the center was used for training programs of staff and villagers, and for regional Ekta Parishad meetings.

(a)	Year of establishment	:	2000
(b)	Registration No	:	JK 5050
(c)	Location	:	Bijaori, Katni, M.P.
(d)	Coverage area	:	8 states, 60 districts and 4,000 villages of India.
(e)	Staff strength	:	45 (33-WOMEN, 12 –MEN)
(f)	Source of funding	:	Christian aid, FORD foundation, Shashi Association Support Group, Switzerland, Gandhi peace Initiative – Germany.
(g)	Approximate population served	:	Two lakhs
(h)	Target groups	:	Rural India
(i)	Objectives	:	

- The pursuit of livelihood resources for marginalized individuals- most notably, scheduled castes, adivasis (tribals), women and landless agricultural workers.
- Loss of control over livelihood-resources, such as arable land, water and forest, is a major root of poverty, migration and other related social problems.
- Assisting and empowering individuals and communities to regain control of the resources that are rightfully theirs.
- To organize women's self-help groups, initiating economic programs, promoting self-governance, teaching improved agricultural methods, and empowering people to help themselves.

Details of activities: The center is currently used for a variety of programs including:

- Sustainable agriculture training for local farmers.
- Cultural and political empowerment of villagers.

(j)	Research	:	On Panchayat Institutes
(k)	Vocational training	:	Nursery, Agriculture
(l)	Skill development	:	Training for Gramin Youth in agriculture

♦ ♦ ♦

Sarvodaya Shikshan Samity

(1)	Contact person	:	Sri Narendra Dubey
(2)	Designation	:	Convenor
(3)	Contact No.	:	0731-2874489, 2489475
(4)	Mobile	:	098274 38575
(5)	E-mail	:	vinobaji1@yahoo.com
(6)	Website	:	N.A.
(7)	Address	:	Sarvodaya Shikshan Samity, Devendrapuram Vill, Machala, Via Kasturbagram, Indore, Madhya Pradesh - 452 020.

About the Organisation: Under the guidance of Dr. Devendra Kumar, B. Tech from Kanpur, a registered society named 'Sarvodaya Shikshan Samity' was established on 3 Dec 1954 on the auspious occasion of the birth day of Dr. Rajendra Prasad, our First President of India. The State Govt allotted three acres of land to samity. The samity constructed class rooms, staff quarters, prayerhall, well and a overhead tank.Sarvodya shikshan samity took up educational, training and developmental programs such as khadi and village industries training center, panchayatiraj training centre, gramswarajya vidyalaya for sarvodaya workers, basic school for village children, non-edible oil research centre, villae soap industry, Oil Ghani research cener, neera and palm gur industry, apiary etc. Gradually these activities were transferred to other governmental and non-governmental organisation.The sarvodya shikshan samity then decided to launch other constructive programms to meet the challenges of present times. In the context of deteriorating environment the samity switched over from chemical farming to organic farming, vermin compost and bullock farming, propagation of environment friendly mudhouses, construction of check dams for water conservation, village sanitation, solar energy and installation of biogas plants etc.

(a)	Year of establishment	:	1954
(b)	Registration No	:	110 dated 31/12/1954
(c)	Location	:	Indore District of Madhya Pradesh State
(d)	Coverage area	:	3 villages, one block, one District
(e)	Staff strength	:	Teaching :4 , Technical : 5, Non teaching: 2.
(f)	Source of funding	:	NCRI, State Government
(g)	Approximate population served	:	10,000 people
(h)	Target groups	:	SC, ST students
(i)	Objectives	:	

1. To generate awareness amongst teachers, parents and NGO workers about Nai Tamlim system of education.
2. To demonstrate and display Bamboo articles produced by tribal.

3. To motivate participants about use of Bamboo in daily life.
4. To provide platform for exchange of ideas and discussion on Nai Talim.

Details of Activities

(j) Research : Bullock Power Project. Waterlifting , Battery charging, floor grinding, Chaff cutting , Simplification of science Education: Published Books from 3rd standard to 8th standard, Tele-medicine appliance research: The project is funded by M.P.Council of Science & Technology., Eco-Sanitation project: Night soil compost making by using minimum of water.

(k) Vocational trainin : Running Half- Yearly course in Animal Husbandry.

(l) Skill development : Training in readymade garments

♦ ♦ ♦

MAHARASHTRA

Appropriate Rural Technology Institute

(1)	Contact person	:	Dr. A. D. Karve
(2)	Designation	:	Chairman
(3)	Contact No.	:	91-20-24390348 / 24392284
(4)	Mobile	:	N.A.
(5)	E-mail	:	contact@arti-india.org
(6)	Website	:	www.arti-india.org
(7)	Address	:	2nd Floor Maninee Apartments, Survey No. 13, Dhayarigaon, Pune, Maharashtra, India-411 041.

About the Organisation: Appropriate Rural Technology Institute (ARTI) is an NGO based in Maharashtra, founded by a group of scientists and social workers in 1996. The mission of the organization is to serve as an instrument of sustainable rural development through the application of scientific and technological knowledge. ARTI is a registered scientific society, established in April 1996 by a group of scientists, technologists and social workers, to develop and transfer innovative, sustainable technologies to rural people for income generation and to improve their quality of life.

Under the leadership of Dr. A. D. Karve, the institute started off with 9 research projects at different stages of completion, transferred from the project 'Centre for Application of Science and Technology for Rural Development (CASTFORD). To date, ARTI has completed over 50 projects sponsored by various funding agencies - both national and international. It has emerged as one of the internationally acclaimed R & D institutions working in the field of rural development through innovative appropriate technologies

(a)	Year of establishment	:	1996
(b)	Registration No	:	The institute is registered under the Societies Registration Act of 1860 under registration number Maharashtra/4703/Satara, and under the Bombay Public Trusts Act of 1950 under registration number F-4674.
(c)	Location	:	Pune
(d)	Coverage area	:	All Over India
(e)	Staff strength	:	90
(f)	Source of funding	:	National and International
(g)	Approximate population served	:	90,000
(h)	Target groups	:	Rural India
(i)	Objectives	:	

- To serve as an instrument of rural development through application of scientific knowledge and technology.
- The primary objective of ARTI is to develop, standardise, popularise & commercialise innovative rural technologies aimed at improving the quality of life and standard of living of the rural inhabitants of India.
- Special emphasis would be laid on making traditional rural business more profitable and on generating new business and employment opportunities in the rural sector through introduction of novel technologies.

Details of Activities

The sphere of ARTI's research activities and ideas is reflected in its projects and training activities undertaken since its inception in 1996. Many of these projects have culminated into successful technologies for rural areas.

(j) Research : Commercialisation of Improved Biomass Fuels and Cooking Devices in India, Standardisation and commercialisation of compact biogas plants for domestic use, establishing norms for kitchen architecture and cooking devices for pollution free cooking in Maharashtra.

Many of ARTI's developed technologies have resulted in eco–friendly and energy efficient products. These products are being promoted by ARTI's commercial partners and have enjoyed huge popularity and success.

- Bamboo and Agri–horticultural technology products-Sugarcane seedlings,Bamboo seedlings,Miniature flowering plants.
- Energy technology Products-Compact Biogas System Kit (includes plumbing material and single burner biogas stove),Charcoaling Technology Kit (including 20 Charring Kilns and Briquetting Machine), Char Briquettes, Sarai Cooking System, Wax sticks, Vivek Sawdust Stove, Sampada Gasifier Stove, Agni Gasifier Stove, Improved Laxmi stove kit, Improved Laxmi stove mould, Compact urban leaf litter Charcoaling Kit.

(k) Vocational Training : Nursery Techniques,Crop production on permanent raised beds, Treatment of bamboo and wood and their use, Biomass burning chulhas and fuel from light biomass, Plant tissue culture.

(l) Skill Development : Production of root mat by rural women, Monitoring indoor air quality in households with and without improved Cookstoves.

♦ ♦ ♦

Indian Institute of Education

(1)	Contact person	:	Smt Yogini Sagade
(2)	Designation	:	Office Superintendent
(3)	Contact No.	:	020-25436980,
(4)	Mobile	:	98906 20073
(4)	E-mail	:	iiepune@vsnl.com
(5)	Website	:	www.iiepune.org
(6)	Address	:	Indian Institute of Education, 128/2, J. P. Naik Path, Kothrud, Pune - 411038.

About the Organisation: The Institute is a non-government organization, a Public Trust of which the dominant intention is public service through 'Education for All' and 'Health for All'. Its activities cover basic as well as action-research, teaching, extension and publications, with emphasis on planning, policy-formulation, and management of education. The inter-relationship between education and development is underscored. It is more inclined towards non-formal education and innovations as measures for counteracting the rigidities of the formal education system. It invests interdisciplinarity into educational research and teaching so as to interlink education with the goal of sustainable development.Based in Pune City which is known as a leading academic centre in India, the Institute appears in the International Encyclopaedia of Education, as one of the two major organizations established in India for educational research and policy-making, the other organization being the National Council for Educational Research and Training. The Institute was affiliated to Bombay University for post-graduate work in education. But its programmes required more facilities and it was shifted to Pune on 1st August, 1976. Its activities have subsequently grown, with greater thrust on the rural education sector.

(a)	Year of establishment	:	1976
(b)	Registration No	:	083930109
(c)	Location	:	Rural
(d)	Coverage area	:	Villages : 8, Mandals: 2 , District : 1
(e)	Staff strength	:	N.A.
(f)	Source of funding	:	ICSSR . Deptt. of Science and Technology, CAPART, IIE Trust, NCRI.
(g)	Approximate population Served	:	16000
(h)	Target groups	:	Youth, women, others
(i)	Objectives	:	

To improve the quality of life of the villagers for sustainable. Development and to empower the rural women through non-formal Education.

Details of Activities

(j) Research : Educational Policy, planning and finance, management of education. Personnel, structures and practices, education and development, Teacher education and learning processes, comparative education.

(k) Vocational training : Rural Technology, Training of farmers, training of rural women and SHG Groups in arts and crafts, Orientation of science teachers.

(l) Skill development : Livestock raising, agriculture, horticulture, growing medicinal plants, making 'masalas' and sun-dried foods, jams, jellies, advanced cuisine, Making vermicompost, bio-manure.Grading, packaging, marketing of fruit and vegetables, Tailoring, sewing embroidery, making rexin and Cloth bags, Soft skills.

(m) Organisations under establishment :

1. Centre for Educational Studies
2. Gram Shakti Vardhini (Rural Institute)
3. Vigyan Ashram (Science Hermitage)
4. J. P. Naik Centre for Development of Rural Women
5. G. D. Parikh Centre
6. J. P. Naik Centre for Education and Development
7. STRIDE Centre (Science and Technology for Rural Integrated Development and Education)
8. Dr. B. D. Tilak Memorial Community Education Centre, Shivapur

♦ ♦ ♦

Institute for Integrated Rural Development

(1)	Contact person	:	Joy Daniel
(2)	Designation	:	Executive Director
(3)	Contact No.	:	+91-02431241534 240-2376336/2376828 FAX +91-240-2376866
(4)	Mobile	:	9822431391, 9823067272
(5)	E-Mail	:	jdaniel@iird.org.in , info@iird.org.in
(6)	Website	:	www.iird.org.in
(7)	Address	:	Institute for Integrated Rural Development (IIRD), P.Box 562, Kanchan Nagar, Nakshatrawadi, Aurangabad, Maharashtra 431002.

About the Organisation: Institute for Integrated Rural Development (IIRD) was established in 1987 as a development organization committed to empowerment of the rural poor particularly in Marathwada region of Maharashtra. IIRD and associated development volunteers at the village level believe that social justice and care of the environmental resources is intertwined. Over the past two decades, IIRD has established its presence in the Marathwada region in areas of non-formal education, Vocational training, support for the aged, rural housing, environmental awareness, women's empowerment, and organic agriculture. IIRD is also actively involved in national networking in organic agriculture and environmental conservation. Besides the establishment of a national network of organic bazaars spread over 14 different towns and cities in different parts of India based on alternative guarantee systems for organic produce, IIRD is also a member of several national and international networks that include International Federation of Organic Agriculture Movements (IFOAM), Participatory Guarantee System (PGS) India Council, World Conservation Union (IUCN), and ASPBAE. IIRD has emerged out of the need to strengthen grassroots development initiatives for promoting sustainable livelihoods. It is also emerged as an institution, which provides national and international training and exposure programmes on rural development and organic agriculture.

(a)	Year of establishment	:	1987
(b)	Registration No	:	AF-1486
(c)	Location	:	Kanchan Nagar, Nakshatrawadi, Aurangabad
(d)	Coverage area	:	Marathwada region of Maharashtra State, National and International.
(e)	Staff strength	:	IIRD currently has about 30 staff and 90 volunteers with expertise in different areas that include biodiversity, affordable construction, vocational skills, organic agriculture, community mobilization, water management, care of the elderly, health, and biodynamic farming. IIRD works closely with

network partner NGOs in Marathwada region and in four other states of India particularly for the promotion of organic agriculture.

(f)	Source of funding	:	DESWOS, HIVOS, EED, Government of India - Ministry of Agriculture, MISEREOR, GTZ, and HelpAge.
(g)	Approximate population served	:	1 lakh
(h)	Target groups	:	Women farmers, rural youth, destitute
(i)	Objectives	:	IIRD has a long-term role of shaping itself into a regional organization with a vision of expanding the PEACE programme at the national, regional and international level. The vision also includes developing a global partnership for the grassroots development movements, establishing an alternative marketing system of organic produce at the regional level and development of Asian Academy for organic agriculture.

Details of Activities

(j)	Research	:	Organic agriculture in KOBI University of Japan, Development and promotion of the concept of community based guarantee system or Participatory Guarantee System (PGS) which has created an impact at the national level resulting in emergence of the concept of PGS in the National Scenario, Development of a Register for Bio-diversity Conservation, Development of Organic production Manual in local language (Marathi) in cooperation with the agricultural universities of Maharashtra.
(k)	Vocational training	:	Provided livelihood opportunities for over 10000 small organic farmers in six states of India, Vocational training of school drop out youth – more than 3000 trained youth in technical education and employment opportunities for these trained youth, Initiating rural women's groups in the 94 villages which are able to manage local development activity on a self reliant basis.
(l)	Skill Development	:	Tailoring, organic agriculture, carpentry, and domestic wiring . Promotion of appropriate low cost housing programmes through training of women masons – 150 rural women have been trained in masonry, Environmental education programmes in 94 villages of Paithan Taluka.

♦ ♦ ♦

Magan Sangrahalya Samiti

(1)	Contact person	:	Dr. Vibha Gupta
(2)	Designation	:	Chairperson
(3)	Contact No.	:	07152-245082
(4)	Mobile	:	09766697311
(5)	E- Mail	:	vibha@womentech.org
(6)	Website	:	www:gandhifootprints.org
(7)	Address	:	J. C. Kumarappa Road, Wardha, Maharashtra, India-442001.

About the Organisation: Magan Sangrahalaya was inaugurated by Gandhiji on 30th December 1938. It is the first museum of Rural Industries and Khadi. Gandhiji wanted it to be a dynamic window on evolving techniques in rural industrialization and a centre of education for the common person to impart information on new modes of production which could help the poor of the land. The museum showcases 32 rural industries including - Food processing, Agriculture tools for small farmers , Honey from the wild rock-bees, Non-violent Leather (goods from fallen hides), Pottery, Hand made paper, oil from edible & Non-edible seeds. It also exhibits industries based on Palm, Bamboo, Lac, Grasses, Jute, Wood, Metal, Glass, Stone, Mud, Horn, Cow dung and Cow urine. The main objective of Magan Sangrahalaya Samiti (MSS) is to bring to the fore indigenous skills of the village artisans, stemming from the accumulated traditional knowledge, and facilitate its interaction with the recent knowledge of science and technology. To innovate technologies that could be converted into sustainable business opportunities at the grassroots level.

(a)	Year of establishment	:	1938
(b)	Registration No	:	Bombay Public Trust Act 1950 Reg.No. F-102. Societies Registration Act 1860 Reg. No. 187/68.
(c)	Location	:	Wardha, Maharashtra
(d)	Coverage area	:	Wardha district, Vidarbha Region, Maharashtra
(e)	Staff strength	:	40 persons
(f)	Source of funding	:	HRD Ministry, NCRI , DST, CAPART, NABARD
(g)	Approximate population served	:	7000 Rural Women – SHGs & Rural Enterprises 3000 Farmers - Natural Farming 200000 Artisans - Rashtriya Karigar Panchayat 200 Artisans – Khadi & Natural Dyes Watershed Development & Rural Sanitation
(h)	Target groups	:	Rural Area
(i)	Objectives	:	

- Research, demonstration and extension of Khadi, Village Industries, Agriculture, Dairy, Rural Technical Education etc..

- Display and demonstration of tools, raw materials, production processes of various village based industries.
- Study and research on Gandhian Holistic Economic Development; produce, publish and organise sales of such books.
- Programmes to bring the artisan and indigenous skills of the villagers resulting from accumulated traditional knowledge to the fore and help its interaction with recent knowledge of science and technology.

Details of Activities

Magan Sangrahalaya Samiti is working on

1. Khadi
2. Natural Dyes
3. Rashtriya Karigar Panchayat
4. Rural Enterprises
5. Alternative Cure
6. Self Help Groups
7. Technology for women
8. Natural Farming
9. Watershed Development
10. Rural sanitation
11. Health Awareness Generation
12. Gandhi Museums, Museum of Rural Technology.

(j) Research : The institution has a small documentation unit with 6000 books on subjects like Gandhi, Vinoba, Kumarappa, Rural Technology, Organic farming, Environment etc. The centre has 300 archival documents published by All India Village Industries Association during 1930 to 1960.

To increase the productivity and earnings of thick-yarn weavers using traditional Charkha, MSS developed a Four-spindle Magana Charkha, an improvised spinning wheel. The critical intervention here is the replacement of the costly multi-national 'Top Arm' by an indigenous 'Top Arm', which can be easily fabricated and repaired in any village workshop. With this appropriate device, the spinner can earn and produce four times more than before.

(k) Vocational training : Presently, this self-reliant Khadi unit of MSS is providing employment to 150 artisans including sliver plant workers, spinners, weavers, tailors, dyers and sales persons. With the collective effort of MSS team and artisans, the institute annually sells 50 Lakh Rupees worth of Khadi.

Using the decentralized, sliver plant developed by Dastakar, Andhra Pradesh, MSS is producing the best quality eco-friendly organic sliver. At the same time, it is also recycling the organic cotton seeds back to the organic farmer since the process keeps the seeds intact.

Converting Forest Refuse into color - MSS has developed new improved tools and techniques of natural dyeing and effective ways of recycling the effluents of a natural dyeing unit. As a low cost alternative to block printing, MSS has also developed an innovative printing technique by using fresh leaves where by from a single leaf 200 motifs can be printed.

Promoting Self Reliance through Natural Farming- The Natural Farming practice is low cost organic agriculture that protects environment, earth, water, bio-diversity, livelihood, and promises sustainability. It focuses on increasing soil humus by scientific introduction of cow dung, cow urine, and biomass. The organic inputs, Indigenous seeds, bio-diversity and multilayer cropping help earthworms, bees, and birds to contribute in controlling pests, enhancing pollination and improving soil health, combats water waste and contamination.

Conserving Preserving Soil Erosion- MSS is introducing water and soil conservation structures in an area of 2500 hectare, covering eight water scarcity villages. Farm bunds and drains brought 200-acre additional land under cultivation. A total of 5602 Metric Ton soil is also saved from erosion.

(l) Skill Development : The SHG program assists in capacity building of rural women, raising their technical skills and creativity; accounting and management skill; general confidence and interactive capacity; thereby raising their social, economic and political status. The enthusiasm and confidence of the trained skilled women groups lead to establishment of 50 new enterprises in 40 villages of Seloo and Samudrapur blocks of Wardha district. Thirty members have opened their own shops to sell products of women enterprises along with other daily use items.

These enterprises produce products such as vermi-compost, herbal pesticides, banana fibre, solar dried food products, soyabean products, spices, brooms, milk chocolates, wooden toys, utility products, soaps, detergents, Liquid Blue, phenol, lantana furniture, agro-waste briquettes, paper products, neem and cow dung products, leaf cups, Khadi (cotton) yarn, carpets (Dari) from waste cloth, herbal medicines and products from forest produce like Amla, Imli, Ber, Bel, Mahua, Mango, Chili, Papaya, Tomato & seasonal vegetables.

(m) Organisations under establishment : Karigar Panchayat -An Artisan Movement

Through a network of volunteers the Karigar Panchayat (artisan movement) is spread out in 21 states of in India covering 200000 artisans including wood worker, black smith, bamboo worker, leather artisans, honey gatherers, potters, metal worker, weavers, mat makers, grass artisans etc.

◆ ◆ ◆

Mahatma Gandhi Institute for Rural Industrialization

(1)	Contact person	:	Dr. T. Karunakaran
(2)	Designation	:	Director
(3)	Contact No.	:	07152-253512, 253513, Fax: 07152-240328.
(4)	Mobile	:	N.A.
(5)	E- Mail	:	director.mgiri@gmail.com
(6)	Website	:	www.mgiri.org
(7)	Address	:	Mahatma Gandhi Institute of Rural Industrialization, Maganwadi, Wardha Maharashtra, India - 442 001.

About the Organisation: MGIRI is a National initiative under Ministry of MSME, Govt. of India. The initiative in the form of setting up an autonomous National Institute named Mahatma Gandhi Institute of Rural Industrialization (MGIRI) at Wardha, together with a number of 'technical interfaces' in the major S&T institutions in different regions of the country is a significant step in the direction of creating such a mechanism. Through this network, it is expected to harness the available R&D expertise as well as facilities in the country to provide a strong backup of Science, Technology & Management to the Rural Industry sector. MGIRI has been developed through a project sponsored by KVIC to IIT Delhi in 2001 resulting in the development of appropriate vision, methodology, and adequate infrastructure facilities as well as model R&D projects. The infrastructure development work envisaged by this project was completed in January, 2006. The collaboration between KVIC and IITD continued during 2007-08 and the advisory role of IIT Delhi has been extended till the end of XI five year plan.

(a)	Year of Establishment	:	2001
(b)	Registration No	:	1602 dated 4 Dec 2003
(c)	Location	:	Wardha
(d)	Coverage Area	:	National
(e)	Staff Strength	:	35 - 6 departments ; khadi and textile, bio-processing and herbal,chemical industries division,craft and engineering, Energy & infrastructure, management and systems.
(f)	Source of Funding	:	Partially self, Central Govt.
(g)	Approximate population served	:	Across the Nation.
(h)	Target Groups	:	Micro, Small and Medium Entreprenuers
(i)	Objectives	:	

- Creating a mechanism to provide the best possible Science, Technology and Management inputs in a comprehensive manner to promote this sector.
- Creating an ethos to motivate professionally trained youth as well as senior 'experts' to work towards developing indigenous models of decentralized and eco friendly Rural Industries in tune with the Gandhian vision of development.

- Empowering the traditional craftsmen and artisans to upgrade their skills and production methods in tune with modern imperatives by providing closer interaction with Scientists, Designers, Technical and Management experts to foster creativity, innovation and quality consciousness.
- To indigenously develop and disseminate commercially viable technology packages by integrating traditional strength with modern methods to promote rural entrepreneurship at a large scale and in a sustainable way.
- To develop and disseminate appropriate HRD modules for rural entrepreneurs, field agency functionaries, RI institution trainers and Govt. officials enabling them to promote Rural Industrialization with professional rigour.
- To create/adapt innovative models of marketing, co-operative management and modern methods of quality assurance and standardization to augment the competitiveness and saleability of RI products.
- To create an active liaison with the major funding agencies such as KVIC, CAPART, DST etc. as well as with CSIR, NIRD and other rural development institutions to give a boost to the sponsored R&D as well as Technology Dissemination efforts in the RI sector.
- To setup and monitor in a co-ordinated way the network of technical interfaces in major technical institutions in the country creating an ethos for R&D dedicated to Rural Industrial sector.
- To collectively visualize and recommend important policy initiatives to facilitate the process of sustainable rural industrialization in the country.

Finally, to provide a sound platform for the NGOs, artisan clusters as well as individual entrepreneurs to interact with the above network for technical support and training.

Details of Activities

(j) Research :

- To develop tools and machineries suitable for optimization of different craft work methodologyTo create quality enhancement and quality guidance methods for different craft sector.
- To disseminate technologies developed at MGIRI through modern methods of training including incubation and creation of sustainable model of technology /methodology of transfer to the artisans.
- Identification of sustainable energy technology alternatives-The following set of activity – directions initiated during the project period of MGIRI in collaboration with IIT, Delhi-biogas cleaning, packaging and use in engines, micro hydel based workstations, briquetting systems on community scale, energy conservation in potter's kiln etc., Infrastructure related areas like: storage system, water recycling, housing, waste recycling, transport & communication with focus on the design of 'housing-elements'.

(k) Vocational Training : Innovative designs & technical development training are given at MGIRI craft division in terracotta, metal crafts, wood & bamboo crafts, textile craft, leather craft etc.

(l) Skill Development :

- To upgrade the skill, creativity & productivity of rural artisans and to provide science and technology support for value addition & quality improvement of their products by providing closer interaction with scientists, designers, technical and management experts to foster creativity, innovation, quality consciousness & ready marketability of products.
- To provide support in the design and fabrication of prototypes and machines and in the development of new products.
- To develop entrepreneurs among the educated rural youth through advanced scientific training in available rural craft practices.

♦ ♦ ♦

People's Institute of Rural Development

(Grameen Vikas Loksanstha)

(1)	Contact person	:	Machhindra Gojame
(2)	Designation	:	President
(3)	Contact No.	:	022- 262339, 262243
(4)	Mobile	:	94230 77848
(5)	E-Mail	:	president_pird@yahoo.com grameenvikas@gmail.com
(6)	Website	:	http://pirdlatur.blogspot.com/
(7)	Address	:	Karad Nagar, Nanded Road PO. Ahmedpur, dist. Latur, Maharashtra-413515.

About the Organisation: People's Institute of Rural Development (PIRD) was started on 15th August 1983, to initiate a process of comprehensive development of rural people, especially poor, marginalized and landless. Drawing strength from Mahatma Gandhi's call - 'March to villages' - the organization began its work in Ahmedpur, district Latur from Marathwada region. During last twenty years the scope of work is widened to include 6 talukas from Latur, Osmanabad and Parbhani districts, where we have direct contact and intervention activities. The organization is also recognized as one of the leading organizations in the Marathwada region.

Mobilization and organization of deprived sections in the society, particularly women, children, agricultural labourers, has remained PIRD's core strategy to address their issues and to uphold their rights. Awareness led to mobilization and it further led to action. In this process PIRD initiated constructive activities without ever expelling its confrontative measures. It worked on immediate strategies, thinking side by side upon long-term solutions for the problems. The conscious understanding of root causes of social issues and interrelation between them enabled the organization to start series of developmental programs and interventions. The primary motivation, however, throughout remained the same - commitment to rural people.

(a) Year of establishment : 15th August 1983

(b) Registration No :

1. Societies Registration Act 1860 Reg.No.MH/44/83/Latur, Dt 21.12.1983
2. Under Bombay Public Trust Act 1950. Reg No.F - 509, Dt.24.01.1984
3. Foreign Contribution (Regulation) Act 1976. Reg No. 083910015, Dt 12.08.1985
4. Regi.Under 80-G Income Tax act. 1961 .No. A,bad/IT.C./80-G/24/12/2005-06

(c) Location : Ahmedpur, dist. Latur, Maharashtra

(d) Coverage area : 6 talukas from Latur, Osmanabad and Parbhani districts.

(e) Staff strength : 12

(f) Source of funding : Maharashtra Foundation, New york, DRDA,-latur, Govt. of India., United way of Mumbai, SEVA international –USA.

(g) Approximate population served : 1 lakh

(h) Target groups : Rural people, especially poor, marginalized and landless.

(i) Objectives :

- Committed with Rural People
- Active for Rural Development
- Advocates Rights of Rural People

Details of Activities

In its journey for over two decades, PIRD has been able to initiate several developmental programmes. Among them are sustained campaigns and activities to draw attention towards deserving issues of working children and women. Employment forms a critical issue with regards to rural development. We worked towards demanding employment as well as seeking alternative ways of creating employment opportunities for rural people, with focus on landless and small landholders. We also participated in relief and rehabilitation work of earthquake afflicted with a purpose to ensure just and appropriate measures in disaster management. In coming years, we would take up these and such developmental issues, with same vigor and commitment.

(j) Vocational training :

- Employment through EGS
- Campaign against Child Labour
- Womens development Programme
- Water resources for drinking & irrigation purpose
- NRM / Watershed Development Programme
- Rehabilitation of destitute women in EQ Area

(k) Skill development : We also perceive the need to understand emerging issues and get ourselves equipped with innovative strategies to address them. Some of future projects include:

- Rehabilitation Center for Child labourers:
- Rural Development Training Center:

• • •

Sampoorna Bamboo Kendra

(1)	Contact person	:	Sunil Deshpande
(2)	Designation	:	Secretary
(3)	Contact No.	:	07226-202772
(4)	Mobile	:	0942125925,0942825970
(5)	E- Mail	:	sampoornabk@rediffmail.com
(6)	Website	:	N.A.
(7)	Address	:	Lawada, P.O. Duni, Ta. Dharani, Amaravathi Dist., Maharashtra -444702.

About the Organisation: Sampoorna Bamboo Kendra is an organization of the individuals and artisans working on various aspects of bamboo.Late Shri Vinnoo Kaleji, a architect and follower of Gandhiji devoted his life for upliftment of bamboo artisans. As Bamboo is one of the instruments of low capital, labour intensive, they feel that they could produce a self- reliant and regionally interdependent society.

(a)	Year of establishment	:	1988
(b)	Registration No	:	MAH – 3994/97 (YAVATMAL)
(c)	Location	:	Amaravathi, Maharashtra
(d)	Coverage area	:	Melghat tribal region of Maharashtra
(e)	Staff strength	:	15
(f)	Source of funding	:	From NCRI since three years
(g)	Approximate population served	:	3000
(h)	Target groups	:	Tribals in Melghat region
(i)	Objectives	:	The objective of Sampoorna Bamboo Kendra is rural employment through training and skills upgradation in the Melghat tribal region, an interior area of Maharashtra where such training does not exist.

Details of Activities

(j)	Vocational training	:	To make decorative items, educational toys, furniture, articles of house hold use
(k)	Skill development	:	Promoted seven udyogshalas in the remotest villages of Melghat. More than 50 tribal youth are earning from Rs.50 to Rs. 200 per day and developed marketing skills.

♦ ♦ ♦

Sanskriti Samvardhan Mandal

(1) Contact person : Sri. Promod Deshmukh

(2) Designation : Chairman

(3) Contact No. : 091-2465-227848, 227834
Fax: 227848

(4) Mobile : 91 9823989997

(5) E-Mail : deshpramod@gmail.com

(6) Website : www.ssmandal.net

(7) Address : Sharadanagar, Sagroli dist.
Nanded, Maharashtra– 431731.

About the Organisation: S.S.M., a rural voluntary organization was founded in 1959 by Mr. K.N. Deshmukh, who donated 100 Acres of his own land as he was craving to remove the darkness of ignorance, poverty and superstitions. A school was initially setup for educating and enlightening children in the area, which had then no school in the radius of 50 k.m. The school, which started with 36 students and a few huts has now grown enormously into a two storey, well equipped school building and a hostel accommodating 1600 rural boys and girls .SSM, though a dream child of one person, has evolved in to the present position not without the support of a great team of devoted volunteers, members of the staff and advisers. The entire activities of SSM are co-ordinated by various committees with a say in the implementation of dreams in to reality.

(a) Year of establishment : 1959

(b) Registration No : B- 118/59(vidarbha) Dated 14-12-1959

(c) Location : Nanded, Maharashtra

(d) Coverage area : Maharashtra State

(e) Staff strength : Full time: 260, Part time: 009, Volunteers: 080

(f) Source of funding : NABARD, Govt. of Maharashtra.

(g) Approximate population served : 3000 students

(h) Target groups : Women and children

(i) Objectives : To attain general rural development through Education, Health Care, Empowerment of women and watershed development.

Details of Activities

(j) Research : Water shed Development programme.

(k) Vocational training : In sports, trained the atheletes to qualify for National Games, as well as Asian games and olympic 2008.

(l) Skill development : **S. S. M. supports the groups training programmes in various fields, conducting training programmes, arranging excursions and guiding women in starting income generation programmes.**

(m) Organisations under establishment :

1. Shri Chatrapati Shivaji Pre-primary, Primary, High school & Jr. Collage
2. Millennium English School
3. Shivrai Vidyapeeth
4. Rajarshi Shri Chatrapati Shahu Sainiki Vidyalaya (Military School)
5. N.S.B. Pre-service recruitment training centre
6. Maharshi Vedvyas Sanskrit Vidyalaya
7. Shri Dhunda Maharaj School for the Deaf and Dumb
8. Technical School (Vocational courses.)
9. Sagroli Sunrise
10. Bonny Shah Sponsorship Programme & Computer Training Center

♦ ♦ ♦

Shirdi Sai Rural Institute

(1) Contact Person : Dr. B. K. Salalkar

(2) Designation : Director

(3) Contact No. : (02423) 243892

(4) Mobile : 9766767125

(5) E-mail : ssripravara@rediffmail.com

(6) Website : pravarassri.org.in

(7) Address : Shirdi Sai Rural Institute, Pravaranagar, Arts, Science and Commerce College Campus, Rahata, Tal- Rahata, Dist-Ahmednagar. (423107).

About the Organisation: Shirdi Sai Rural Institute was established through the vision of Hon'ble Padmabhushan Shri. Balasaheb Vikhe Patil (Ex-Minister, Govt. of India, Founder Managing Trustee, SSRI and is based on the ideas and philosophy of Mahatma Gandhi, particularly concerning Agriculture and Rural Development. The envisioned role of SSRI is to function as a catalyst for promoting priority to rural development in the region and the country. The objectives of rural education are to develop the human resource base to continuesly study and search for solution to problems in social, economic and productive sectors. The institute recognized the need to advance social justice and to include human values in education, scientific knowledge and technology which are the major bases for transformation have to properly harnessed and modified if required. SSRI also recognized the need to promote the sanctity of rural life of rural life, which embodies affection for each other, self less ness and mutual trust help and co-operation. SSRI aims to setup forums of people who think in terms of rural development. It also aims to in calculate the sprite of self reliance among the rural communities with special emphasis on rural youth and women.

(a) Year of Establishment : 1997

(b) Registration No. : B.P.T. Act No. E-16710 (Bombay)

(c) Location : Rahata Tahasil in Ahmednagar District.

(d) Coverage area : Ahmednagar District

(e) Staff strength : 104

(f) Source of funding : From different Government Agencies and other NGOs and nominal charges from trainees.

(g) Approximate population served : Thousands of People.

(h) Target groups : Un-employed rural youth, SHGs Women, Farmers, Students.

(i) Objectives :

- To develop improved method of crop based agriculture in food grains, non-food grains, commercial crops and tree crops.
- To develop improved methods of animal husbandry and fishing.
- To develop knowledge of agro-processing and distribution.

- To develop in selected areas capabilities for research advanced technology creation and diffusion for agricultural and rural development.
- To acquire capabilities for developing social and organisational skill for technology generation and diffusion.
- To act as catalyst and facilitator for promoting priority to rural development concerns in the region and the country.
- To consciously strive for developing methods for supporting marginal farmers, landless labourers, women, children and deprived sections of rural society.
- To provide relevant education and training to artisan draftsman. Professional so as to equip them will recent technologies for rural development.
- To undertake in-depth studies into problems and complaints relating to the whole camp of rural development and evolve strategies for their resolution.
- To educate and motivate people to use natural resources economically.
- To raise consciousness and realisation of soil and water as the most important natural resource and to protect conserve and use non-renewable resource in a sustainable manner by good management based on improved social organisation and technology.
- To promote the spirit of self-reliance for development and to sustain a widespread base for Agricultural and rural development.

Details of Activities

Towards achieving this objectives SSRI, to introduce a variety of activities such as resource mobilization, education, training, extension, monitoring and research which support usage of appropriate technology in agriculture with minimum damage to environment, promote rural human resource development, employment generation and motivation for self employment and promote sustainable development through micro planning.

(j) Vocational training : Fitter, Electrician, Wireman, Mech. Motor Vehicle, Welding, Comp. Operation under National Council for Vocational training Scheme D.G.E.T.(Affiliated).New Delhi.

(k) Skill development : Incense Stick Making, Candle Making, Chalk Making, Washing Soap Making, Pedha, Kaju Preparation and Making, Beauty Parlour and Cosmetics, Photography and Video-Shooting, Tailoring and Fashion Designing , Computer Education, Rexine Bag Making, Repair and Maintenance of Cell Phone

(l) Organisations under establishment : SSRI Consist of...

01. Arts, Science and Commerce College, Rahata.
02. Industrial Training Centre, Rahata.
03. Rural Institute, Rahata. (Sponsored by HRD Ministry, Govt. of India, Hyderabad)
04. Sai Rural Entrepreneurship Development Centre, Rahata.
05. Pragati Project

♦ ♦ ♦

Shri Kishan Das Jajoo Grameen Sewa Mahavidyalaya

(1)	Contact person	:	Dr N. Y. Khandait
(2)	Designation	:	Principal
(3)	Contact No.	:	07152-230518, Fax: 07152-230518
(4)	Mobile	:	09850591099
(5)	E-Mail	:	sjgs_pw@redffmail.com
(6)	Website	:	www.shikshamandal.org/skdj.html
(7)	Address	:	PIPRI-WARDHA, (Maharashtra)

About Organisation

Conceived in 1961 as basically an institute to take care of higher education of the rural youth with an apt designation of RURAL INSTITUTE, Shrikrishnadas Jajoo Gramin Sewa Mahavidyalaya has now entered into the 50th year of its existence. Now, with 50 years of glorious track record, we have not only justified our existence but also are in a position of defining new bearings that rural education should take for the betterment of the rural youth in Maharashtra proper through our constant endeavours.

(a)	Year of Establishment	:	1961
(b)	Registration No	:	Affiliated to Nagpur University UGC during 1991
(c)	Location	:	PIPRI-WARDHA (Maharashtra)
(d)	Coverage Area	:	WARDHA District (Maharashtra)
(e)	Staff Strength	:	12
(f)	Source of Funding	:	UGC
(g)	Approximate population Served	:	2 lakhs
(h)	Target Groups	:	Rural youth and farmers
(i)	Objectives		

(1) To provide higher education to rural students.

(2) To encourage students to study rural life.

(3) To conduct the course on the basis of education, extension and research.

(4) To arouse the feelings of patriotism, nationalism and dignity of labour.

(5) To prepare students for healthy competition.

Details of Activities

To fulfil the hopes and aspirations of these young faces is our greatest motivating factor and therefore we are chalking out a fresh path for us to achieve our new goals which include the creation of more job opportunities for our students with an added focus on self-employment. In this connection, we are planning to enter into some kind of arrangement with a few NGO's who are active in RD.Our ultimate goal, thus, is to become a self-sufficient autonomous institute like Gandhigram before we try to gain the status of a deemed university.

(j) Research : Environment and water conservation

(k) Vocational Training :

- Farmers for compost, Crops and Cattle, demonstrated and constructed compost pits for the environmental awareness among the villagers.This project involves earthworms which are provided ideal conditions for breeding and growth. The worms' excreta act as an organic fertilizer.
- Cleanliness drive, compost pits at Pandharkawda
- Water conservation scheme at Vidyavihar colony

(l) Skill Development : Marketing for promoting sales and Khadi spinning Community development and extension. Farmer counseling, Vermi compost.

♦ ♦ ♦

Society for Education in Values & Action

(1)	Contact person	:	Sri K. S. Deshpande
(2)	Designation	:	Secretary
(3)	Contact No.	:	0242335411 / 2343215
(4)	Mobile	:	94227 01250, 98239 70009
(5)	E-Mail	:	maitree_inst@yahoo.com, ks_deshpande@yahoo.com
(6)	Website	:	www.sevaindia.org
(7)	Address	:	291, Pushpak, Samarthenagar, Aurangabad, Maharashtra - 431 001

About the Organisation: SEVA is a non profit, non-political & non–governmental social action group endeavoring to serve the poor & downtrodden of the society with active participation of the people through social. Educational interventions & survival oriented programmers.

The origin of SEVA is of grass root level, action oriented voluntary organisation, touching the entire –linked grass root problems, came into existence after a long interaction with the poor & marginal sections of society.

(a)	Year of establishment	:	1992
(b)	Registration No	:	E- 432, Aurangabad
(c)	Located	:	Rural, Urban, Backward area
(d)	Coverage area	:	Villages –500, Mandals-35, Districts – 5
(e)	Staff strength	:	Teaching/Technical: 5
(f)	Source of funding	:	BMGF-USA through AIAP – Hyd, Ministry of women & Family Welfare – Hyd.
(g)	Approximate population served	:	4 to 5 Lakhs
(h)	Target groups	:	Children, youth, women, Farmers, Teachers, etc.
(i)	Objectives	:	The main focus of the organisation is to transform rural areas through our various development programmes.

Details of Activities

(j)	Research	:	Evaluation of all Rural Development Programmes, Impact Assessment Studies of Backward Class Development Corporation, Concurrent Evaluation & Monitoring of IRDP/JRY, Evaluation of NREGA, Rural Water supply& Sanitation
(k)	Vocational training	:	Sanitation & Health, SHG Groups Awareness Try, Women Empowerment & Panchayat Raj, Child Labor.

(l) Skill development : Women Empowerment, Child Youth Empowerment, SHGTraining Programme, Computer training, Water quality, personal hygiene, watershed development, Organic farming.

♦ ♦ ♦

Shri Mouni Vidyapeeth

(1)	Contact person	:	C. D. Chougule
(2)	Designation	:	Director
(3)	Contact No.	:	02324-220011, 220030 +91-2324-220075, 220076
(4)	Mobile	:	9423280090
(5)	E-Mail	:	khcollege@sanchrnet.in
(6)	Website	:	Smvicregargoti.org
(7)	Address	:	Shri. Mouni Vidyapeeth, Murlidharnagar, Gargoti, Dist. Kolhapur.

About the Organisation: Shri Mouni Vidyapeeth was established in the year 1951 with following Motto,"Rural reconstruction through education and education through rural reconstruction." Shri Mouni Vidyapeeth is educational laboratory where new techniques & methods of educational are evolved. These methods and techniques are experimented to educate the rural masses. A new vision for development is provided by Shri Mouni Vidyapeeth to rural masses all along from its inception and still wishes to provide it under the changed scenario through its huge infrastructure in the area of information and technology. In the last two decades there have been many changes in the educational field. Reconstruction of education and reconstruction of educational techniques have been the main objectives of these changes. Shri Mouni Vidyapeeth is all along it's development has contributed substantially towards these changes. Shri Mouni Vidyapeeth is not just located in rural area, but is also working hard for surrounding area. The shortage of funds, insufficient infrastructure, and remoteness of its location in comparison to other institutes never stood between Shri Mouni Vidyapeeth and development of its surrounding society.

(a)	Year of establishment	:	1951
(b)	Registration No		...
(c)	Location	:	Murlidharnagar, Gargoti, Dist Kolhapur
(d)	Coverage area	:	93 villages in Bhudargad taluka.
(e)	Staff strength		...
(f)	Source of funding	:	UGC
(g)	Approximate population served	:	Maharastra
(h)	Target groups	:	Rural masses in existing area.
(i)	Objectives	:	

- To provide Quality Education to all by means of sheer hardwork, dedication devotion
- Education to inculcate cultural values into students & to make them better citizens of India.
- To promote scientific temper, vision & values.
- To attain community & social development through infrastructural facilities of the college
- Responsibility & nationality through sports, cultural activities, NCC, NSS & other events
- To help the students for the job training & placement of jobs whenever possible.

- To provide a platform to the students to enhance their skills/potentials as well as a sense of socialism.
- To ensure values like truth, honesty, character, science & sacrifice into the students.

Details of Activities

To improve Social awareness among the students, we organise Social Service Camps, Medical Camps, Blood donation Camps, AIDS Awareness, Superstition Eradication, Hutatma Din, Jata Nirmulana, Environment Awareness etc. through rallies, exhibitions, lectures, slide shows, camps, Yuvati munch and so on. We plan our activities accordingly to achieve these aims and objectives.

The programs such as debate, elocution competitions, discussions, seminars etc. are often arranged by the institution.

(j) Organisations under establishment :

1. Laximibai Korgoankar Shishu Bhavan
2. Jawahar Bal Bhavan, Gargoti
3. Shri Shahu Kumar Bhavan, Gargoti
4. Doulat Vidyaa Mandir , Madilage(Bk)
5. Kumar Bhavan , Shengoan
6. Shri.Mouni Maharaj Highschool, Patgoan
7. Koor Highschool, Koor
8. Kumar Bhavan , Kardwadi
9. Kumar Bhavan , Sheloli
10. Shri. Udajirao Jr.College Of Education, Gargoti
11. Primary School Extension Centre
12. Karmveer Hire Arts,Commarce, Science & Education College , Gargoti
13. Acharya Jawadekar Shikshan Shastra Mahavidyala, Gargoti
14. Govindrao Korgaonkar Rural Educational Research Centre
15. Institute of Civil & Rural Engineering, Gargoti
16. Community Polytechnic, Gargoti
17. Panchyat Rajya Training Centre,Gargoti
18. Gramsevak Training Centre, Gargoti
19. Composite Training Centre , Gargoti
20. Anganwadi Training Centre , Gargoti
21. Mouni Vidyaapeeth Sevakanchi Sha.PatSanstha, Gargoti
22. Mouni Vidyapeeth Sahakari Bhandar, Gargoti
23. Kai. Amarnath Kamble Backward Student Hostel
24. Backward Girls Hostel .

Vanarai Foundation

(1)	Contact person	:	Sri. Shriram Gomarkar
(2)	Designation	:	Secretary
(3)	Contact No.	:	020-2444935, 24440351 Fax: 020-24445299
(4)	Mobile	:	09850585628
(5)	E-mail	:	varanasitrust@rediffmail.com
(6)	Website	:	N.A.
(7)	Address	:	498, Parvati, Aditya Residency, Pune, Maharashtra -411009.

About the Organisation: Vanarai organisation was formed by Dr. Mohan Dharia in the year 1982 and after securing success it was registered under the Charitable Trust Act in 1986. Since 2006 it has been converted into Vanarai Foundation.During last 24 years Vanarai has reached all parts of Maharashtra and also to other states. Vanarai Foundation is now recognised as one of the major Voluntary Organisations both at the state and national level.

(a)	Year of establishment	:	1982
(b)	Registration No	:	E 1060 dated 10/7/1986
(c)	Location	:	Maharashtra
(d)	Coverage area	:	Maharashtra and Union territories
(e)	Staff strength	:	30
(f)	Source of funding	:	Corporate offices, Hindustan UnileverLtd, HSBC,Commence India, CTR corporation, pune.
(g)	Population served	:	1 crore
(h)	Target groups	:	Rural and Urban weaker sections of society
(i)	Objectives	:	Making more than 250 villages self-reliant.

Details of Activities: Afforestation, environment, scientific watershed development to develop all lands, generate employment to millions and create additional new assets for the country. Healthy planned urban areas with parks, gardens and other amenities. Empowerment of women and youth. Use of modern software for speedier development.

(j)	Research	:	Reverse migration of labour from cities to villages.
(k)	Vocational training	:	Dairy farming, tailoring, vermi composting, skill upgradation of village computer literacy.
(l)	Skill development	:	Home industries like papad making, agarbathis, candles etc.
(m)	Organisations under establishment	:	Formation of Confederation of NGOs of Rural India (CNRI): Dr. Mohan Dharia is Chairman of CNRI also which has more than 6,000 member organizations spread all over India. Through CNRI the name of Vanarai has reached all corners of India.

• • •

Vigyan Ashram

(1)	Contact person	:	Ram Pakole
(2)	Designation	:	Chairman
(3)	Contact No.	:	+91 2138-292326
(4)	Mobile	:	09730005027
(5)	E-Mail	:	vaibt100@gmail.com
(6)	Website	:	www.vigyanashram.com
(7)	Address	:	Vigyan Ashram, Pabal Dist, Pune–412403.

About the Organisation: This organization is spread over an area of 5 acres, Vigyan Ashram was founded eighteen years ago, with the help of Consortium of Agencies for Promotion of Appropriate and Rural Technology, to educate the village Youth in rural technology – and also to help spread such technology to the surrounding villages. The Ashram believes that rural development can be brought about by developing appropriate rural technologies. Presently 15 schools around Pabal are receiving training in rural technology related to agriculture, dairy farming, energy and environment, health and sanitation. This organization believes is philosophy of "Learning while doing".

(a)	Year of establishment	:	January 1983
(b)	Registration No	:	F-1852
(c)	Location	:	Village Pabal, Rajgurunagar, Shirur Road, Pune
(d)	Coverage area	:	Maharashtra, Karnataka, Andhra, Goa and Assam
(e)	Staff strength	:	29
(f)	Source of funding	:	Department of Science & Technology, self funding, Donations from volunteers.
(g)	Approximate population served	:	50 students per year
(h)	Target groups	:	School students of age group 14 to 16 yrs ofVIII, IX and X classesand youth in the villages.
(i)	Objectives	:	

- To conduct innovative experiments in education.
- To provide non-formal training in rural technology to school dropouts.
- To develop a net-work of village schools and provide such training to rural youth.

Details of Activities

(j)	Research	:	Agriculture, energy environment, food science and education. It is the first institution to have developed a tractor known as "Mac Bull" – Another innovation is the construction of an

			instrument to test the quality of the soil as well the level of underground water.
(k)	Vocational training	:	Agriculture, dairy farming, energy and environment, health and sanitation.
(l)	Skill development	:	All technical matters related to production, maintenance and repair of agricultural implements and other equipments required daily in the villages
(m)	Organisations under establishment	:	Lokamanya Tilak Mandir, Chikalgram, Ratnagar Dist, Maharashtra and Jyana Probodhini Vidyalaya, Saloombre, Pune Dist, Maharashtra.

• • •

MANIPUR

Diocesan Social Service Society

(1)	Contact person	:	Fr. Dominic Kanmi
(2)	Designation	:	Director
(3)	Contact No.	:	0385-2427633;2427818
(4)	Mobile	:	9612001613; 9436022830
(5)	E-Mail	:	dsssimphal @gmail.com kkanmi@gmail.com
(6)	Website	:	dsssimp.org
(7)	Address	:	Diocesan Social Service Society, (DSSS) Mantripukhri, Imphal 795002 Manipur, India
	Mailing address	:	Diocesan Social Service Society, (DSSS) Mantripukhri, P.B. No. 275, Imphal 795001 Manipur, India.

About the Organisation: Diocesan Social Service Society, Imphal (DSSS) is the development wing of the Archdiocese of Imphal which initiates, co-ordinates, plans, formulates, implements, monitors and evaluates all the development projects. The Diocesan Social Service Society has its humble beginning since 1st April 1981. The objectives for which the society is established are to provide technical and vocational training, to promote scientific method of agriculture, horticulture, pisciculture, to establish farms, to perform works of charity and relief, to train development workers in the state, to improve quality of life, to arrange seminars, workshops, conferences and programmes relating to one or more of its objectives.

(a)	Year of establishment	:	1980
(b)	Registration No	:	253/M/SR/1991
(c)	Located	:	Imphal, Manipur
(d)	Coverage Area	:	Entire State of Manipur. At present, operating in 1. Chandel Dist 2. Churachandpur Dist. 3. Imphal E/W, Senapati, Tamenglong, Thoubal
(e)	Staff Strength	:	87 116 volunteers
(f)	Source of Funding	:	Caritas Germany, Caritas Denmark, Caritas India, MESEREOR, NABARD, NCRI, UNITRANS.
(g)	Approximate population Served	:	12,80,280
(h)	Target Groups	:	The Poor and marginalized, underpriviledged rural polulation, School dropouts, Unemployed Tribal Youth, poor and marginalized Women, Small Farmers, People affected by Violence, People

living with HIV/AIDS, Drug users, Teachers, Students, Mother & children.

(i) Objectives : The objectives for which the society is established are to provide technical and vocational training, to promote scientific method of agriculture, horticulture, pisciculture, to establish farms, to perform works of charity and relief, to train development workers in the state, to improve quality of life, to arrange seminars, workshops, conferences and programmes relating to one or more of its objectives.

Details of Activities

- Animation, Formation of People's Organization, Saving, Credit and Income Generation
- Natural resource Management
- Prevention, Control and Care of HIV/AIDS, alcoholism and drug abuse
- Early Childhood education and strengthening Primary Schools
- Disaster management and Emergency response
- Community Health
- Peace Building
- Access to safe drinking water

(j) Research: Three Research fellows undertook Research on Conflicts **for** a Diploma from Catholic Relief Services (CRS) in 2005.

(k) Vocational training

- Tailoring, weaving & embroidery course
- Exercise book binding training & production.
- Handicrafts training

(l) Skill development

- Entrepreneurship Development Programme on Food
- Processing &Spices production
- Detergent powder & Dish wash production training
- Enhanced dress designing& embroidery
- Pest & disease management
- Soil & nutrient management
- Bench terracing
- Promotion of ITKs (Indigenous Technology Know–how) in Organic Farming for sustainable Agriculture.

♦ ♦ ♦

Kasturba Gandhi Seva Ashram

(1)	Contact person	:	N. Medhabati Devi
(2)	Designation	:	Secretary
(3)	Contact No.	:	0385-229666
(4)	Mobile	:	9862269385
(5)	E-Mail	:	N.A.
(6)	Website	:	N.A.
(7)	Address	:	Khongman Zone - III, Imphal East District, Manipur, Pin Code - 795001.

About the Organisation

Kasturba Gandhi Seva Ashram, since its establishment in 2002 has been striving to promote overall development of women and children through vocational training, health awareness programmes and SHG promotion etc. The institute has been networking with leading NGOs in the rest of the country towards achieving their objective.

(a)	Year of Establishment	:	2002
(b)	Registration No	:	8/M/SR/2002
(c)	Located	:	Imphal
(d)	Coverage Area	:	Bishnupur, Chandel, Churachandpur, Imphal East, Imphal West, Senapati, Tamenglong, Thoubal, Ukhrul.
(e)	Staff Strength	:	32
(f)	Source of Funding	:	ACTION AID and UNICEF
(g)	Approximate population Served	:	30,000
(h)	Targert Groups	:	women & children

(i) Objectives :

- To promote the over all development of women and children.

Details of Activities

Integrated Agriculture Development Farming under CAPART, Guwahati, Inter Personal Communication on HIV/AIDS, Naturopathy Awareness Programme for Women under NIN, Punei, Environment Awareness programme under EEWing, Manipur. Polio Immunisation programme, Five days Awareness generation programme, Firm Management on Banana Plantation with collaboration Horticulture Deptt., Govt. of Manipur, Construction of Poly House for Nursery Plantation, Gardening, Orphanage/Street children welfare programme, Yoga and Naturopathy Awareness programme, horticulture development programme, Free health camp, SHG promotion etc.

(k) Vocational Training : Embroidery and tailoring, computer, agriculture development, vermi compost, health counselling.

(l) Skill Development : training the unemployed in Naturopathy

• • •

Self Employment Voluntary Association

(1)	Contact Person	:	Kh. Chinglen Singh
(2)	Designation	:	Chief Functionary / Secretary
(3)	Contact No.	:	0385-2056189
(4)	Mobile	:	9856288250 / 977406914
(5)	E-mail	:	seva_naoremthong@yahoo.com / sevamanipur01@gmail.com
(6)	Website	:	www.sevamanipur.com
(7)	Address	:	North Babupara, Behind MLA Flat, Imphal-West, Manipur – 795001.

About Organization: Self Employment Voluntary Association (SEVA), Manipur was established in the years 12th January 1991 by a groups of Social Worker with a view to undertake various activities for the welfare of the disadvantaged and valuable groups of the society. The Association was registered in the year 13th February 1991 under the Manipur Societies registration Act 1989 and bearing registered No. 1279 of 1991 and the Association was also registered FCRA in the year 14th December 2004 under the Foreign Contribution (Regulation) Act. 1976 and bearing registration No. 194130268 and as a non-political, non-profitable making, non-sectarian, non-religious and non-governmental organization. Self Employment Voluntary Association (SEVA), Manipur is absolutely secular in nature without discrimination of caste, creed and religion. It is a non-profit Voluntary Association dedicated to the cause of bringing about a more "SELF EMPLOYMENT VOLUNTARY ASSOCIATION" worth-living for all through selfless efforts for peace Solidarity and programme of the World Fraternity.

SEVA is working mainly with "Non-Violence and Conflict Transformation through Capacity Building of Civil Societies" in order to bring to Peace and Harmony in the present society of Manipur and also worked as Microfinance institution for the upliftment of the rural masses for their economic empowerment.

(a)	Year of Establishment	:	1991
(b)	Registration No.	:	Registration No. 2173 / ID / SR / 1991 (M) on 13-02-1991.
(c)	Location	:	North Babupara, Behind MLA Flat, Imphal-West, Manipur – 795001
(d)	Coverage Area	:	Whole State of Manipur
(e)	Staff Strength	:	13 (Thirteen)
(f)	Source of Funding	:	BASIX, RGVN, NCRI.
(g)	Approximate population Served	:	500 individual SHGs members and 600 villagers are covered.
(h)	Target Groups	:	Rural masses and weaker section of the society.

(i) Objectives

- To run and maintain Education Institution from Pre-School stage upto higher level with inclusion of vocational trades and jog oriented streams and to established and run Youth Hostel in feasible places and to provide adequate facilities in the field of vocational and physical education.
- To organized Awareness Programme, Seminars, meetings workshops for human rights and work camps, exhibition, study tours, excursion for accelerating the work on rural and urban development.
- To take up different schemes of computer, embroidery, weaving knitting, tailoring, craft centre, hostel/school, typewriting shorthand, video, T.V., audio, screen printing, press printing, shoe making and leather production and training for SC, ST and OBC and other economically backward classes below poverty line and to conduct and impart training of rural artisans and landless labourers.

Details of Activities

(j) Research: We are mainly working with the Rural masses so, we are conducting various research work on How to developed Rural mass, socially economically and politically as well. Therefore it is a continuous process for us.

(k) Vocational Training: So far we had conducting various Vocational Training Programme, Some of them are given below:

- Piggery Rearing Training Programme for SC and OBC people.
- Crafts Training Programme for Women Societies.
- Poultry Rearing Training Programme for BPL / AYY families.
- Weaving training programme especially for young ladies.
- Tailoring Training Programme for Women especially for BPL / AYY families.

(l) Skill Development: Above mention programme are also conducted under the skill development programme that is, weaving skill development programme, Tailoring skill development programme, Crafts skill development programme. Most of the skill development programmes are conducted for women.

♦ ♦ ♦

ODISHA

Gandhi Vidya Mandir Sanghatan

(1)	Contact person	:	Gaurang Mahapatro
(2)	Designation	:	Secretary
(3)	Contact No.	:	0674-2740564
(4)	Mobile	:	9040135842
(5)	E- Mail	:	gvmsrural@gmail.com
(6)	Website	:	N.A.
(7)	Address	:	Qr. No. FR-37/6, Ph-II, Housing Board Colony, Sailashree Vihar, Bubaneshwar, Pin-751021

About the Organisation: GVMS is an organisation formed in inspiration with Gandhian ideology and the patronship of Pro. Dr. Satrughna Nath, the eminent Gandhian teacher of Odisha in 1996. From the day of inception, this institution has dedicated to establish Basic Education and Gandhian activities in the State by organising Schools under the banner of the Gandhi Vidya Mandir Sangathan .The schools have to be named as SADVABANA SCHOOL or GANDHI VIDYA MANDIR as the School committee decided. This is an infrastructure of minimum 50 nos. of schools in the State with capacity of Organisational affiliation. This organisation is recognised by the D.I. of Schools, Bhunaneswar in the year 1999 in its registration year.It is a forum of the Gandhian Workers , who are engaged in individual level for social changee in rural plckets to bring them to one platform for united activities and establishment of positive non-violent ,non-exploitative PRI institutions by introducing Gandhi-Vinoba policy for accountable and responsible peoples representatives.GVMS has involved in peace process.

(a)	Year of Establishment	:	1996
(b)	Registration No.	:	259-90/99-2000
(c)	Location	:	Odisha
(d)	Coverage Area	:	Khurda district
(e)	Staff Strength	:	10- part time
(f)	Source of Funding	:	Public donation, Rotary Club & BBSR
(g)	Approximate population Served	:	1050 families
(h)	Targert Groups	:	Down trodden families,slum dwellers.
(i)	Objectives	:	

- To encourage the rural social activists and organisations to establish and organise Gandhi Vidya Mandir(Sadbhabana School)for Gandhian Basic Education and Nai Talim.
- To introduce activities for world peace and international brotherhood.
- To organise vocational training centres for women ,age care centres, Balwadi and child labour schools for the down trodden classes.

- To establish and encourage the child library, child camp, mobile library, study tour and youth exchange (Gandhian work camp).
- To conduct refresher courses for teachers at regular interval with assistance of Gandhian Basic Education trained research scholars for bettter implement of Gandhian ideology in General education system.
- To endeavour research, training and re-orientation network.
- To organise speeches through the eminent Gandhian professors in variouis Educational streams on Gandhi-Vinoba ideology to make the society an accountable and responsible in future.

Details of Activities

(j)	Research	:	Socio economic development through Nai-Talim is under going.
(k)	Skill Development	:	Skill development approach is introduced in respect of PRI Members and SHG.

♦ ♦ ♦

Indian Institute of Youth and Development

(1) Contact person : P. C. Misra

(2) Designation : Director

(3) Contact No. : 0674-2350259,

(4) Mobile : 9437961821

(5) E- Mail : iiyd@hotmail.com

(6) Website : N.A.

(7) Address : 65-Pawani Complex, Jagamohan Nagar, Khandagiri Bhubaneswar, Odisha-751030

About the Organisation: IIYD was founded during 1978 with a view to promote youth groups, strengthen them and through them take up and development work. During first few years it devoted its time in promoting youth groups and providing training. Ministry of Human Resource Development (MHRD) and Viswa Yuva Kendra (VYK) New Delhi supported for training at the state level. After few years of its operation it has undertaken field projects within a cluster of 200 villages covering major area of Kandhamal and some parts of Ganjam district. It is recognized by Ministry of Human resource Development (Deptt. Of education) has accepted IIYD as All Inca organisation .It has affiliated organizations in 5 states i.e. West Bengal, Andhra Pradesh, Kerala, Tamilnadu and Odisha. The institute has established 33 water source in the water scarcity area and 30 traditional spring water sources (chuans). It has about 35 Publications on rural development till date and more than 50 NGOs have come up in Odisha as a result of training / capacity building programme of IIYD.

(a) Year of Establishment : 1978

(b) Registration No : 14439/1288/78-79/Dt. 2.12.78

(c) Location : Kandhamal / Khurda - Odisha

(d) Coverage Area : 15 districts of Odisha

(e) Staff Strength : Ten

(f) Source of Funding : GOI / International /Membership

(g) Approximate Population Served : 50,000

(h) Target Groups : Tribal / Rural

(i) Objectives :

- Promoting youth groups to think for themselves and for the communities to which they belong.
- Enable tribal / rural mass to join the main stream of development

Details of Activities

During 32 years of its operation it has helped mostly disadvantaged sections of the communities to join the main stream of development.

(j) Research : 35 Publications on topics Scientific explanation of so-called miracles, charcoal preparation, labour saving devices, Banana, Soil, Vit(A) manual, Now technology and employment of disabled persons, Cooperative farming , Bee keeping, Child labour a project design, groundnuts, management of group feeding, guidelines for training organization for group feeding.

(k) Vocational Training :

- Certificate in computer technology (CIT)and Computer Literacy Programme (CLP)
- Carpeting, Gardening, Health education, Kitchen, Tailoring
- Providing profession/education though IGNOU a national university of Govt. of India.
- Its health centre at Koinjhar is catering is catering to the needs of the tribal's mostly far diarrhea control malaria control and MCH Care. It also conducts health education activities in the surrounding area. From time to time it educates people through IEC activities.
- It has conducted training on nutritional deficiency and vitamin 'A'.
- An orientation an Advocacy action was conducted for NGOs working on Water Sector invited and given orientation about Govt. schemes for PRIs
- SHG leaders were given orientation leadership development.
- PRIs were oriented on Government schemes.

(l) Skill Development : Promotion of Youth NGOs across Odisha.

(m) Organisations under Establishment : Networking with water, Sanitation and Hygiene NGOs of 12 districts. About 450 NGOs are affiliated with the institutes from 30 districts of Odisha.

• • •

Lok-Shakti Vikash Kendra

(1)	Contact person	:	Mrs. Gitanjali Behera
(2)	Designation	:	Gen. Secretary
(3)	Contact No.	:	06758-255093
(4)	Mobile	:	9861650347, 9040470324
(5)	E-Mail	:	gitanjali.lsvk@mail.com
(6)	Website	:	N.A.
(7)	Address	:	AT/PO: Nayahat, Dist; Puri-752107

About the Organisation: The institute has been majorly focusing on empowering women and children with a prime focus of motivating the community towards participatory planning process. Over last decade, LSVK has promoted about 215 SHGs and 5 farmer groups and played a tremendous role in empowering women.

(a)	Year of Establishment	:	2000-2001
(b)	Registration No	:	5892-105 /2002-03 on dated 18/08/2002-03
(c)	Location	:	At/po: Nayahat, Gop, Puri (Odisha)
(d)	Coverage Area	:	Gop, Kakatpur, Astaranga, Nimapada, Pipli
(e)	Staff Strength	:	9
(f)	Source of Funding	:	Govt. of Odisha & Govt. of India
(g)	Approximate Population Served	:	70,000/-
(h)	Target Groups	:	Women, farmer, children, SC, Minority, Youth, Disability & Backward Class.
(i)	Objectives	:	

- People's action for participatory sustain community development make common platform for humanitarian objective of self rule and socio-economic power towards peaceful living.

Details of Activities

Developing youth in sports & culture.

- Sensitising women on micro legal literacy.
- Cultivation under SRI.

(j)	Research	:	Women issue. PDS. water & sanitation issue, agriculture technology
(k)	Vocational Training	:	Appliqué, Coir, Mushroom, Readymade garment, Dairy, Poultry
(l)	Skill Development	:	Women, youth & farmer, sensitized women on micro legal literacy.

• • •

Janasahajya

(1) Contact person : Ratna Swar Nath& Basanta Routray

(2) Designation : Secretary

(3) Contact No. : N.A.

(4) Mobile : 09437839951

(5) E-Mail : janasahajya@rediffmail.com

(6) Website : N.A.

(7) Address : Kuchejore, PO-Santpur, Narla Road, Bhawanipatna, Kalahandi-766110 Odisha.

About the Organisation: Janasahajya is actively involved in advocacy process for the development of forest rights act from the beginning with state level and national level forums. With the facilitation of the organisation the local activists and leaders from the operational area have participated in different programmes like workshops, demonstrations and satyagrahas.Janasahajya by its experience in working with the community has identified some other major gap areas of attention for which a major chunk of the population are deprived of in securing their rights over natural resources like land, water, forest, etc. and lack of participation in the decision making process by majority of the population is one of the major cause of the poverty and under development. Taking this in to account, in the later part of intervention the focus area became the conservation of natural resources like land, water and forests, etc., protection of people's right over these resources and small enterprise promotion through women groups.

(a) Year of Establishment : 1986

(b) Registration No. : Societies Registration Act. XXI of 1860 in the year 1989 and registered under the FCRA in the year 1991

(c) Location : Kalahandi

(d) Coverage Area : The organization empowers deprived communities in 206 villages in 5 blocks of 3 Districts, covering a total population of 46000 from socially excluded community of different categories.

(e) Staff Strength : 22

(f) Source of Funding : Government of Odisha, Action India Village, London, UK, NABARD and CARE, Indo Global Social Service Society,. Shanti Odisha, France

(g) Approximate population Served : 46000

(h) Target Groups : Poor and deprived sections of the community, especially socially excluded groups like Schedule tribe, Schedule Caste, Women & Children, older persons and people with different categories of disabilities.

(i) Objectives : To work for the rural poor, by improving their health, sanitation their surroundings and helping them during the times of natural calamities.

Details of Activities

(k) Vocational Training : Capacity building of CBOs to ensure their participation in development processes at village and panchayat levels like pallisabha, Gram Sabha, Forest protection committees etc., watershed development, Rural sanitation programme, SHG formation and Capacity building.

(l) Skill Development :

- PEARL (people empowerment for accessing rights to livelihood): The major focuses in this project are enhancement of income through proper implementation of MGNREGS, social security schemes of government, forest land right act, women SHG formation and capacity building of the members to undertake micro enterprise and bank linkage for the credit requirement, promotion of eco-friendly agriculture practices and sustainable land and water management practices.
- SURAKHYA: The focus of the project is housing, sanitation, kitchen garden development, agriculture development and exploring the scope for the micro enterprise development.

♦ ♦ ♦

Organisation for Rural Reconstruction & Integrated Social Service Activities

(1)	Contact person	:	Shri Biswamohan Mohanty
(2)	Designation	:	Secretary-cum-Director
(3)	Contact No.	:	91-674-2587243
(4)	Mobile	:	91 94370 04697
(5)	E-mail	:	info@orrissa.co.in, orrissabbsr@gmail.com, biswamohanm@gmail.com
(6)	Website	:	www.orrissa.co.in
(7)	Address	:	ORRISSA, Plot No 40/570,Laxmi Vihar, Po-Sainik School, Bhubaneswar-751005. Odisha, India. P. O. Box No. 51, GPO, Bhubaneshwar, Odisha.

About the Organisation

A culmination of the questions, aspiration and philanthropic spirit led a group of committed young Social Worker's to establish the 'Organization for Rural Reconstruction & Integrated Social Service Activities' or in short 'ORRISSA' in the year 1987. The first hand community development experience with international exposure of the founder members led by the founder Secretary Mr. Suresh Chandra Bisoyi took the team to build a farm base in the sector. Under the leadership of Suresh Bhai, the group initiated small community based initiatives in most trying conditions in the year 1987. The preserved and practiced values of the Kondh and Koya adivasi's are the guiding principles in the interventions of the team. In its mission of finding out alternatives for the disadvantaged and neglected, the group operates in some of the interior pockets of the state of Odisha. Over these years, ORRISSA team has been successful in issue-based intervention on tribal rights over Health, Land, Water and Forest through People's Organizations.

(a)	Year of establishment	:	1987
(b)	Registration No	:	Society Registration ACT XXI of 1860 Regd. No – 1838-102 of 1988-89 , Dt. 1st July 1988; FCRA No 104830005 dated 31.07.1991
(c)	Location	:	Bhubaneshwar, Odisha
(d)	Coverage area	:	Tribal villages of Malkangiri and Kandhamal districts of Odisha
(e)	Staff strength	:	42
(f)	Source of funding	:	Trocaire/DC, Ireland ; KZE, Germany; CAPART (Ministry of Rural Development, Govt. of India) New Delhi; National Council of Rural Institutes (NCRI), Hyderabad; Dept. of Youth under Ministry of Youth and Sports, Govt. of India; National Child Labour Eradication Project (NCLP);

National Alliance of Women (NAWO), New Delhi; Project Director (RKVY), Malkangiri and many other sources.

(g) Approximate population served : 15000

(h) Target groups : Farmers, Dalits and tribals.

(i) Objectives :

- To achieve positive health and development of women and children and promote sustainable change process at grassroots
- To rejuvenate the traditional tribal organizations and empower them to sustain their life support systems.
- To facilitate the process of women empowerment.
- To work on community based Natural Resource Management and promote Scientific and Traditional Knowledge.
- To facilitate advocacy and campaigns on emerging issues and strengthen the Panchayati Raj Institutions.

Details of Activities

The following activities are undertaken by the institution:

- Women & Child Rights
- Micro-credit & Micro-Enterprises
- Reproductive & Child Health
- Disaster Mitigation
- Research, Advocacy & Networking

(j) Research : Action Research on Village self Reliance through development of Village Micro Plans; Training on Fruits Process and Pickle Making;

(k) Vocational training : Supported by NABARD, ORRISSA has facilitated two entrepreneurship development programme on Pickle making and Amla Quash for 30 adivasi women in Kandhamal district. The trainees were successfully linked to the bank and availed loan for regular production and marketing.

(l) Skill development :

- The project supported by UNICEF, Bhubaneswar identified a total of 150 traditional Dai's operating in Chakapada block and oriented them on the skills of safe delivery.
- Capacity building of 'Asha' Workers under Brahmanpad PHC area in Chakapad block of Kandhamal district. The project was supported by CDMO, Kandhamal, under NRHM Progamme, Govt of Odisha, continuing since June 2008.

(m) Organisations under establishment :

1. Maa Bhabani Chasi Sangathan, Gangala and Pedawada G.P., Malkangiri
2. Banabasi Chasi Unnyana Samiti, Udupa and Padmagiri G.P., Malkangiri

3. Mahalaxmi Krusak Sangathan, Tikabali of Tikabali Block
4. Nilanchal Krusak Sangathan, Chahali GP, Chakapad Block
5. Trisambhu Krusak Sangathan, Chakapad, Chakapad Block
6. Mahila Krusi Oh Swastya Samabaya Ltd, Chahali, Chakapad Block
7. Mahalaxmi Chasi Sangathan, Vejaguda and Nayakguda G.P.Mathili
8. Saberi Chasi Sangathan, Tandbai, Bhubanpali, Lugal G.P. of Padia and Kalimela block.

♦ ♦ ♦

Sachetana

(1)	Contact person	:	Sri Umesh Mohanty
(2)	Designation	:	Secretary
(3)	Contact No.	:	Tel: 0674-2430916
(4)	Mobile	:	09853188993
(5)	E-Mail	:	umeshpmn@yahoo.com
(6)	Website	:	N.A.
(7)	Address	:	Street Address Brp-96, Pandav Nagar, Tankapani Road Bhubaneswar - 751018

About the Organisation: This organization is established by like- minded people gathered for the establishment of the poor and downtroden people of Odisha and formed the organization "Sachetana".The main motto is to educate the poor women and provide the necessary assistance for their earnings to have a good society in projected area.

(a)	Year of Establishment	:	1995
(b)	Registration No.	:	21545/122 of 2002-2003 issued against Khurda District; Reg. No: KRD 6783-465 of 1995-96
(c)	Location	:	Astarang, Puri district Pin 752109
(d)	Coverage Area	:	Puri Distirct
(e)	Staff Strength	:	35
(f)	Source of Funding	:	Central social welfare board and state social welfare board. National Instiute of Naturopathy.
(g)	Approximate population Served	:	3,000
(h)	Target Groups	:	Poor deprived women and disabled women
(i)	Objectives	:	The main object is to educate the poor women and provide the necessary assistance for their earnings to have a good society in projected area.

Details of Activities

(j)	Research	:	Education and livelihood programme
(k)	Vocational Training	:	Tailoring, Bamboo craft, computer training.
(l)	Skill Development	:	Marketing support
(m)	Organisations under establishment	:	1. Sachetana, Astarang. 2. Sachetana, Waligang, Paripada, Dt Mayurghanj

♦ ♦ ♦

Sarvodaya Samiti

(1)	Contact person	:	Akshay Kumar Mohanty
(2)	Designation	:	Secretary
(3)	Contact No.	:	Tel/Fax: 91-6852-251417 (O),
(4)	Mobile	:	9438351393/919437053637
(5)	E-Mail	:	samiti@bsnl.in, sarvodayasamiti@gmail.com
(6)	Website	:	www.sarvodaya.net.in
(7)	Address	:	Sarvodaya Samiti, Gandhi Nagar, Koraput –Odisha State-764020.

About the Organisation: The Sarvodaya Samiti is a non-government, non-political & non-profit making organization committed for the development of tribal, rural and other underprivileged classes of the Society. The Samiti was formed by some eminent freedom fighters and dedicated social workers during the Bhoodan and Gramadan movement initiated by Acharya Binoba Bhave during 1959. The Sarvodaya Samiti was earlier known as Narayanpatna Khetra Samiti, started its operation in Koraput and Kalahandi districts of Odisha. The Samiti was registered under Societies Registration Act in the year 1970-71.

(a)	Year of Establishment	:	1950
(b)	Registration No.	:	Societies Registration No. 5883/83 of 1970-71 under the Act XXI of 1860
(c)	Location	:	Koraput, Odisha
(d)	Coverage Area	:	Odisha
(e)	Staff strength	:	30
(f)	Source of funding	:	Govt of India & Govt of Odisha
(g)	Approximate population served	:	12,000
(h)	Target groups	:	SC/ST/OBC/Women, Children and other economically weaker sections
(i)	Objectives	:	The main objectives of this organization are to create a literate, educated community with improved awareness and decision making capabilities, to develop human resources for effective use of their potential and to promote of Khadi and Village Industries to mobilize local resources and man power.
(j)	Vocational training	:	Tailoring, leaf plates making, khadi, weaving, spinning.
(k)	Skill Development	:	Entrepreneurship development programme
(l)	Organisations under establishment	:	

- Sarvodaya Samiti, Dharamgarh, Kalahandi district, Odisha.
- Sarvodaya Samiti, Nabarangapur, Dabugoan district, Odisha

♦ ♦ ♦

Seva Samaj

(1)	Contact person	:	Sri. Rajeshwari Dalai
(2)	Designation	:	Secretary
(3)	Contact No.	:	06857-250001
(4)	Mobile	:	9437338217
(5)	E-Mail	:	seba samaj@gmail.com
(6)	Website	:	N.A.
(7)	Address	:	At P.O Gunupur, Rayagada Dist., Odisha -765022.

About the Organisation: The Seva Samaj is a voluntary organization grew out of the Bhoodan-Sarvodaya movement in undivided Koraput District. A team of Sarvodaya workers who ere dedicated to the cause and welfare of the down-trodden, decided to form an association with the objective to eliminate the condition under which the tribals, harijans and the down trodden were facing exploitation. The broader objective was to initiate a social change through the methods of Mahatma Gandhi and Vinobaji.

Accordingly seva samaj was formed with an objective to educate the future generation of the down-trodden, so that they could be able to fight out their own problems and join in the main stream of the society. The seva samaj has been concentrating in the education of the tribal girls since 1964 up to this date. In 1964, a small tribal girls hostel was started at Rayagada with only eight girls. In these years it was expanded to hostels, orphan homes, residential schools, and crèche centes in which services are rendered to 286 tribal-orphan girls and 280 children, mainly tribals. So the present strength of totals comes to 566.

(a)	Year of Establishment	:	1964
(b)	Registration No	:	Regd no: 3350/44 of 1965-66
(c)	Location	:	Rayagada district
(d)	Coverage Area	:	Odisha
(e)	Staff Strength	:	11
(f)	Source of Funding	:	State government, Women and Child welfare Department
(g)	Approximate population Served	:	131 per year
(h)	Target Groups	:	Tribal children
(i)	Objectives	:	The object of this association is to promote social, educational and economic advancement of the tribals and depressed communities by selfless service through truthful and nonviolent means.

- To make peaceful efforts for the establishment of classless, casteless and unexploited society.

- To promote the social welfare of the tribals and the backward communities etc. and to diffuse useful knowledge in them, with a view there to start, establish, conduct and maintain educational centres, social welfare centres, dispensaries, maternity centres, technical training centres, hostels and boarding houses.
- To run social service centre in backward areas of the state in order to fulfil the objectives of the seva samaj.
- To start orphanages and shelter homes for the widows and depressed women.
- To prevent, suppress and abolish all kinds of diseases and epidemics and also all kinds of social vices including intemperance, prostitution, gambling, exploitations and other evils by all legitimate and peaceful means.
- To spread among the people the cooperative movement in the form of coop societies.
- To organize and take up all constructive programmes expounded by Mahatma Gandhi and Vinobaji including Khadi and Village Industries.
- To organize labour welfare centres for the agricultural and industrial labourers.
- To provide, establish, endow, manage, control and aid schools and educational institutions of all kinds and in particular spread literacy to open adult educational centes and night school etc.,

Details of Activities

(k) Vocational Training : Painting and music

(l) Skill development : Spinning Charkha

♦ ♦ ♦

Social Association for Rural Development and Health Action

(1)	Contact person	:	Sukanta Sethi
(2)	Designation	:	President
(3)	Contact No.	:	Ph: 06853-245814
(4)	Mobile	:	9439545524
(5)	E-Mail	:	sardha.1@gmail.com,
(6)	Website	:	N.A.
(7)	Address	:	Social Association for Rural Development and Health Action (SARDHA), At/P.O – Muniguda, District – Rayagada, Odisha.

About the Organisation: The Organisation SARDHA had made its noble effort of a group of youths and intellectuals with an aim of nurturing the under-privileged rural mass and undeveloped urban slum in our society. The organisation with its trained, experienced, skilled and determined team of professionals has always aspired and struggled to actualize its dream to reality. The creative and innovative pursuits of the organisation have helped its action to be realised till today and the management is confident that this process will continue in future.

(a)	Year of establishment	:	1996
(b)	Registration No	:	2011
(c)	Located	:	Rural area
(d)	Coverage Area	:	5- blocks, 200 Villages, Rayagada District.
(e)	Staff strength	:	3 Teaching Staff, 16- Non-teaching, 2- technical, 6- Non technical, 3- Peon.
(f)	Source of funding	:	NABARD- Bhubaneswar, NCRI- Hyd, NIN- Pune, RCDC-Bhubaneswar, UNDP, Water and sanitation, Donations from the NGOs and People, Vedanta foundation-Bombay.
(g)	Approximate population Served	:	10,000 People
(h)	Target Groups	:	Particularly on ST Children, Women, Women's SHG, Tribal Girls.
(i)	Objectives	:	The aim of this centre is to promote this initiative in the areas to secure the food problems faced by the state and on the other hand, it is a process to restore the interest of labour and the attraction of agriculture as a source of meaningful livelihood.

Details of Activities

SARDHA activities are in the areas of Health and Nutrition, Disaster Mitigatio, Women Development, Health Camp, Road Safety, AIDS awareness camp, Naturopathy and Yoga, Vocational training, SHG promotion, Cultural activity, Polution Control etc.

(j)	Vocational training	:	Pickle training, Phenyl making, Tailoring, Cotton weaving, Spinning, Organic Farming, entrepreneurial development.

♦ ♦ ♦

Social Organisation for Voluntary Action

(1)	Contact person	:	Udayendu Mishra
(2)	Designation	:	Director
(3)	Contact No.	:	06722228745
(4)	Mobile	:	9437361026
(5)	E- Mail	:	sovadkl@rediffmail.com
(6)	Website	:	N.A.
(7)	Address	:	Social Organisation for Voluntary ction, Ranapasi, Gengutia (P.O.), Denkanal District-759013

About the Organisation: This Institute was established on 02 Oct 1989 . It is awarded by State level humanitarian service award from Govt of Odisha and outstanding youth club award from the district admin of Denkanal district. The institute works towards empowerment of women and youth, community health and livelihood project of socio economic backward.

(a)	Year of Establishment	:	1989
(b)	Registration No.	:	2846/210 dt 19/9/1992
(c)	Location	:	Ranapasi, Gengutia (P.O.), Denkanal district
(d)	Coverage Area	:	Denkanal district of Odisha
(e)	Staff Strength	:	42
(f)	Source of Funding	:	Ministry of Textiles, Ministry of Youth affair sports, and Ministry of Health and Family Welfare.
(g)	Approximate population Served	:	1 lakh
(h)	Target Groups	:	Dalits , backwards & tribals, SHGs
(i)	Objectives	:	The main object of this Institute is empowerment of women and youth, community health and livelihood project of socio economic backward.

Details of Activities

(j)	Vocational Training	:	Skill upgradation training in traditional crafts(bamboo production) computer & screen printing, handicraft training and youth club development training.
(l)	Skill Development	:	SHG promotion, Youth Activities like National Integration Camp, Health Activities like RCH, AIDS awareness, eye care, gender issues, adolescent issues, Rural Sports & Cultural Programme like promotion of rural sports talents & formation of a cultural team towards organizing cultural shows in different issues.
(m)	Organisations under establishment	:	SOVA, Jagannathpur P.O, Angul District, Odisha.

♦ ♦ ♦ ♦

Vinoba Seva Pratisthan

(1)	Contact person	:	Mr. Manoj Jena
(2)	Designation	:	General Secretary
(3)	Contact No.	:	0674-2595973
(4)	Mobile	:	09437178921
(5)	E-Mail	:	info@vspodisha.org, vspOdisha@gmail.com
(6)	Website	:	www.vspodisha.org
(7)	Address	:	298, Ganga Nagar, Unit-6, Bhubaneswar, Odisha - 751003.

About the Organisation: Vinoba Seva Pratistan (VSP) is a Non Political, Non Profit Voluntary Organization working with the poor and deprived communities of the state of Odisha (India). Vinoba Seva Pratisthan (VSP) has been formed and inspired by the pragmatic and humanistic work-ethics and values of Mahatma Gandhi and his number one disciple Vinoba Bhave .The organization is a common platform for the like-minded people to work together for human development. VSP envisions a just and equitable society based on self-reliance, social well-being and sustainable development following Gandhian and Sarvodaya principles.

(a)	Year of Establishment	:	2004
(b)	Registration No	:	Registration under SRA Regn. No.: 21834/12
(c)	Location	:	Bhubaneshwar
(d)	Coverage Area	:	Entire Odisha
(e)	Staff Strength	:	...
(f)	Source of Funding	:	Donations
(g)	Approximate population Served	:	Odisha
(h)	Target Groups	:	Poor and deprived communities of Odisha
(i)	Objectives	:	Upliftment of poor and deprived communities & enabling of visually-impaired women .

Details of Activities

- Strengthening of Panchayati Raj Institutions (PRIs)
- Issue based campaign for burning problems of Odisha
- Youth mobilization for Peace & Development

(j) Vocational Training: Imparting training to 300 Youth Volunteers for Emergency Response

- Training to 600 Youth Club members on
- community development

- Providing self employment assistance to 50 visually impaired women ,Advocacy & Lobby for the betterment of disabled

(k) Skill Development : Conducting trainings & Intervention on human rights issues

♦ ♦ ♦

Voluntary Action for the Rural Reconstruction

(1)	Contact person	:	Mrs Gitanjali Rout
(2)	Designation	:	Chairman
(3)	Contact No.	:	09437865563
(4)	Mobile	:	09777992975
(5)	E-Mail	:	info@varr.org, varr_dkl@yahoo.com varrdkl@gmail.com
(6)	Website	:	www.varr.org
(7)	Address	:	VARR, Dhenkanal, At/PO-Anlabereni Dist. Dhenkanal State-Odisha, Pin- 759026.

About Organisation: This is Institute is a registered voluntary organization working for the rural women, dalit, tribal since last 17 years in the Dhenkanal District of Odisha. It is a secular of political philanthropic organization solely committed to the cause of rural generation. This organization works at true level, first it carries out community development programme in the direct partnership with the poor and marginalized in the remote tribal areas of the Dhenkanal District of Odisha.

(a)	Year of Establishment	:	1993
(b)	Registration No.	:	3106/23 Registered in Odisha ,under the Societies Act 1860
(c)	Location	:	Anlabereni, Dist.- Dhenkanal, State-Odisha
(d)	Coverage Area	:	131 villages in 4 blocks
(e)	Staff Strength	:	17
(f)	Source of Funding	:	NABARD, CAPART, Govt. of India
(g)	Approximate population Served	:	20,000
(h)	Target Groups	:	women, Children, SC/ST
(i)	Objectives	:	First, it carries out community development programmes in direct partnership with the poor and marginalized in the remote tribal areas of the district. Its grass root level activities are aimed at enabling people to create their own institutional means for fulfilling their needs and securing their entitlements. Second, it extends its support to primary level community based organisation (CBO) and other development organisation and networks to accelerate the process of social changes. Third, it carries out policy research and advocacy on issues concerning the poor and tries to reorient development policies and paradigms

along their needs and aspiration.Details of Activities Stabilising people's livelihood has been the major thrust of VARR's poverty eradication strategy.

(j). Research : Rural farmers in sheer paddy

(k) Vocational Training : Bamboo, metal craft, mushrooms, agriculture vegetable cropping, food processing, spices making., Increasing environmental awareness of the target community, Teacher's sensitisation programmes to promote equitable learning opportunities among the Disabiled, Micro Finance, Capacity Building of SHGs,Micro enterprise and marketing, Water Harvesting / Management, Bio-Fertilisers, Organic Vegetable Cultivation, Organic Vegetable Cultivation.

(l) Skill Development : Capacity building of self help groups, capacity building of acquitted social health activity, handicrafts, Leaf Cup Plate making, Soft toys making, Tailoring.

♦ ♦ ♦

RAJASTHAN

Banasthali Vidyapeeth

(1)	Contact person	:	Prof. Diwakar Shastri
(2)	Designation	:	President
(3)	Contact No.	:	01438 228341 (12 Lines) Fax: 228365
(4)	Mobile	:	N.A.
(5)	E- Mail	:	dshastri@banasthali.ac.in
(6)	Website	:	http://www.banasthali.org
(7)	Address	:	Banasthali University, P. O. Banasthali Vidyapith, Rajasthan – 304022, Jaipur Campus, Banasthali Vidyapith, C-62, Sarojini Marg, C-Scheme, Jaipur (Raj.) - 302001.

About the Organisation: The Banasthali Vidyapith was established originally in 1935 and became a deemed to be university in 1983. Originally established as a school for girls in the memory of their departed daughter, Shantabai, by her parents, Smt. Ratan Shastri and Pandit Hiralal Shastri, in course of time, it began to offer undergraduate and graduate courses for women. Originally an "Approved Institution" of Rajasthan University, which gave it some degree of autonomy, it subsequently sought university status and became a deemed university in 1983, so that, it could enjoy greater autonomy to achieve its educational goals. It is a women's university and the only one in the northern states of the country.

(a)	Year of Establishment	:	1935
(b)	Registration No.	:	Deemed to be university under Section 3, UGC Act December 9 to 11, 2002
(c)	Location	:	Rajasthan
(d)	Coverage Area	:	North India
(e)	Staff Strength	:	196
(f)	Source of Funding	:	UGC
(g)	Approximate population Served	:	Rajasthan
(h)	Target Groups	:	women

- The Vidyapith is a unitary university with certificate, diploma and degree programmes and also has a school attached to it. It is situated on 610 acres of land.
- The Vidyapith has different undergraduate, postgraduate, diploma and certificate courses of traditional, unconventional, professional and vocational nature. It has nine (9) Faculties, viz. science, mathematical science, social science, management, home science, education and fine arts. The programmes encompass a wide spectrum of disciplines from computer science to biological and physical sciences to business management, humanities including

arts, fine and performing arts, home science and foundation courses including Indian Cultural heritage, Women's Studies and one vocational course.

(i) Objectives : The Banasthali Universities aim of a full and balanced development of students' personality got concrete expression in the form of 'Panchmukhi Shiksha' which evolved out of initial experimentation. ' Panchmukhi Shiksha ' attempts a balance of the five aspects of education, namely Physical, Practical, Aesthetic, Moral and Intellectual.

The Banasthali University's aims at the synthesis of spiritual values and scientific achievements of the East and the West. Its educational programme is based on the concept of " Panchmukhi Shiksha " and aims at all round harmonious development of personality. Emphasis on Indian culture and thought and simple living including khadi wearing are hallmarks of life at Banasthali.

Details of Activities

(j) Research : Research has been a component of the Vidyapith's higher education even before its attainment of Deemed University status. However, earlier it concentrated mainly on Doctoral research but over the past ten years, the efforts have expanded to include institutional and individual research projects.

Nineteen departments in the Vidyapith have research programmes leading to M.Phil and Ph.D. degrees. There are 12 full time and 76 part time research scholars and more than 34% of the faculty members are involved in research activities in their disciplines. Quite a few teachers have authored books and have a number of research publications to their credit.

In the last five years nineteen departments have reported around 10 research projects. As research work is almost absent in some of the departments it is necessary that a plan for development of research be initiated.

♦ ♦ ♦

Barefoot College

(1)	Contact person	:	Sanjith Roy
(2)	Designation	:	Director
(3)	Contact No.	:	+91 (0)1463- 288204, +91 (0)1463-288206
(4)	Mob	:	No
(5)	E-mail	:	barefootcollege@gmail.com
(6)	Website	:	www.barefootcollege.org
(7)	Address	:	The Director, Barefoot College Tilonia, Rajasthan, Tilonia vill, via Mdanganj, Ajmeer Dist, Rajasthan-305816.

About the Organisation: Established in 1972, the Barefoot College is a non-government organisation that has been providing basic services and solutions to problems in rural communities, with the objective of making them self-sufficient and sustainable. These 'Barefoot solutions' can be broadly categorised into solar energy, water, education, health care, rural handicrafts, people's action, communication, women's empowerment and wasteland development.

(a)	Year of establishment	:	1972
(b)	Registration No	:	Social work & research centre 5292, 1971, 1860 Act, Society
(c)	Location	:	Tilonia, Rajasthan
(d)	Coverage area	:	15 states affiliated & sub centres
(e)	Staff strength	:	180 (or) 200
(f)	Source of funding	:	NABARD, Ministry of Labour, Education, Youth & Sports
(g)	Approximate population served	:	50 lakhs
(h)	Targert groups	:	Rural men and women
(i)	Objectives	:	

- The College believes that for any rural development activity to be successful and sustainable, it must be based in the village as well as managed and owned by those whom it serves. Therefore, all Barefoot initiatives whether social, political or economic, are planned and implemented by a network of rural men and women who are known as 'Barefoot Professionals'.

Details of Activities

Barefoot College draws on the same philosophy when it selects members of the rural community to provide education in its rural schools. This is done to reduce dependency on external aid as well as reduce migration by generating employment within the rural communities.

(j) Research : The Barefoot College has been pioneering solar electrification in rural, remote, non-electrified villages, since 1989. The College has demystified solar technology and is decentralizing its application by making it available to poor and neglected communities.The Social Work and Research Centre had a media centre, where film strips and slides were developed for using in the educational camps for the adults.

(k) Vocational training : Rain Water Harvesting, Clothing and accessories, decorative home furnishings, furniture, rugs, textiles, handmade paper products, puppets, educational toys, metalwork, and leather goods, making puppets, writing the scripts, and presenting the programmes.

Rural men and women irrespective of age, who are barely literate or not at all, and have no hope of getting even the lowest government job, are being trained to work as day and night school teachers, doctors, midwives, dentists, health workers, balsevikas, solar engineers, solar cooker mechanics, water drillers, hand pump mechanics, architects, artisans, designers, masons, communicators, water testers, phone operators, blacksmiths, carpenters, computer instructors, accountants and kabaad-se-jugaad professionals

(l) Skill development : The Barefoot College creates livelihoods directly as well as indirectly, through its programmes such as Solar Energy, Water, Education, Health Care, Rural Handicrafts, People's Action, Communication, Women's Empowerment and Wasteland Development, Sewing, fabricating at the mechanical workshop, candle-making, chalk-making and carperntry.

♦ ♦ ♦

Gram Vikas Seva Sansthan

(1)	Contact person	:	M. L. Choudhary
(2)	Designation	:	Chairman
(3)	Contact No.	:	9414499337
(4)	Mobile	:	9414499337
(5)	E- Mail	:	gvsspiparcity@rediffmail.com
(6)	Website	:	gvssjdr.org
(7)	Address	:	Adrash Colony, Silari Road, PIPARCITY-342601, District-Jodhpur (Raj.) India.

About Organization: Gram Vikas Seva Sansthan is registered in 1997-98 under Rajasthan Society act 1958, Registration under Foreign Contribution Regulation Act of 1976, 12 A Registration Certificate & Valid 80G.

(a)	Year of Establishment	:	1997
(b)	Registration No	:	206/Jodhpur/1997-98
(c)	Location	:	Jodhpur
(d)	Coverage Area	:	Jodhpur, Jalore, Jaisalmer, Barmer, Pali & Nagaur
(e)	Staff Strength	:	Full Time- 97, Part time-80, Self Employ- 250
(f)	Source of Funding	:	Govt. Department
(g)	Approximate population Served	:	1 lac above
(h)	Target Groups	:	SC/ST/OBC/General Women, Child Labour & Others

(i) Objectives

- To work for poor, Dalit and backward classes of the people for social upliftment.
- Poor disabled, helpless women and youth employment for income generation.
- Maternal and child health services in remote and distance places.
- Land and water conservation programmes.
- Health, Education Environment and Social Evils Eradication and Awareness.
- Community mobilisation.
- Strengthening of community structure.
- Social mobilisation for fulfilling the local needs.
- Poverty Alleviation programmes.
- Adult Education, Balbari Programmes.
- Strengthening Panchayat Raj Institutions.
- Economic upliftment of women of poor classes.

- Women empowerment, especially in slums.
- Research and analytical work relating to socio-economic projects.
- To work for upliftment of dalits.
- To Co-ordinate programmes on rural development and Panchaytiraj.

Details of activities

Present Activities run by GVSS- BPL SHG Formation & Credit Linkage ,Non BPL SHG Formation & Credit linkage, Asha- Sahyogni Block Level Training, Total Sanitation Campaign, Targeted Intervention Project (FSW), Short Stay Home,Jeevan Aadhar Community Care Centre, Family Counselling Centre, Male Sex Worker Project (MSW), Rajiv Gandhi National Creche Scheme, Non BPL SHG Formation & Credit linkage, Inter State Youth Exchange Program Non BPL SHG Formation & Credit linkage, Rajiv Gandhi National Creche Scheme, Targeted Intervention Project (FSW)

(j) Vocational Training : REDP Training in Jodhpur, Jaisalmer & Jalore District.

♦ ♦ ♦

Jagran Jan Vikas Samiti

(1)	Contact person	:	Ganesh Purohit
(2)	Designation	:	Founder Director
(3)	Contact No.	:	+91 294 2441322
(4)	Mobile	:	N.A
(5)	E- Mail	:	jagraqn@jjvs.org, jagranudr@gmail.com
(6)	Website	:	www.jjvs.org
(7)	Address	:	Sapetia Road, Bedla, Udaipur Rajasthan India 313 011

About the organization: Jagran Jan Vikas Samiti (JJVS) is a non-governmental organization that focuses on the socio-economic improvements of the rural and tribal communities in Rajasthan, India.

"Jagran Jan Vikas Samiti" means an association dedicated to public awareness and self-development through cooperative efforts. JJVS was established in 1985 and founded by a group of people from Valī and its surrounding villages. The organization is based in Udaipur and operates in tribal villages of southern Rajasthan while expanding its activities related to promotion of traditional system of medicines in 7 states. JJVS has own Field offices in Jaisamand, Vali, Kurabar and Dhariyawad in Udaipur and Pratapgarh district of Rajasthan.

(a)	Year of Establishment	:	1985
(b)	Registration No	:	21/udaipur/1987-88 under society Regd.act.
(c)	Location	:	Udaipur.
(d)	Coverage Area	:	JJVS operates in more than 130 villages in the 8 development blocks of Udaipur District of Rajasthan state.
(e)	Staff Strength	:	JJVS has 21 full-time and 12 part-time employees; We also have more than 250 volunteers from all around the world.
(f)	Source of Funding	:	NCRI, Misereor, Germany, UNDP, Ministry of Environment & Forest, Govt. of India, Department of AYUSH, Ministry of Health & Family Welfare, Govt. of India, Catholic Relief Services, India, CAPART, Govt. of India, Misereor, Germany, Department of science & technology Govt. of India.
(g)	Approximate population served	:	30,000
(h)	Target Groups	:	Rural and Tribal Communities.
(i)	Objectives	:	

- Supporting appropriate rural development and agriculture-based industries

- Creating a clearinghouse of local solutions to local problems
- Increasing awareness of health and education opportunities
- Improving the effectiveness of government plans and programs
- Conserving the environment and natural resources
- Organizing the community for coordinated campaigns

Details of Activities

(j) Research : Design and implement innovative projects during their time at Jagran and provide crucial research used for lobbying and community planning.

(k) Vocational Training : In arts, personality development, games, competitions in general knowledge.

(l) Skill Development : 2500 households from 10 villages benefited by strengthening govt. schemes or programme and getting ownership right on livelihood resources

- Through watershed programme 6700 households from 15 villages became self-sufficient in managing their natural resources and are using best agricultural practices for changing their lives
- 90 Self Help Group and 70 Joint Liability Group members are using micro loans to establish small scale village based industries for their income generation

(m) Organisations under Establishment : 4 regional level community organizations constituted for lobbying and advocacy of different development policy issues

- Jhameshwar Majdoor Kisan Sangh under Jhamari Bachao Andolan for industrial pollution and Mine displacement issues
- Jangal Jameen Jan Andolan regulation of forest right act, 2006 in tribal area for allotment of cultivable forest land
- Jaisamand Vikas Manch for giving preference to local people for water supply from Jaisamand lake; sustainable conservation and utilization of natural resources in catchments area of Jaisamand lake
- Chadreshwar Kisan Sangharsh Samiti for Mansi – Wakal dam displacement issue.

♦ ♦ ♦

Mahila Evam Paryavaran Vikas Sansthan

(1)	Contact person	:	R. C. Saini
(2)	Designation	:	Chief Functionary
(3)	Contact No.	:	01428-680843
(4)	Mob	:	9829142013
(5)	E-mail	:	mepvs.dudu@gmail.com
(6)	Website	:	N.A.
(7)	Address	:	Mozamabad, Laporiya Village (Dudu) Jaipur, Rajasthan-303008

About the Organisation: Mahila Evam Paryavaran Vikas Sansthan (MEPVS) is anon-government development organization that was established by a few like-minded village youth groups with a vision of holistic development of the local villages. The Organisation has been implementing integrated rural development programs in twenty villages of Dudu and Phagi blocks of Jaipur district in Rajasthan since 1998. MEPVS believes that all human beings have innate potential, which can be developed by providing proper learning environment and opportunities.

(a)	Year of establishment	:	1998
(b)	Registration No	:	Regd.no.706 March 5th.
(c)	Location	:	Jaipur
(d)	Coverage area	:	Dudu, phagi district, 25 villages in Jaipur
(e)	Staff strength	:	8
(f)	Source of funding	:	NCRI
(g)	Approximate population served	:	2,050 people
(h)	Target groups	:	School children and women
(i)	Objectives	:	

- Integrated development of women and girls from vulnerable and disadvantaged communities.
- Better education, health, agriculture and natural resource management of rural community.Initiating and implementing plans and programs at various level to reduce social and gender disparities in the rural communities and to bring the deprived communities in the the mainstream of development.
- Implement and collaborate in social welfare and development programs of central and state governments.
- Upliftment of rural poor, Buniyadi sikshan to the drop outs.

Details of Activities

(j)	Research	:	Awareness on buniyadi sikshan, training for govt teachers on Nai Talim education.
(k)	Vocational Training	:	Anganwadi, cultural programmes, and puppet shows.
(l)	Skill Development	:	Embroidery, artificial flowers.

♦ ♦ ♦

Manav Pragati Sansthan

(1)	Contact person	:	Pradeep Poonia
(2)	Designation	:	Chief Executive
(3)	Contact No.	:	01562-258054
(4)	Mobile	:	91-9414665855
(5)	E-mail	:	mpsrajgarh170@yahoo.co.in
(6)	Website	:	www.mpsraj.org
(7)	Address	:	Usmanabad Colony, Behind New Bus Stand, Churu (Rajasthan)-331001

About the Organisation: Manav Pragati Sansthan (MPS) means "Society human development" and is a non government organisation founded in 1996. In addition to its health & educational presentation activities, MPS works improve and project the Govt., provided vocational training to rural women, rural youth and uplift those who are backward about their socio-economic situation. The organization is a pioneer in self employment sector and has been working on these issues since its inception. The organization has been implementing rural health, education, environmental conservation, self employment through vocational training project and organize EDP programme from time to time .

(a)	Year of Establishment	:	1996-97
(b)	Registration No	:	91/churu/96-97
(c)	Location	:	Churu (Rajasthan)
(d)	Coverage Area	:	All Rajasthan State
(e)	Staff Strength	:	31
(f)	Source of Funding	:	Grant-in Aid, Donation & Contribution, Membership fee, Foreign Funding
(g)	Approximate population Served	:	1 Lakh
(h)	Target Groups	:	Women, youth, children, oldage, rural population
(i)	Objectives	:	Education, health, self employment promotion, rural development and social welfare.

Details of Activities

(j) Vocational Training: 360 youth along with women have been trained in different kind skill trade like Readymade garments –cum-embroidery, computer literacy, electrical- cum-electronics, Motor vehicles driving, beautician, rural young professional etc.

(k) Skill Development: 360 youth have been trained in skill development training.

• • •

Sahaj Sansthan

(1)	Contact Person	:	Sri Baburam Bishnoi
(2)	Designation	:	Chairman
(3)	Contact No.	:	02925-222651,
(4)	Mob.	:	094144 12367, 099502 22895
(5)	E-mail	:	sahajkhichan@rediffmail.Com, b.rambishnoi@rediffmail.Com, sahajsansthan@gmail.com
(6)	Website	:	N.A
(7)	Address	:	Sahaj Sansthan, B-182, Jawahar Colony, Khichan (Phalodi), Jodhpur, Rajasthan - 342 308

About the Organisation

Over a decade, Sahaj Sansthan is dedicated to the fulfillment of requirements and aspirations of people. The institute has been developing suitable techniques for rural development resulting in the growth, enhancement and progress in the fields of agriculture, drinking water, environment, protection of wild-life, education, health, women development and cattle-life in order to strengthen the rural economic system. The SAHAJ SANSTHAN is dedicated to the fulfillment of requirements and aspirations of people.

(a)	Year of Establishment	:	1999-2010
(b)	Registration No	:	191/2000
(c)	Location	:	Jodhpur (Rajastan)
(d)	Coverage Area	:	Two Block (Jodhpur District) One Block (Jaisalmer District)
(e)	Staff Strength	:	15 Person staff and 25 volunteers
(f)	Source of Funding	:	Central Govt./State Govt./Trust
(g)	Approximate Population Served	:	25000
(h)	Target Groups	:	Youth/Women/student and SC/ST
(i)	Objectives:	:	

- To develop a suitable technique for rural development resulting in the growth, enhancement and progress in the fields of agriculture, drinking water, environment, protection of wild-life, education, health, women development and cattle-life in order to strengthen the rural economic system.
- To prepare and implement development plans on the basis of balanced use of human resources and overall participation of people.

Details of Activities

- Rural Education Training and Awareness Programme
- Participatory Rural Appraisal Camp
- Nirmal Gram Abhiyan
- Total Sanitation Campaign
- National Programme Medicinal Plants Traditional Knowledge and Enhancing.
- Residential Gunni Training
- National Environment Awareness Campaign
- National Child Labour Education Programme
- Awareness Generation for Rural and Poor Women
- Workshop on Prevention of HIV-AIDS
- Sensitization Programme on Prevention of female Feticide / Infanticide
- Workshop on Women Empowerment and Sensitization
- Training of Child Right Policies and Legislation
- Animal Husbandry Treatment and Awareness camp
- Woman self help group Training
- Drawback Deaf- Dumb Boys-Girls Residential Educational Camp
- Reproductive Child Health Programme
- Inter State Youth Exchange Programme
- Panchayat Election Voters Awareness Campaign
- Condensed course of Education for Adult Women

(k) Vocational Training : Women Self Help Group Training

(l) Skill Development : Barefoot Veterinarian Training, Pri Training, Staff Capacity Building, Core Team Training .

♦ ♦ ♦

Society to Uplift Rural Economy

(1)	Contact person	:	Magraj Jain
(2)	Designation	:	Secretary
(3)	Contact No.	:	02982- 230801, 231103, 260123
(4)	Mobile	:	9414107501
(5)	E-Mail	:	surebmr@rediffmail.com
(6)	Website	:	www.sure.com
(7)	Address	:	Gurdwara Road, Po. No. 29 Barmer, Rajasthan

About the Organisation: 'Society To Uplift Rural Economy or SURE as it is popularly known ,is the outcome of the vision of Padama Shri Magraj Jain-a vision that has matured over six decades of work with the poor and destitute in Barmer district. In the beginning SURE started work with women folk of the refugees from Pakistan of the Indo-Pak war of 1971.In 1992 SURE started work in education with the Shiksha Karmi programme of the Rajasthan Government. SURE has been active in providing relief in the face of the prolonged drought that the region has been facing since 1999.

The working area of SURE has been the Barmer district. To begin with SURE wanted to work in an area that was remote, inaccessible and devoid of any facilities.

(a)	Year of Establishment	:	1992
(b)	Registration No.	:	55/Barmer/89-90 dated 22/2/1990
(c)	Location	:	Barmer
(d)	Coverage Area	:	Rajasthan
(e)	Staff Strength	:	150
(f)	Source of Funding	:	Government of India

1. Indian Council of Agricultural Research (ICAR), Ministry of Agriculture, GOI
2. Department of Science & Technology, Ministry of Science & Technology, GOI
3. Ministry of Forest and Environment, GOI
4. Ministry of Textile, GOI
5. Ministry of Social Welfare Department, GOR

Foreign

1. Action Aid
2. EZE, Germany (Voluntary Health Association of India)
3. Save the Children fund UK
4. Sight Savers International

5. CASA
6. Christian Aid
7. Capitalization of Livestock Programme Experiences India (CALPI)
8. INTERCOORPORATION/SWISS DEVELOPMENT CORPORATION

Other Agencies/Trust

1. Aravali, Jaipur
2. Unnati, Ahemdabad
3. CAIRN Energy India PTY. Ltd.
4. Chetna, Ahemdabad
5. Shri Nakoda Trust, Balotra

(g) Approximate population Served : 13,265

(h) Target Groups : poor, marginalized

(i) Objectives : "To ensure the participation of the poor and marginalized in sustainable development processes through collective decision making and facilitating the emergence of democratic leadership and institutions among people."

Details of Activities

(j) Research : Report on sensitizing urban youth to enhance dignity of the girl child (Girl Child Project I - IFES/USAID) Posters and Book of slogans on NREGA, PDS, ICDS and Mid-day meal programs "Haq Ki Ladai" – a book for neo literates Report on workshop conducted in collaboration with Divisional Forest office, Tonk on Environment Conservation.

(k) Vocational Training : 3 day Training Module for training of NSS POs (Girl Child Project I - IFES/USAID)

- 1 day Training Module for training of NSS PEVs (Girl Child Project I - IFES/USAID)
- Resource-kit for the PEVs consisting set of 2 books (Girl Child Project I - IFES/USAID):
- PEVs handbook titled 'Mere Samajik Sarokar-Meri Diary' (My Social Responsibilities My Diary).
- Book of Slogans against sex selection titled 'Dekho Ladki Ka Vishwaas' (Look at the Confidence of the Girl Child).
- Adaptation of 3 day Training Module for training of NSS Pos, 1 day Training Module for training of NSS PEVs and Resource-kit for the PEVs consisting set of 2 books (Girl Child Project II - UNFPA/WPC)

(l) Skill Development : 'The Handicraft programme of SURE was initiated with 224 women artisans. Today SURE is successfully running 15 production centre supporting over 600 atisans. Women are involved right from the production of Handicrafts to the marketing of these. Action aid, VHAI, DCH have been some of the main institutions that have supported the handicraft

(m) Organisations under establishment : 1. Society to Uplift Rural Economy Jasalmeer, Rajasthan.
2. Society to Uplift Rural Economy Jaipur, Rajasthan.

♦ ♦ ♦

Sucheta Kripalani Gram Vikas Sansthan

(1) Contact person : Mr Inder Singh Solanki

(2) Designation : Secretary

(3) Contact No. : N/A

(4) Mobile : 09414247158, 09461223363

(5) E-Mail : skgvsnewra@gmail.com

(6) Website : N/A

(7) Address : Registered Office: Vill. & PO Newra, via Osian-342303, District Jodhpur, Rajasthan
Administrative Office:
'Matrachhaya', 3, Shiv Colony
Chainpur, Mandore-342016
Jodhpur (Rajasthan)

About Organization: Visionary and freedom fighter Acharya J.B. Kripalani Founded of Secheta Smarak Nidhi in the year 1975 having its headquarters at Sucheta Bhawan, 11/A, Vishnu Digambar Marg, New Delhi .The Smarak Nidhi was founded in the memory of Sucheta Kripalani for propagating her mission to uplift the poor and needy in the society. Later, Sucheta Kripalani Shiksha Niketan was established in Jodhpur in 1979 aiming at welfare of people around the Thar desert. For further expansion of the mission Sucheta Kripalani, Sucheta Kripalani Gram Vikas Sansthan having its head office at Newra in Jodhpur district was founded as a registered society in the year 1996 bearing registration number 152/Jodhpur/1996-97 on October 16, 1996. The organization is involved in desert village / areas of Jodhpur district, Rajasthan. The organization closely works poor, dalit and tribal communities on the issues such as environment, water harvesting, agriculture development, women's empowerment, youth training and support programmes. SKGVS is concerned on livelihood opportunities to the rural poor and it has been closely working to aware the poor communities for food security and organic farming.

(a) Year of Establishment : 1996

(b) Registration No : 152/Jodhpur/1996-97 dated 16th October 1996

(c) Location : Jodhpur (Rajasthan)

(d) Coverage Area : Thar Desert area of Jodhpur, Rajasthan

(e) Staff Strength : 7

(f) Source of Funding : The organization has been getting financial support from state government, departments at district level, foreign funding sources, and local contribution. Recently, NCRI has sanctioned a project on micro-planning.

(g) Approximate population Served : 3.5 lacs

(h) Target Groups : Socially and economically marginalized communities including Poor, scheduled caste, scheduled tribal, other backward castes, small & marginal formers, women, children etc

(i) Objectives :

- To ensure the restoration of a sustainable environment by initiating efforts from local people.
- To enhance the level of awareness and capability of the needy people.
- To organize and mobilize the weaker section enabling them to solve their problem collectively.
- To initiate and sustain skills and resource-based appropriate income generation programme.
- To promote people-based development interventions.
- To ensure social justice for the target group in general and women in particular.
- To mobilize youths for creative purpose.
- To establish linkages with GOs and NGOs working for similar causes.
- Providing proper education to children and women and imparting health awareness.
- To render every possible efforts for promoting the socially and economically downtrodden especially women, aged, handicapped and destitute.
- Planning the enforcement of a team work in the event of a natural calamites or mishap.

Details of Activities

(k) Vocational Training : Tailoring, Embroidery, Agro Farming etc.

(l) Skill Development : Training for CBO - SHG, VDC, Communities leaders .

♦ ♦ ♦

Vidya Bhawan Society

(1)	Contact person	:	Dr. H. K. Dewan
(2)	Designation	:	Educational Advisor
(3)	Contact No.	:	0294-2451332
(4)	Mobile	:	09414160815
(5)	E- Mail	:	vbsudr@yahoo.com
(6)	Website	:	www.vidyabhawan.org
(7)	Address	:	Dr. Mohan Sinha Mehta Marg, Dewali Road, Fatehpura, Udaipur - 313 004 (Raj.)

About the Organisation: Vidya Bhawan started off as a small middle school with only four classes, way back in 1931 when the percentage of literacy in Mewar State was only 4.9. The school was allotted a plot of four acres the larger part of which was rocky, uncultivable and widely overgrown with cactus bushes. Although this plot was at that time useless and desolate, it lay in wild, healthy and picturesque surroundings about a quarter of a mile from Fatehsagar Lake. Vidya Bhawan drew its inspiration from the tenets of the Boy Scout Movement with an emphasis on community services. Founded at a time of great national ferment, when India was at the height of her struggle for political self government, Vidya Bhawan could not but be affected by the social climate in the country. However, the founders of Vidya Bhawan chose social reconstruction, which they felt was of as great value for national freedom and regeneration as (though less spectacular than) the political struggle. In keeping with the progressive character of the effort Vidya Bhawan was probably the first to introduce co-education in feudal Rajasthan.

(a)	Year of establishment	:	1931
(b)	Registration No	:	5079/1941 Date : 10th Sept., 1941
(c)	Location	:	Udaipur, Rajasthan
(d)	Coverage area	:	Mewar in Rajasthan directly but with many other States through Govt. institutions including SCERT, DIET, Colleges, schools, etc.
(e)	Staff strength	:	528
(f)	Source of funding	:	State Govt., Central Govt., MSDF, NCRI, Azim Prejmji, Foundation, WIPRO, ICEE, SDTT, NRTT, UNICEF, DFID, ICAR
(g)	Approximate population Served	:	In Udaipur Division – 25,000 1. Outside Udaipur influence many lakhs teachers 2. and students in some way.
(h)	Target Groups	:	Children, youths, women, farmers, Panchyatiraj elected representatives, girls.

(i) Objectives :

- To promote sound education which implies the full and harmonious development of the individual according to his or her aptitude with a sense of social responsibility;
- to develop a broad and open-minded outlook on life and a healthy sense of citizenship;
- to disseminate sound ideas on education among parents, teachers, guardians and people in general;
- to conduct and promote educational experiments and research; and
- to promote vocational and professional education based on employment needs of the society at large.

Details of Activities

(j) Research

- Research work is being conducted at our V.B. G.S.T. Teachers Training College for Ph.D., M.Ed. and on In-service Teachers Training Programmes.
- Research conducted by our Education Resource Centre on Baran Study, Study of Secondary Boards Evolution System (Rajasthan, Chhattisgarh, Uttrakhand and CBSCE Board), Study being conducted on Learning Guarantee Programme in collaboration with Azim Premji Foundation.

(k) Vocational Training

- Provides training in agricultural innovative and better practices to men and women farmers from 5 rural and tribal block of Udaipur, Kherwara, Jhadol, Gogunda, Girva and Badgaon.
- Short term vocational courses for young unemployed rural youth from rural habitation around Udaipur.
- Technical training in civil engineering, electronics, computer science, information technology and electrical engineering for rural youth.
- Capacity building of representatives of local self govt. institutions like Ward Panch, Sarpanch, member of zilla parished. Special attention is paid to training to women representatives.
- Vocational training to our students through Handmade paper making, carpentry, tailoring, food processing. electrical home appliance repairing. agriculture.

(m) Organisations under establishment

1. Vidya Bhawan Senior Secondary School, Udaipur
2. Vidya Bhawan Public School, Udaipur
3. Vidya Bhawan Secondary School, Ramgiri, Udaipur
4. Vidya Bhawan Secondary School, Jhamarkotra, Udaipur
5. Vidya Bhawan G.S.Teachers College -Institute of Advanced Studies in Education, Udaipur
6. Vidya Bhawan S.T.C., Udaipur
7. Vidya Bhawan Rural Institute, Udaipur

8. Vidya Bhawan Polytechnic College, Udaipur
9. Vidya Bhawan Krishi Vigyan Kendra, Udaipur
10. Vidya Bhawan Institute of Local Self-government and Responsible Citizenship.
11. Vidya Bhawan Cellulose Waste Recycling Education Project,Ramgiri,Udaipur.
12. Vidya Bhawan Gandhian Institute of Educational Studies,Udaipur.

♦ ♦ ♦

TAMILNADU

Centre for Experiencing Socio-Cultural Interaction

(1)	Contact person	:	Dr. S. Jeyapragasam
(2)	Designation	:	Vice-President & Director
(3)	Contact No	:	0452 2478359 / 255
(4)	Mobile	:	98430 40226
(5)	E-Mail	:	majabetsy@gmail.com
(6)	Website	:	www.cesci.ch
(7)	Address	:	CESCI, Majagram, Chatrapatti P.O., Madurai 625 014 City address: 4/2A Upstairs, Dr.Thangaraj Salai, Madurai 625 020.

About the Organisation: CESCI is situated near Madurai in Tamil Nadu in South India. It was founded in 1993 by the Swiss psychiatric nurse and photographer, Maja Koene, in collaboration with the well-know human rights activist, Rajaghopal PV, the initiator of the land rights movement, Ekta Parishad.As its name suggests, CESCI exists to promote socio-cultural exchange. But it is also a place where the activists of Ekta Parishad can reflect on their work, receive training and regenerate their energies for the social struggle.CESCI's primary function is hosting training for the activists and providing an environment in which they can recharge their energies after a spell in the field. For the activists, all of whom are committed to living according to Gandhian principles.

(a)	Year of establishment	:	1994
(b)	Registration No	:	44/1994 (under the society's Act)
(c)	Location	:	Majagram, Kadavur, Chatrapatti P.O., Madurai
(d)	Coverage area	:	Seven villages around the head quarters two villages in Tiruchi and two villages in Nagapatinam,Participants from local, state and national levels in our programmes.
(e)	Staff strength	:	Permanent 9, consolidated 4, Part-time 15, Hony (volunteers) 5
(f)	Source of funding	:	Self-generating, Individual donars, Govt. Sources, International sources
(g)	Approximate population served	:	Direct - 10,000; Indirect - 10,00,000
(h)	Target groups	:	Women, children, tribals & scheduled castes,social workers, students, youth & public
(i)	Objectives	:	Reaching and empowering the unreached,sustainable rural development, Environmental protection, Nonviolence and Peace Education.

Details of Activities: A resource and training centre for social change located in a village setting in a village style. CESCI has launched through its wing (International Gandhian Institute for Nonviolence and Peace - IGINP) a Diploma Course in Nonviolence and Peace (DNP) through open and distance learning (DOL) with support from NCRI. A quarterly Journal (both in English and in Tamil) Ahimsa Nonviolence is also published.

(j) Research : Documentation, case studies & research library& publication

(k) Vocational training : Tailoring, Food Processing, Oil and Oil cake, Soap making, honey.

(l) Skill development : Folk theatre for rural education; Accounting andmicro-level planning for women & children, Nonviolence and Peace Education.

♦ ♦ ♦

Gandhi Niketan Ashram

(1)	Contact person	:	Mr. Venkata Swamy
(2)	Designation	:	President
(3)	Contact No.	:	91 -04549 270521
(4)	Mobile	:	9500003510
(5)	E-Mail	:	gnashram@yahoo.co.in
(6)	Website	:	www.gandhiniketan.org
(7)	Address	:	Gandhi Niketan Ashram T. Kallupatti Post, Peraiyur Taluk Madurai District, Tamilnadu, India, Pin. 625 702.

About the Organisation: Gandhi Niketan Ashram which has a long history and rich tradition behind it is the brain child of a young man of 21 burning with the desire of helping to create an independent India and reconstructing Rural India as envisioned by Mahatma Gandhi. In 1930 at the age of twenty one, the well known Gandhian and freedom fighter Mr.G.Venkatachalapathy had the golden opportunity of spending one evening and night with Mahatma Gandhi while touring Tamilnadu and under the Mahatma's magic spell he decided that his life's ambition would be to follow the Mahatma in thought, deed and action. Nothing else in the world mattered to him. The result was the founding of the Gandhi Niketan Ashram in 1940 by him with the sole aim of rural reconstruction and imparting basic education as spelt out by Mahatma Gandhi to rural children.

(a)	Year of establishment	:	1940
(b)	Registration No	:	125/2005
(c)	Located	:	Madurai District, Tamilnadu
(d)	Coverage area	:	All India
(e)	Staff strength	:	175
(f)	Source of funding	:	State govt,Khadi & Village commission- Mumbai
(g)	Approximate population served	:	3 lakhs population & 3000 Students
(h)	Target groups	:	Students, Farmers, NGO's, Ghandhian Institutes
(i)	Objectives	:	

- To operationalise the Gandhian vision of Gram Swaraj by promoting constructive training, demonstration and development programmes
- To enable the villagers to produce their own clothing by spinning and weaving with hand spun yarn.
- To promote an appropriate educational system suited to rural realities based on the Gandhian concept of Basic Education

- To eradicate the evil of untouchability and to propagate Adult Literacy
- To train the rural people to keep their villages clean.
- To improve agricultural practices and to teach villagers to produce nutritive food grains
- To educate people on the dangers of alcoholism and wean them away from liquor.
- To achieve all of the above to create a village reconstruction army.

Details of Activities: The Gandhiniketan Ashram has adopted a village by name Thambipatti located 6 kms from T.Kallupatti. It is one of the tiny hamlets wherein the people are very enthusiastic to participate in the overall development of their village. We plan to have the following activities.

- Technology Development Programmes
- Creating awareness of their rights and duties as citizens of this country
- Nutritional advice for the pregnant mothers and children and practical demonstrations of nutritious food with what is available locally.
- Improve the sanitation facility for the individual houses as well as for community.
- Employing a teacher to give supplementary teaching to the children of the village who do not have access to extra coaching and adult literacy will be part of this program.
- Conducting periodical medical camps
- To facilitate for them to get various developmental schemes adapted by the government.

(j) Research : Socio-economic surveys

(k) Vocational training : Training programmes for school teachers, covering values related to national integration, secularism, self-reliance, ecology, social responsibilities and community living are imparted.

(l) Skill development : Hand Spinning, Learning by Cleaning, kadhi production, echo friendly tannery and leather products, Detergent soap making, honey processing, tailoring, vermi composting, pottery, electrical and electronic works related to agricultural pumps, television and two wheelers.

(m) Organisations under establishment : Dr. J.C. Kumarappa Institute of Khadi and Rural Industries and Sustainable Development.

• • •

Gandhigram Rural University

(1)	Contact person	:	Dr. N. Narayana Swamy
(2)	Designation	:	Registrar
(3)	Contact No.	:	0451-2452371/2452375
(4)	Mobile	:	9442626369
(5)	E-Mail	:	grucc@ruraluniv.ac.in
(6)	Website	:	www.ruraluniv.ac.in
(7)	Address	:	Gandhigram Rural University Gandhigram - 624 302, Dindigul District Tamil Nadu, INDIA

About the Organisation: With undying faith and deep devotion to Mahatma Gandhi's revolutionary concept of 'Nai Talim' system of education, Gandhigram Rural Institute has developed academic programmes in Rural Development, Rural Economics and Extension Education, Rural Oriented Sciences, Cooperation, Development Administration, Rural Sociology, English and Communicative Studies, and, Tamil and Indian Languages. Students who emerge from its portals tend to meet the personnel needs for rural development under various governmental and non-governmental schemes. To teaching was added, the dimensions of research and extension in course of time. This three-dimensional approach became a pioneering model which earned appreciation from all over the country. The work of the Institute invited national attention and the Government of India (Ministry of Education), on the recommendation of the University Grants Commission, conferred the status of a Deemed University on the Institute under Section (3) of the UGC Act of 1956, on 3rd August, 1976. Today, it has become a nationally and internationally recognised Institute for its contribution to rural education, so much so that the New Education Policy of the Nation reflects the principles evolved here in developing the rural university concept.

(a)	Year of establishment	:	1976
(b)	Registration No	:	20/1976
(c)	Located	:	Dindigul, Tamil Nadu
(d)	Coverage area	:	All India
(e)	Staff strength	:	375
(f)	Source of funding	:	UGC
(g)	Approximate population served	:	2 lakhs population & 3000 Students
(h)	Target Groups	:	Students, Farmers, NGO's, Gandhian Institutes

(i) Objectives :

1. To provide for instruction and training in such branches of learning as it may determine to promote a classless and casteless society and integrated rural development;
2. To provide for research and for the advancement of and dissemination of knowledge;

3. to function as a centre for extension work towards Integrated Rural Development;

Details of activities

Gandhigram Rural University offers courses in

- Tamil, Indian Languages & Rural Arts
- English And Foreign Languages
- Rural Social Sciences
- Rural Oriented Sciences
- Rural Development
- Agriculture And Animal Husbandry
- Rural Health And Sanitation
- Education
- Library
- Energy Centre
- Physical Education
- Computer Centre
- Krishi Vigyan Kendra
- Rural Extension And Evaluation Cell
- Information Development And Resource Agency (Idara)
- Rural Technology Centre

(j) Research : Centre for Jatropha and Bio fuels Promotion proposed by Dr. G. S. Kannan, Reader in the Faculty of Agriculture and Animal Husbandry to act as a resource centre for the Promotion, Research and cultivation of Jatropha plants and Bio-fuel usage in south India.

(k) Vocational training : Degree Courses , Short term courses in Rural Health, Integrated rural development, sanitation, agriculture, pre- school education

(l) Skill development : Computers & Software Training

♦ ♦ ♦

Kasturba Gandhi Kanya Gurukulam

(1)	Contact Person	:	Mr.Vedaratnam
(2)	Designation	:	Managing Trustee
(3)	Contact No.	:	+91 (04369) 250227, 250027
(4)	Mobile	:	N.A.
(5)	E-Mail	:	gurukulamvdm@yahoo.co.in
(6)	Website	:	www.gurukulam.org
(7)	Address	:	P. B. No. 2, Vedaraniam, Dist. Nagapattinam, Tamilnadu, India-614 810.

About the Organisation: With the kind blessings of Mahatma Gandhi, Late Sardar A.Vedaratnam Pillai, the veteran freedom fighter and pioneer of the Vedaraniam Salt Satyagraha in the Southern India launched by our beloved Rajaji in the year 1930 devoted his entire attention to the constructive programs of Mahatma Gandhi. He started the Gurukulam in the year 1946 to educate the girls in villages which is one among the constructive programs of Mahatma Gandhi and named it as Kasthurba Gandhi Kanya Gurukulam.

From 1946, till today the institution has grown up with the munificence of philanthropists and well wishers. Now it has a higher secondary school for girls from Standard I to XII, a school of printing to develop the printing skill to rural women. An electronic production unit to enable women to be self reliant and a cottage industry unit for the production of Agarbathi, Indian incense sticks. The institution is run on Sarvodaya lines. This is a living and learning cooperative community.

(a)	Year of establishment	:	1946
(b)	Registration No	:	184/ 9th January, 1950, Public Trust.
(c)	Location	:	Nagapattinam, Tamilnadu
(d)	Coverage area	:	Whole of Tamil Nadu
(e)	Staff strength	:	70 Teaching Staff, 30 Administration Staff
(f)	Source of funding	:	State Government of Tamilnadu Educational Grants aid
(g)	Approximate population served	:	2,500 Students & Trainees
(h)	Target Groups	:	Destitute, Orphan and Refugee Girls.
(i)	Objectives	:	To educate the girls in villages which is one among the constructive programs of Mahatma Gandhi.

Details of Activities

(j)	Vocational training	:	Training is given in the various activities connection with printing. Agarbathi unit (perfume sticks), Radio Tv Assembly Training.

(k) Skill development : Hand Pounding of Rice

(l) Organisations under establishment :

1. Basic School
2. Higher Secondary School
3. Sri Thayumanavar Vidyalayam Middle School
4. Teachers Training School
5. Printing Press -Training and Production
6. Electronic Unit / Training Cum Production Centre in Tv Assembly
7. Agarbathi Unit / Training Cum Production Centre
8. French Frienship Hospital
9. Siddha Dispensary (Native Medicine) Handed Down By Saints
10. Dairy Unit/Biogas
11. Ireland Aided Bakery Training Centre
12. Home for the Destitute

♦ ♦ ♦

Peoples Upliftment in Rural Areas

(1)	Contact person	:	R. Kalaiselvi
(2)	Designation	:	Office Incharge
(3)	Contact No.	:	43534554534
(4)	Mobile	:	9842695348 / 93677 79692
(5)	E-Mail	:	pura1993@rediffmail.com
(6)	Website	:	www.epondicherry.com
(7)	Address	:	33 Green Street, South Railway Gate, Nagapattinam, Nagercoil, Tamil Nadu-611 001.

About the Organisation: PURA-People's Upliftment in Rural Areas was established in the year 1993 by 7 active women who were inspired by the sufferings of women and children in the soicty. The organization is run and managed by women. In view of this, they established a children's home to protect the rights of orphan, semi-orphans, destitute and sexually abused girl children. We have 47 girl children in our home. We have also organized children collectives in 24 centres with 20-30 children in a group. The organization is running a women counseling centre in which they take up the issues of family and individual women and sorting out the problems. So far we have sorted of 73 family issues in last 3 years.The organization has been working among the tribals(Adivasis) of Kanayakumari district. We have established 10 Tribal groups in 10 tribal settlements and there are 48 settlements in the district which will be covered in the coming year.We have organized 211 women self help groups and 13 men groups in 6 blocks of the district. We are motivating and training the women in self employment perspectives and assisting them to obtain loans from the government.

(a)	Year of establishment	:	1993
(b)	Registration No	:	Society Act No.31 / 1993 Income Tax Act
(c)	Location	:	Nagercoil,Tamil Nadu
(d)	Coverage area	:	Tamil Nadu, Pondicherry
(e)	Staff strength	:	21
(f)	Source of funding	:	Nandri help for South India; Unnati Foundation, Siemenpuu Foundation, Through Network of NGOs.
(g)	Approximate population served	:	12,000
(h)	Target groups	:	Depressed and marginalized women in SC, ST and General communities.
(i)	Objectives	:	

- To construct a children home and to accommodate minimum 150 beneficiaries each.
- To organize the entire tribal people in the district under Grama panchayats and providing income generation activities to the youth who have no access Construction of permanent building for Children's home and Old age home to employment.

- To provide training to the Self Help Group members in technology based programme such as mushroom cultivation, Piggery and Poultry farming.
- To organize the village children under children collectives and training them in developing mind body and soul leading to Self development of children.

To construct low cost houses to the widows and disadvantaged women through out the district.

Details of Activities

(j)	Research	:	Done research in water management and finalized it in a report.
(k)	Vocational training	:	To the children of our children collectives on book binding, envelope making, and handicraft works using glass papers.
(l)	Skill development	:	Solar dry fish processing to coastal women,-Coir processing units for most disadvantaged women,Tailoring training for young girls, Handicrafts out of banana fiber and sea shells to filariasis affected women.
(m)	Organisations under Establishment	:	Children collectives, Adivasi Groups, Self help Groups of women and men.

♦ ♦ ♦

Sarada Ashram

(1)	Contact Person	:	Nitya Vivekapriya Amba
(2)	Designation	:	Director (Rural Develop)
(3)	Contact No.	:	04149 – 222432,
(4)	Mob.	:	94432 20362, 09443221452
(5)	E-Mail	:	info@srisaradaashram.org ashram@srisaradaashram.org
(6)	Website	:	www.srisaradaashram.org
(7)	Address	:	Sri Sarada Ashram (Sri Ramakrishna Sarada Trust), New Edaikkal, Villupuram Dist., Tamilnadu-606 107.

About the Organisation: Sri Sarada Krishi Kendra is one of the most important activities of the vivekananda seva pratishtan. Agriculture still is the mainstay of rural india and no rural development activity can be achieved without addressing the problems of agriculture. It has been found that traditionally indian farmer practiced time tested farming system and practices and could lead life in plenty and prosperity.

The ashram is convinced that unless the wisdom of the traditional farming system and practice is revived amidst the farmers, there are very few chances for them. However, the re-discovery of the value of the traditional farming system and practice in the current circumstance is neither affordable by the farmer nor convincing enough for him. The strength to try new - even if it is traditional - things is lost in the farmers and the fear of failure is too strong for him to even attempt any change in the status quo.

(a)	Year of establishment	:	1992
(b)	Registration No	:	619/ 92; Dt. 30-11-1992 (Sri Rama Krishna Sharada Trust)
(c)	Location	:	Villupuram District, Tamilnadu
(d)	Coverage area	:	120 Villages; 4 Blocks In Tamilnadu.
(e)	Staff Strength	:	250
(f)	Source of funding	:	Govt. of India, Tamil Nadu- Dept. of Women, Corporation of Tamil Nadu and individual donors.
(g)	Approximate population served	:	1 Lakh
(h)	Target groups	:	Women, Children, Farmers, Students, Youth.
(i)	Objectives	:	The Ashram is the home for many initiatives in the worship of the God in man through educational, agricultural, rural development, natural resource management, health and emergency relief activities.

Details of Activities: Sri Harathi agricultural consultancy services has been especially set-up to train farmers in the traditional organic agricultural methods. The trial plots have been carefully developed for different crops and each stage has been documented to prove the distinct advantage of practicing organic farming on the soil, plant, pest control, yield and profits. All attempts are made to understand the farmer's unique problems and provide him with a solution package to not just make profits but also to convince him and re-claim his strength - the wisdom of traditional organic farming.

(j) Vocational training : Organic farming: Sri Sarada krishi kendra was started with the objective of creating a model farm guided by traditional wisdom. The kendra practices traditional organic farming utilising the best of traditional and modern methods and is today an organic farming learning centre for the villupuram district.

The kendra has developed farm to showcase to the farmer the benefits of organic farming and also trains him in the various techniques and tools required for organic farming. The kendra also has developed various farm inputs, viz. Vermi compost, bio compost, panchagavya and bio-pesticides which farmers in the neighbourhood can buy for their fields.

♦ ♦ ♦

Shanti Ashram

(1)	Contact Person	:	Sri P. Parthipan
(2)	Designation	:	Youth Coordinator
(3)	Contact No.	:	0422-2605550
(4)	E-Mail	:	shanti@eth.net, katrukatru@gmail.com
(5)	Website	:	www.shantiashram.org
(6)	Address	:	Shanti Ashram, Shanti Ashram Road, Koraipudur, Coimbatore, Tamil Nadu - 641 042

About the Organisation: "Shanti Ashram is a creative laboratory where the problems faced by our communities can be both identified and provided with constructive solutions. We need to think and act and globally locally" Dr.M.Aram, Founder President.

The Ashram has its headquarters at Kovaipudur, Coimbatore. Shanti Ashram believes that rural children, like all other children, have a right to first call—not only to our love and care, but also to our resources. Dr. M. Aram and Mrs. Minoti Aram, were the founders of Shanti Ashram.

(a)	Year of establishment	:	1986
(b)	Registration No	:	91 6.5.88 Document No. 244 Of 1998 Booc 4
(c)	Location	:	Peri-Urban
(d)	Coverage area	:	40 Villages of Perur and Madukkarai Blocks
(e)	Staff strength	:	Full Time -38, Volunteers - 50
(f)	Source of funding	:	International / National / Local Project Funders, Interest from Seed Capital, Community Contribution, Rotary / Lions Club / Inner Wheel / Local financial Institutions, Donations
(g)	Approximate Population Served	:	200,000
(h)	Target groups	:	Women, Youth & Children.
(i)	Objectives	:	

- To promote Peace and Development in the Country and the World and to take goodwill mission Projects.
- To take up literacy mission projects and to work for the transformation of education system.
- To take up Rural development Programs.
- To promote Micro Level Planning including Village, Block and District Planning.
- To take up service projects for the welfare of Women, Children and Economically backward classes.
- To take up programs on Sanitation, Hygiene, Youth welfare and Environment.
- To work towards solution for various problems keeping with the Gandhian Principles of Non Violence and Sarvodaya.

- To undertake Khadi and Village Industries Program
- To publish books, periodicals, bulletins and monographs

Details of Activities

Program Areas: Shanti Ashram works in the following eight program areas since its inception

- Bala Shanti Kendra
- Community Health
- Environmental Restoration
- Panchayat Raj Research and Training
- Peace and Inter Faith Collaboration
- Poverty Alleviation
- Women's Development
- Youth Leadership

(j) Research : Shanti Ashram has so far carried out the following Research / Evaluation studies for Union Planning Commission / State Planning Commission / Shanti Ashram Village Community

- A study on Building Child development Indicators in Rural Panchayats of Tamilnadu
- Ensuring Human Development – Studying the Gender impact of Government Programs in Perur and Madukkarai Panchayats
- Iodine Deficiency Disorder – Salt Testing

(k) Vocational training :

- Tailoring
- Computer
- Beautician
- Preparation of Masala Powder
- Preparation of Nutritious Fast Food
- Bridal Make up and Mehandi

(l) Skill development :

- Capacity Building for Children on environmental Restoration
- Personal Hygiene for Adolescent Girls
- Program on Life skill Education for School Children
- Practicum on Rural Community Health to the Students of Harvard School of Public Health
- Practicum on Integrated Rural Development to the students of Michigan State University
- Course on Participatory Rural Appraisal to the students of Master of Social Work of local Colleges
- Youth development programs to the interns of Master of Social Work of local Colleges

♦ ♦ ♦

Sri Ramakrishna Mission Vidyalaya

(1)	Contact person	:	Swamy Ramanda
(2)	Designation	:	Secretary
(3)	Contact No.	:	(0422) 2692676, 2692676, 2695451, 2695453,2695452
(4)	Mobile	:	9894084458
(5)	E-Mail	:	srkvcoe@md3.vsnl.net.in
(6)	Website	:	www.srkv.org
(7)	Address	:	Sri Ramakrishna Mission Vidyalaya Sri Ramakrishna Vidyalaya (P.O) Periyanaickenpalayam Coimbatore - 641 020

About the Organisation: Ramakrishna Mission Vidyalaya, Coimbatore, is a major educational centre of the well-known Ramakrishna Mission. It is 19 km from the Coimbatore City on the highway to Ootacamund,and situated in a serene environment spread over about 300 acres. The Institution was founded by Sri T.S. Avinashilingam in 1930 with an investment of just Rs. 5.75 and with one harijan boy on its roll.

* Give me a few men and women who are pure and selfless, and I shall shake the world *
Swami Vivekananda

Over a period of 70 years, the Vidyalaya has grown into a comprehensive and reputed educational complex with nearly 4000 students, offering them facilities for education ranging from the pre-school to the doctoral levels. As a support service, there are eight hostels in the campus, with a total strength about 1500 boys.

(a)	Year of establishment	:	1930
(b)	Registration No	:	138/1909
(c)	Located	:	Periyanaickenpalayam, Coimbatore - 641 020
(d)	Coverage area	:	All over India
(e)	Staff strength	:	1200
(f)	Source of funding	:	Govt. self
(g)	Approximate population served	:	2 lakhs population & 3000 Students
(h)	Target groups	:	Students, Farmers, NGO's, Ghandhian Institutes
(i)	Objectives	:	The Vidyalaya strives to infuse the educational and spiritual ideas of Bhagavan Sri Ramakrishna and Swami Vivekananda into the daily lives of its students. Universal values such as self-reliance, self-control, patriotism, service and dedication to duty are taught in various practical ways.

Details of Activities

(j) Research : Education, rural empowerment

(k) Vocational training : Diploma in Civil Engineering, Mechanical Engineering, Electrical and Electronics Engineering , Information Technology, Diploma in Agriculture and Rural Development

English Communication Skill, Value Education, NCC / NSS / Sports and Cultural Education, Yoga, Special Education, Computer and Internet Training (25 Hours).

(l) Skill development : Spinning, weaving.Courses offered on developing skills of fitter, mechanic, turner, Draughtsman Mechanical, Wireman, Electrician, Welder (Gas & Electric), Computer Operator and Programming Assistant (COPA), Computer Hardware, Floriculture and Landscaping, Horticulture.

Bakery, Beauty culture, Candle Making, Embroidery, Farm Management, Food Presentation, Four-Wheeler Mechanism, handicraft Courses, House Wiring, Irrigation System, lathe Operator, Multi Mechanic, Mushroom Cultivation, Radio and Television Mechanism, Screen printing, Tailoring, Toys Making.

(m) Organisations under Establishment : Gandhi Teacher Training Institute, Polytechnic College, College of Arts & Science, Agriculture Institute, Maruthi College, College of Education.

♦ ♦ ♦

Tribal Health Initiative

(1)	Contact Person	:	Dr. Regi & Lalitha
(2)	Designation	:	Managing Director
(3)	Contact No	:	+91-4346-258611/299061/ 025/ 333
(4)	Mobile	:	N.A.
(5)	E-Mail	:	thisittilingi@gmail.com office@tribalhealth.org
(6)	Website	:	www.tribalhealth.org
(7)	Address	:	Tribal Health Initiative Sittilingi PO, Dharmapuri Dist. Tamil Nadu, India.

About the Organisation: Tribal Health Initiative is a public charitable trust located in the Sittilingi valley in Dharmapuri district, Tamil Nadu. We are dedicated to working for the health and welfare of the tribal communities located around us. We run a 24 bed hospital, a community health programme, an organic farming initiative and a craft initiative, all predominantly staffed by people from the surrounding villages.

(a)	Year of establishment	:	1993
(b)	Registration No	:	147/92
(c)	Location	:	Sittilingi In Dharmpuri District, Tamil Nadu.
(d)	Coverage area	:	21 Villages In Sittilingi Valley
(e)	Staff strength	:	55
(f)	Source of funding	:	BCF [Business and Community Foundation], SK [Skillshare International], Tansacs [Tamil Nadu Aids Control Society], Aid [Association for India, Development], Fos [Friends of Sittilingi], NCRI [National Council for Rural Institutes], IIT [Indian Institute of Technology], MMKCMT [Manmohini Kaul Charitable Medical Trust], DRRT [Dwaraknath Reddy Ramana Trust] and Many Others.
(g)	Approximate population served	:	10,000 Tribals
(h)	Target groups	:	Village Women, Age Old, Youth, Farmers And Infants
(i)	Objectives	:	Our vision is that the people of Sittilingi valley lead a better quality of life.

- To attain the highest possible level of physical, mental and social health
- To enhance their socio-economic status while retaining their pride, self-respect and self-reliance and ensuring their active participation in programs meant for their welfare

- To create an atmosphere highly conducive for the growth and development of local cultures and customs

THI seeks to work with tribal people in a spirit of peace, understanding, trust, and justice.

Details of Activities

(j) Research : Creation of Seed Banks, ensuring the survival of various minor millets and other traditional seeds, which were at risk of extinction due to the increased demand for rice and decreased demand for other similar sources, Creation of the SVAD (Sittilingi Valley Agricultural Valley) brand, under which 25 organic products are sold in various cities in south India

(k) Vocational training : Formation of SOFA (Sittilingi Organic Farmers Association), an association of farmers currently practicing organic methods, and is in the process of receiving organic certification from the government, Organization of Farming Collectives, giving farmers better bargaining power in buying seeds, and better prices for their goods,-Formation of Women's Self-Help Groups (SHGs), which perform value-addition processing, increasing the profit margin for specific products, training in agriculture and non-profit management, increasing our organization's level of expertise in those fields

(l) Skill development : Education Initiative- This has been promoting village libraries for the tribal children. The health auxiliaries keep a number of easy to read books which the young children can borrow and read. A community worker visits each village once a month to tell stories. He also motivates and helps the children to read as well as do other activities like paper folding to encourage their interest in learning and increasing their depth of knowledge.

Farming initiative: Tribal people have lived by rain fed subsistence farming and the produce of their forests for a very long time. Traditionally they had ample food growing various varieties of about fifteen different crops suited to the environment.

Tribal craft initiative facilitates local people to value their tradition and allows them to bring money into their local economy. Their tradition of embroidery was very nearly lost being remembered by only a few of the older women. This tradition has now been revived by the craft initiative, with the older women teaching the younger women.

♦ ♦ ♦

TRIPURA

Baba Longtarai Sevashram

(1)	Contact person	:	Sri Ratanjoy
(2)	Designation	:	Secretary
(3)	Contact No.	:	+91 Ph. (03824) 268231
(4)	Mobile	:	09436136018
(5)	E-mail	:	blsdhalai@rediffmail.com
(6)	Website	:	N.A.
(7)	Address	:	Vill- Uttar Longtarai, P.O.- Chawmanu, Dhalai, Tripura

About the Organisation: Over last 14 years of existence, the institute has engaged in various development activities and also promoting SHGs and mobilized poor rural women and girls. The institute motivated and supported several tribal children, both boys and girls for taking up higher education. Several skill training programmes on handlooms, handicrafts etc. were conducted for ensuring sustainable socio-economic development of the region. Most of the beneficiaries are now engaged in income generation activities.

(a)	Year of establishment	:	1996
(b)	Registration No	:	2844/1996
(c)	Location	:	Dhalai, Tripura.
(d)	Coverage area	:	Chawmanu R.D. Block, Manu R.D.Block under Dhalai Tripura District
(e)	Staff strength	:	12 including Teachers & Computer Operator
(f)	Source of funding	:	1) Department of Tribal Welfare, Govt. of Tripura, 2) NABARD, 3) SIDBI, 4) Tripura State Social Welfare Board and 5) Tripura State Pollution Control Board.
(g)	Approximate population served	:	3000
(h)	Target groups	:	Poor Rural Tribals with special reference to Women & Girls
(i)	Objectives	:	

- To promote basic Education based in the line of Gandhian Philosophy.
- To promote SHGs amongst poor Tribal Women & Girls
- To conduct Skill Training on various trades for sustainable socio-economic development of the rural tribal communities.

Details of Activities

(j)	Research	: Conducted preliminary survey on socio- economic status of the poor tribals under Chawmanu R.D. Block, Dhalai District.
(k)	Vocational training	: Conducting Vocational Training on Computer Education.
(l)	Skill development	: Conducting Skill Development Training on Tribal Textiles, Handicrafts etc.

♦ ♦ ♦

UTTAR PRADESH

Banwasi Sewa Ashram

(1)	Contact person	:	Mr. Bimal Kumar
(2)	Designation	:	Coordinator
(3)	Contact No.	:	91-5447-285223, 285224, 285396
(4)	Mobile	:	09452159552
(5)	E-mail	:	banwasisevaashram@gmail.com
(6)	Website	:	www.banwasisevaashram.org
(7)	Address	:	Govindpur, Via Turra Sonbhadra, U.P.-231221

About the Organisation: Banwasi Seva Ashram is a voluntary organisation believing in Gandhian principles of life. It develops and implements programmes to achieve Gramswarajya - that is simple productive cooperative self-sufficiency and self-reliance at the village level with the involvement of the beneficiary community. Banwasi Seva Ashram's work strategy is to develop friendship with the target community to understand their basic problems of living and help target community members work out the models that can be managed by them with appropriate training and support service.

As a policy Ashram goes into the depth of the problem faced by its beneficiary community, finds and appropriate solutions and then implements the programmes with the involvement of the beneficiary. The infrastructure developed for the involvement and improvement of the beneficiary is named Gramswarajya Sabha Sangathan.

(a)	Year of establishment	:	1954
(b)	Registration No	:	265/56-57
(c)	Location	:	Govindpur, Via Turra, Sonbhadra
(d)	Coverage area	:	Sonbhadra, U.P.
(e)	Staff strength	:	157
(f)	Source of funding	:	NIRD, Khadi Village, Germany
(g)	Approximate population served	:	3 Lakhs
(h)	Target groups	:	Youth, children & women
(i)	Objectives	:	

- Empowerment of the deprived and oppressed through socio-economic and educational activities in order to develop holistically under privileged village communities.
- Development of a self sufficient, harmonious society by encouraging people to live according to the principles of Sarvodaya (development of all) and Gramswarajya (self-reliance)
- Capacity building of Ashram staff and village functionaries in order to guarantee the success of the development process

- Orientation of new generation adolescents and youth to life situation
- Support to youth volunteers working in other areas of Uttar Pradesh and other states for the work of Gramswarajya

Details of Activities: At present Ashram has 10 departments: Gram Nirman (Village Development), Women's Empowerment, Education, Vocational Training, Khadi and Village Industry, Agriculture, Animal Husbandry, Health, Environment, Support to Other Volunteer Groups, 13 Village Development Centres and 80 Development Forums.

The development activities undertaken so far in Sonbhadra area:

1. Water and soil conservation, land development
2. Whole village development projects
3. Employment oriented apprentice training in crafts and services needed for the development activity and for employment elsewhere
4. Rural health service
5. Women's development and empowerment
6. Securing rural entitlements
7. Public interest litigation in Supreme Court for land rights, rights of the displaced and bonded labour
8. Study and representation of environmental pollution problem in south Sonbhadra at different levels
9. Life orientation of adolescents and youth
10. Gramswarajya Sangathan – People's Organisation
11. Awareness Generation
12. Water Conservation, Irrigation And Land Improvement
13. Agriculture, Horticulture And Forestry
14. Animal Husbandry
15. Khadi and Village Industry
16. Education of Children
17. Health and Medical Care
18. Women Empowerment
19. Rural Entitlement and Legal Support
20. Environmental Health Protection

(j) Research : Education, training, making washing powder, chalk, agriculture.

(k) Vocational training : Education & teachers training.

♦ ♦ ♦

Brij Bhushan Memorial Society

(1) Contact person : Brij Mohan Sharma
(2) Designation : Chief Functionary
(3) Contact No. : 0562-2881747
(4) Mobile : 9917205550
(5) E-mail : bbmsociety_sahyog@rediffmail.com
(6) Website : N.A.
(7) Address : Sector 1/685. Near LIC Building, Suhaag Nagar, Firozabad (U.P)

About the Organisation: The founder of Brij Bhushan Memorial Society was Sri. Brij Bhushan, who was the freedom fighter and social worker.This institute is working since 15 years without any difference of caste/creed/colour. Brij Bhushan Memorial Society, Firozabad based NGO working for the community development for last 10 years. During this decate, with community while working on issues like reproductive and child health, health and sanitation. Self help groups, education and family life education etc, the society had felt the need to address the importance of moral value system for well being of an individual as well as for the social development.

(a) Year of establishment : 1998
(b) Registration No : 2390 (Dated. 15th march 2002)
(c) Location : Agra, Uttar pradesh
(d) Coverage area : Uttar Pradesh, Gujarat, Rajasthan, Madhya Pradesh.
(e) Staff strength : 40
(f) Source of funding : NCRI, other funds, society members, donors
(g) Approximate population served : 15,000
(h) Target groups : Women, illiterate, day labour and child labour
(i) Objectives :

- Equipping children to develop as responsible citizens of country.
- Society for vocational training and literacy Programmes.

Details of Activities

(j) Vocational training : Teaching, tailoring, dolls making, handicrafts, health care centre, and education centre.
(k) Skill development : Communication skills, beauty parlour, decorating bangles.
(l) Organisations under establishment : 1) BBMS 1/685, Suhagnagar, Agra, Firozabad, U.P
2) BBMS, MIG, shaeed nagar, Agra.
3) BBMS, near B. Narayan gate, Bharatpur, Agra.

♦ ♦ ♦

Centre for Rural Education and Development Action

(1) Contact person : Mr. Shamshad Khan
(2) Designation : Secretary
(3) Contact No. : (05442) 220285
(4) Mobile : 09415206651
(5) E-Mail : samshad@sancharnet.in
we@credaindia.org
(6) Website : www.credaindia.org
(7) Address : 490-491, Awas Vikas Colony
Mirzapur-231001, Uttar Pradesh

About the Organisation: Centre for Rural Education and Development Action (CREDA) was founded in 1982 by a group of concerned and dedicated social workers under the leadership of Mr. Shamshad Khan. After its formation, the organization started working on issues like education of deprived children, elimination of child labour and bonded labour, conflict resolution, organizing and empowering women through skill training and literacy, issues related to bonded labour and payment of proper wages to workers, vocational training, Gandhian thoughts, and research and studies on various social, developmental and human rights issues. The organization received international attention for its work on child rights. CREDA believes that empowerment of poor people through sharing of information, training and mobilization activities will help them to fight against corruption and injustice and demand for entitlements. The organization is actively involved in the process of spreading the thoughts of Mahatma Gandhi in working areas of U.P. The concept of national integration and communal harmony is also being propagated among school children, rural community and civil society. CREDA has taken care of issues relating to women and adolescent girls. It has started various programmes/projects to empower them through various need based skill and vocational training for self employment.

(a) Year of establishment : 1982
(b) Registration No : 308/1982-83 dated 14.06.1982
(c) Located : Mirzapur (Uttar Pradesh)
(d) Coverage area : 14 Districts in Uttar Pradesh including Bundelkhand region.
(e) Staff strength : 43
(f) Source of funding : The sources of funds, donations and contribution for CREDA since last few years are as follows:

- Ministry of Labour, Government of India
- Ministry of Textile, Government of India
- Ministry of Rural Development, Government of India
- NCRI, Ministry of Human Resource Development, Government of India

- Department of Education, U.P. State Government
- UNDP-USAID
- UNDP-NORAD
- UNDP-IKEA
- ILO-IPEC
- UNICEF
- Centre for Civil Society
- Canadian High Commission
- Affiliated Network for Social Accountability – South Asia Region and Global Partnership Fund
- Foreign funding agencies like Oxfam, Terre des homes, etc.
- Personal donation / contribution
- Membership Fees
- Agricultural Income
- Interests earned
- Community contribution

(g) Approximate population served : 1.5 million

(h) Target groups : Rural community, women, child labour, bonded labour, elderly, rural youths, dalits, tribals, adolescent girls, MNREGA beneficiaries, school teachers, PRIs, SHGs.

(i) Objectives:

1. To develop backward village and weaker section of the people through integrated socio-economic activities in Agriculture, Horticulture, Community Forestry, Irrigation, Formal and Non-Formal Education, Functional Literacy Classes, Balwadis and support, and organise workshops, seminars, visits, classes and meetings to impart economic, social and family life education including budgeting and saving and knowledge of family welfare.
2. To arrange, promote, develop, extend, improve, support or maintain all types of technical, economic, educational and cultural programmes in the field related to rural development.
3. To arrange youth leadership training programmes and youth-camps and develop amongst the participant a critical awareness of their environment, inculcate an understanding regarding overall development of the community, promote national integration and motivate the youth for taking up social service activities.
4. To inculcate the spirit of co-operation and self reliance among the agriculture and rural workers and help them to promote their socio-economic conditions.
5. To render appropriate services, technological and educational assistance inquired for the development of various types of agricultural, dairy, live-stock and poultry, cottage industry, land improvement activities and do all such act and things so as to improve the living condition of poor and downtrodden.
6. To establish clinics, dispensaries, health services and other such activities which can promote health and health education among poor rural population.

Details of Activities

(j) Research :

Following researches / studies have been done:

1. Community participation eliminates child labour
2. Education and training needs in reduction of hazard to the safety and health of working children in carpet industry
3. Elimination of child labour: role of advocacy campaign and community participation
4. Improvement in health hygiene and nutritional status of child labour: experience of creda
5. Budget analysis of state budget (uttar pradesh) from a child right perspective

(k) Vocational training :

1. Carpet weaving training to women with the support of Ministry of Textiles, Government of India.
2. Durry weaving training to women with the support of UNDP-Ministry of Rural Development. Government of India.
3. Zari (a type of embroidery) training to adolescent girls with the support of Canadian High Commission.

(l) Skill development :

Basket making, wooden work and mud work. Tailoring, Menhadi, Painting (Fabric), Painting (Poster), Ceramic Work, Food Preservation, Bakery, Patch Work, Tie and Dye, Soft Toy Making, Beauty Parlor, Candle Making, Floor Making / Argendy, Jute / Use of waste materials, Embroidery (Hand), Embroidery (Sindhi), Embroidery (Zardoji), and computer literacy training.

♦ ♦ ♦

National Association for Voluntary Initiative & Cooperation

(1)	Contact person	:	Dr. V.K. Singh
(2)	Designation	:	National Secretary
(3)	Contact No.	:	05452-265652
(4)	Mobile	:	09415263277, 09984857000
(5)	E-mail	:	navic@yahoo.com
(6)	Website	:	www.navic.org.in
(7)	Address	:	Spinning Mill Area, Siddiqpur, Jaunpur-22200,Uttar Pradesh.

About the Organisation: Voluntary Initiative and Cooperation (NAVIC) is a non-governmental, non-political and not-for-profit organisation. For the past two decades it is working among unorganised sector in different States of India. NAVIC works on two levels: at the grassroots level and at the voluntary organisations level. Interventions at the grassroots level are concentrated in Varanasi and Jaunpur districts of Uttar Pradesh, while those at the voluntary organisations level are spread all over the country. Grassroots interventions are mainly in the domain of sustainable agriculture and local governance while interventions with voluntary organisations are focused on enhancing their capacities to enable them work in a better way.

(a)	Year of establishment	:	1988-89
(b)	Registration No	:	597/1988-89 under society registration act.
(c)	Location	:	Jaunpur, U.P
(d)	Coverage area	:	All over India.
(e)	Staff strength	:	18
(f)	Source of funding	:	CAPART, JAIKA of Japan, Department of science and technology, Jodhpur, U.P, Ministry of Science and Technology, New Delhi.
(g)	Approximate population served	:	All over India.
(h)	Target groups	:	Civil society organizations, which work for development activities.
(i)	Objectives	:	To provide strength to voluntary organisations in development activities. It seeks to influence the lowest rung of society to develop in terms of securing participation, justice, environment and volunteers and provide a forum the field of volunteerism to discuss developmental issues. It provides training to the voluntary organisations and volunteers to increase awareness and induce new thinking to face new challenges. As a network it brings together development, awareness and induces new thinking to face new challenges.

Details of Activities

Whether it is Capacity Building VOs or Grassroots Interventions, the work involves two-fold intervention strategy: Awareness generation and teaching methodology.Tools for awareness generation are: workshops, rallies, wall writings, puppet shows, magic shows, nautanki, padyatras, hoarding, etc. Innovative methods of awareness generation include: street plays, seminars, audio-visual display, slide projection, pasting of bills, workshops, kiosks, etc.Teaching methodology includes classroom lectures, group discussion, psychological exercises, audio-visual display, role play, field visit and interface with successful entrepreneurs and government officials.

(j) Research : Social Assessment and Social Survey, Organises seminars, workshops, conferences, public meetings as a part of advocacy.

(k) Vocational training : Consumer Awareness, Swarna Jayanti Gram Swarojgar Yojana, Panchayat Strengthening, Project Formulation.

(l) Skill development : Conservation of Neem, Jatropha and Medicinal Plants, and Self-Employment, Organic Farming/ Biodiversity, Self-Employment and Micro Credit, Child Labour , Women Empowerment, AIDS/ Pulse Polio/Health/PNDT .

♦ ♦ ♦

Nehru Gram Bharati Viswa Vidyalaya

(1)	Contact person	:	Dr. K. P. Mishra
(2)	Designation	:	Vice-Chancellor
(3)	Contact No.	:	0532-6453999
(4)	Mobile	:	9838737787
(5)	E-Mail	:	info@ngbu.edu.in
(6)	Website	:	www.ngbu.edu.in
(7)	Address	:	Kotwa-Jamunipur, Dubawal, Allahabad 221505 (U.P.) India

About the Organisation: Government of India has made dream project of Late Pt. Jawahar Lal Nehru a reality by notifying Nehru Gram Bharati Vishwavidyalaya under section 3 of UGC Act 1956. With this notification Rajiv Gandhi Post Graduate College, Kotwa - Jamunipur, Allahabad stands elevated to the status of Vishwavidyalaya from the session 2008-2009.

NGBU's mission is to global, socially conscious and integrated University provide wide rage of courses.

It may be recollected that on 26th July 1962 Late Pt. Jawahar Lal Nehru the then Prime Minister of India laid the foundation stone of the "Nehru Gram Bharati" at village Dubawal near Jamunipur-Kotwa of his Phulpur Parliamentary constituency. On this occasion addressing the gathering, he emphasized the need of vocational, technical and professional education apart from conventional one. He promised his electorate that the childrens of Kisans need not to go to the cities for higher education, instead, would be educated and trained in the rural institutes, which is being setup in the village itself. These boys and girls will also get employment/self employment opportunities in their own villages. He also hoped that such rural institutes would come up in other part of the country also.

(a)	Year of establishment	:	1996
(b)	Registration No	:	1117/2006-2007
(c)	Location	:	Dubawal, Allahabad
(d)	Coverage area	:	All India
(e)	Staff strength	:	200
(f)	Source of funding	:	Self finance
(g)	Approximate population served	:	2 lakhs population & 5000 Students
(h)	Target groups	:	Students
(i)	Objectives	:	

- To work for the educational enlistment of the rural and general public irrespective of caste, creed, sex & religion.
- To make the necessary changes in the prevalent educational system in order to cater to the needs of new vocations that are being created increasingly with explosions in the

areas of Science & technology and to adopt a system in education which would promote and stress on "Learning by doing" inculcated through extension of education and through distance learning mode.

- To impart free education to the poor, helpless handicapped and needy children/students, to carry out teaching activities at the campuses and to award diplomas and degrees at the level of bachelor, master, doctoral & post-doctoral level. To carry out utilitarian, explanatory and informative research activities in various disciplines.
- To carry out extension activities in the area of rural craft (Carpentry, Smithy, pottery, leather work etc.) in order to create employment in the rural sector. To organize short term training programmes for farmers, farm workers and others in various aspects of agriculture sciences.
- To carry out training programmes for the village, block and district level officials/non-officials concerned with agriculture and rural development.
- To carry out extension advisory work through direct as well as through distance mode in villages of U.P. and neighbouring states.

Details of Activities

(j) Vocational training : Teacher's education, special education, rural institute, comprising agricultural science & allied courses. Rural engineering and technology, Rural Business Management Comprising M.B.A. & MCA, Women's Empowerment through Priyadarshini Women's College, Medical and Para - Medical Courses, Mass Communication and Journalism, Distance Education and Extension and any other future important & vocational/ professional courses.

(k) Skill development : Soft skills, computers & Software

♦ ♦ ♦

Sai Gramodyog Vikas Samiti

(1)	Contact person	:	Mr. Girish Sharma
(2)	Designation	:	Secretary
(3)	Contact No.	:	9456491868
(4)	Mobile	:	9410247505
(5)	E- Mail	:	srkvcoe@md3.vsnl.net.in srkvcoe@md3.vsnl.net.in girishsharma1976@rediffmail.com srkvcoe@md3.vsnl.net.in
(6)	Website	:	N.A.
(7)	Address	:	Mil View Colony, Saharanpur, U. P.

About the Organisation: The Sai Gramodyog Vikas Samiti is a non governmental society and working for the promotion of the rural development and natural resources management which has been set up by a dynamic team of social workers who have experienced in diverse fields like apiculture economic, environmental medicinal plants. The institution comprises seven members who are well trained in different fields. Mr. Sunil Sharma is the president of the institution .The institution has all the necessary requirements for undertaking rural development activities and to carryout the aims and objective of the institution.

(a)	Year of establishment	:	2000
(b)	Registration No	:	54 dated 18/5/2008
(c)	Location	:	Saharanpur, Uttar Pradesh
(d)	Coverage area	:	Five districts of western U.P. namely, Saharanpur, Meerut, Muzaffarnagar, Mooradabad and Najibabad and area covered in shivalik foothills of Uttarakhand including district Hardwar, Dehradun and Udhhamsingh Nagar.
(e)	Staff strength	:	5-10
(f)	Source of funding	:	NCRI, donations .
(g)	Approximate population served	:	2 lakhs population & 3000 Students.
(h)	Target groups	:	Students, Farmers, NGO's, Gandhian Institutes.
(i)	Objectives	:	Skill development for the beekeepers regarding research and development in honey .Deals in raw natural Honey in bulk. We mainly cater to the requirement of Bulk Buyers. Our Bees are collecting raw natural Honey (mono floral, multi floral, eucalyptus, mustard, Litchi etc) from different fields/forests at our region.

Details of Activities

(j)	Research	:	Medicinal properties of honey.
(k)	Vocational training	:	Beekeeping, honey packaging, procurement, database creation.
(l)	Skill development	:	Modification of honey boxes for collecting honey, Preparation of honeybee filters.

♦ ♦ ♦

Shram Jivi Sewa Samiti

(1)	Contact person	:	Laljit Singh
(2)	Designation	:	Chief Functionary
(3)	Contact No.	:	0532-2563489
(4)	Mobile	:	09236463516
(5)	E-Mail	:	sjss.allahabad@rediffmail.com
(6)	Website	:	N.A
(7)	Address	:	Village Gumduma, P. O. Saidabad, Handia-221508 (Uttar Pradesh)

About the Organisation: Shram Jeevi Seva Samiti was established in 1993 and is working on several areas like animal husbandry, dairying and fisheries, agriculture, dalit upliftment, drinking water, education, literacy, environment and forests.

(a)	Year of establishment	:	1993-94
(b)	Registration No	:	Reg.no: 693(1993 -94) under society reg. act.
(c)	Location	:	Gumduma village, Handia.
(d)	Coverage area	:	All over Uttar Pradesh
(e)	Staff strength	:	25
(f)	Source of funding	:	10% from Khadi gramodyog products sale. Ministry of Water Resource. Project works on environment, forest, culture and tourism. Social Welfare Board of Govt. of India.
(g)	Approximate population served	:	All over Uttar Pradesh
(h)	Target groups	:	Differently-abled, dalit upliftment, aged, & children.
(i)	Objectives	:	Public awareness on water conservation, consumer protection, women empowerment.

Details of Activities

Public awareness on water conservation, awareness on consumer protection, campaign against child labour in Handia tehsil, women's empowerment through training and awareness, state level workshop on preservation of cultural heritage, environmental education to school children, educational right of poor children, revival of folk art of Allahabad district, promotion of thought and ideology of Mahatma Gandhi, number of activities related to rural development, health and family welfare programme.

(j)	Research	:	Mobilizing Panchayats on gender and child labour issues.
(k)	Vocational training	:	Folk arts of Allahabad district.
(l)	Skill development	:	Dairy development, fisheries, agriculture etc.

♦ ♦ ♦

UTTARAKHAND

Development & Research Institute for Social & Technical Education

(1)	Contact Person	:	Mr. Anup Badola
(2)	Designation	:	Secretary
(3)	Contact No.	:	N.A.
(4)	Mobile	:	09410312426
(5)	E-Mail	:	anupkumarbadola@yahoo.com info@driste.org, anup@driste.org
(6)	Website	:	http://www.driste.org
(7)	Address	:	C/O Arvind Mohan Nautiyal, Kaulagarh, Near Bal Culture Academy, Post-IPE, Dehradun, Uttranchal, India.

About the Organisation: Driste is committed to search new avenues & alternatives of development and to provide a new vision of people's action & initiatives for achieving self-dependence and self-reliance. It aims to serve the downtrodden, vulnerable section and most disadvantaged communities through collective action

(a)	Year of establishment	:	2000
(b)	Registration No	:	145/2000-2001; Dt.23-06-2000; Renewed On 23-06-2005.
(c)	Location	:	Kaulagarh, Dehradun
(d)	Coverage area	:	Dehradun, Pardi, Tehri Gadhwal, Rudra Prayag, Chamoli, Nainital (Uttarakhand) , Meerut (UP), Jharkhand, Delhi & Rajasthan.
(e)	Staff strength	:	324
(f)	Source of funding	:	4,00,000
(g)	Approximate population served	:	Women, Children, Rural Folk, Bpl-Shg
(h)	Target groups	:	Rural Poor
(i)	Objectives	:	

- To provide opportunity and to create an understanding through interaction, and promotion of human , social and cultural values
- To make effort and undertake measures for promoting social justice for especially downtrodden, poor and disadvantaged society covering both urban and rural community.
- To help people's groups, organizations and institutions to make plans and programmes, to achieve the goals and objectives, directly or indirectly through projects, training and studies.
- Help people's groups, organizations and institutions to make plans and programmes, to achieve the

- To enter into agreement with any non-religious, non-political agency, government or otherwise in pursuance of the objectives of the institution to obtain from any such agency all rights, concessions privileges that may be conducive to the promotion of the aims of the institution.
- To create a corpus (capital) of the institution of the revenue earned as institutional charges and the recoveries of all the investments made, that are invested in different projects directly undertaken by the institution. Partly or fully, it will be working as revolving fund and shall be continuously reinvested in new project expenses.

Details of Activities

(j)	Vocational training	:	Health training,. Alternative education with Vocational training to the working girls of slums and Agriculture training.
(k)	Skill development	:	Lantana furniture making training.

♦ ♦ ♦

Kasturba Mahila Utthan Mandal

(1)	Contact person	:	Neema Vaishnava
(2)	Designation	:	Secretary
(3)	Contact No.	:	91 05962 2580 03
(4)	Mob.	:	09761619675
(5)	E-mail	:	neemavaishnava@gmail.com; kmumkausani@ hotmail.com
(6)	Website	:	N.A.
(7)	Address	:	Lakshmi Ashram, P.O. Kausani, District Almora, Uttarakhand – 263639.

About the Organisation: Lakshmi Ashram is a Gandhian Basic Education school for girls, as well as a center for the inspiration and practical training of rural community activists. It is also a base for voluntary work, and a place where women from rural areas can organize themselves to define and solve their own problems. The ashram is located in the North Indian Himalayan state Uttaranchal.

This institution was established to educate women and children of the hills who lead a life of deprivation and ignorance. In 1967 one of the disciples of Sarala Behn, Radha Bhatt took charge of affairs and she in turn handed over the responsibility to her workers in 1989. Lakshmi Ashram attempts to make the women more conscious about their own situation.

(a)	Year of establishment	:	1946
(b)	Registration No	:	64/1947-48(dated 25/08/1947) under societies registration act.
(c)	Location	:	Uttarakhand
(d)	Coverage area	:	Uttarakhand
(e)	Staff strength	:	26
(f)	Source of funding	:	Some of the larger projects is also supported by DANIDA, the Danish state's organisation for supporting development countries, and the corrosponding Norwegian and Swedish organisations.
(g)	Approximate population served	:	2000
(h)	Target groups	:	Girls of kumaon hills and women.
(i)	Objectives	:	

To spread education among the women in the hills of Kumaon on the lines of Mahatma Gandhi's philosophy of education

Details of Activities

(j) Vocational training : Manual and productive labour such as Spinning and weaving. Cooking, Environmental actions and campaigns on social causes. Balwadis, Community library, Khadi Centre, Organising women and youth, Anti-liquor campaigns

(k) Skill development : Agriculture, Dairy, Community Living, Spinning for self sufficiently in clothes, Cooking Collecting firewood and fodder from the jungles, Tending to the sick.

♦ ♦ ♦

Society for Integrated Development of Himalayas

(1)	Contact Person	:	Pawan Kumar Gupta
(2)	Designation	:	Director
(3)	Contact No.	:	0135-2631304
(4)	Mobile	:	0-9760049414
(5)	E-Mail	:	pawansidh@gmail.com
(6)	Website	:	www.sidhsri.com
(7)	Address	:	P.O. Box 19, Hazelwood, Landour Cantt., Mussoorie 248179.

About the Organisation: SIDH is an educational institute. It is in existence since 1989. We run several village schools 4 are from the pre-primary level up to class II, 4 are from pre-primary to class V level, and there is one school. Bodhshala, which runs up to class VIII. All these school are located in the tribal area of Jaunpur in Tehri Garhwal district of Uttarakhand. The school initiative started 21 years ago at the request of the villagers as there were no government or private school in the region before the SIDH schools started functioning.

SIDH has focused more on learning from the community about the real problems faced by society, and incorporating this learning back into the schools. So we strive to find answers in the face of the onslaught of modernity and "development". We conduct research studies from time to time with an objective to bring out the assumptions of our mainstream education system that need to be challenged, thereby creating a debate in the country around these serious but neglected issues. We also publish reading material and teaching-learning material for both the teacher and the student. We have programs for teachers to sensitize them to certain philosophical foundations of education and to encourage them to make teaching learning experience more contextual to the local environment instead of making it only textbook oriented. We organize workshops, seminars and conference with teachers, educators, economists, scientists and scholar- philosophers to discuss issues of importance mainly focused on education, society and philosophy. Our attempt is to integrate education with real life experiences and right livelihood to make it more broad based and relevant.

We derive our inspiration from the vision of Mahatma Gandhi and other Indian philosophical traditions and thought.

(a)	Year of establishment	:	1989
(b)	Registration No	:	S/20611 of 1989
(c)	Located at	:	Mussoorie
(d)	Coverage area	:	Our schools cater to the children from 40 villages of Jaunpur Block of Tehri District but our research, publications and training programmes, workshops etc. reach out to most states in India.
(e)	Staff strength	:	About 50 people, teachers and others.

(f) Source of funding : * Own funds through corpus earning.
* Room to Read
* NCRI, Hyderabad.
* Several individual donors and local community.

(g) Approximate population served : About 5-6 thousand people in 40 villages but through our teachers network we touch a large number of schools throughout the country.

(h) Target groups : Children and women from 40 villages. Youth, teachers and others from all over the country.

(i) Objectives : 1. Working on modules for teachers to be used both in class room and for their own understanding.

2. Working on different models to improve the education system.

3. Working with women to make every village family healthy, happy and prosperous.

Details of Activities

(j) Research : 1. A Matter of Quality— Expectations and perceptions of schooling in rural and urban areas of Uttarakhand.

2. Child and Family—A study of the impact of family structure upon the children of the rural Uttaranchal.

3. Text and context.

(k) Vocational training : 1. Cottage industries of masala, baking, weaving and organic farming

2. Recycling of paper. Maintenance- plumbing, electricity, tailoring.

(l) Skill development : In our schools we integrate the skill training with subject teaching. Training of teachers. Eclectic workshops, training, seminars and conferances.

(m) Organisations under establishment : Running 9 schools in different villages of Jaunpur block catering to about 500 children. Schools upto primary level and one upto class VIII.

♦ ♦ ♦

WEST BENGAL

Development Research Communication and Service Centre

(1)	Contact person	:	Shri Anshuman Das
(2)	Designation	:	Secretary
(3)	Contact No.	:	033-24427311, 24411646, Fax: 033-24427563.
(4)	Mobile	:	9433079847
(5)	E-Mail	:	drcsc@vsnl.com, drcsc.ind@gmail.com, dasanshuman@yahoo.com
(6)	Website	:	www.drcsc.org
(7)	Address	:	58 A Dharmatola Road, Bosepukur, Kasba, Kolkata – 700042.

About the Organisation: DRCSC is a non-government development organization working in 12 districts of West Bengal and other states. Our major concern is food and livelihood security of the rural poor through sustainable management of natural resources on the basis of principles and actions, that are environment friendly, economically appropriate, socially just and developed by mutual cooperation.

Development Research Communication and Services Centre (DRCSC) was formed in 1982 as a resource centre for collection, collation and dissemination of information on various socio-economic issues and to highlight the struggles of various NGOs, CBOs and individuals to ensure social justice; especially for informal sector workers, indigenous communities and small & marginal farmers/landless labourers as well as self employed artisans. Along with that, since 1992, the centre focused on Sustainable Agriculture & Natural Resource Management for improving food & livelihood security of the rural poor. The resource centre started to expand its services through a Network of local NGOs and Development Cooperation Groups.

(a)	Year of establishment	:	1982
(b)	Registration No	:	Regn. No.S/39363 of 1982-83].under the Registration of Societies, West Bengal Act XXVI of 1961
(c)	Location	:	Kolkata
(d)	Coverage area	:	N.A.
(e)	Staff strength	:	N.A.
(f)	Source of funding	:	Christian Aid, London; Karl Kubel Siftung, Germany; Department of Science and Technology, Govt. of India; Carlton University, Canada, AEON foundation, Japan; IndienHilfe, Germany; Shaplaneer, Japan; Oxfam, India; WE21 Japan; ABA, Japan; NCSTC/DST, Govt. of India., DFID, UK; Christian Aid, London

(g) Approximate population served : N.A.

(h) Target groups : We work with small local organizations, clubs, farmer & women groups, panchayat & govt. departments and individuals with a purpose.

(i) Objectives :

Details of Activities

1. Enhancing production of food, fodder, fuel etc. through training, demonstrations and collaborative field trials on sustainable utilization of natural resources.
2. Assisting rural communities, especially social exclusion groups to conserve and regenerate common property resources through group based management.
3. Enabling school teachers and educational workers to promote environmental awareness and activity based participatory learning among children and adolescents and to take up agro based enterprises.
4. Arranging and supporting documentation of overall developmental issues, rights, indigenous technologies & knowledge especially in the areas of food production & processing, seed selection etc.
5. Assisting and capacitating small organizations to develop and maintain libraries, documentation centres, seed centres & nurseries, revolving fund, grain banks, bio-labs publication design & production units etc. and also to develop food security & environmental protection related projects.

(j) Research : Field research on several crops and techniques of sustainable agriculture

(k) Vocational training : Trainings on several subjects like nursery raising & management, preparing vermicompost, palm juice & value -added production, Fishery of indigenous species including fish feed making, Bio – Input production, Raising and managing vegetable garden, pond management etc. are given to the youths and women of the villages so that they can be self employed. We also help in making linkages with banks, cooperatives etc..

(l) Skill development : We capacitate the self help groups regarding its management, book keeping etc. We try to enhance the skills of the rural youth as entrepreneur through different trainings. We try to enhance the skills of school students' environment and ecological education.

♦ ♦ ♦

Majhihira National Basic Educational Institution

(1)	Contact person	:	Prasad Dasgupta
(2)	Designation	:	Executive Secretary
(3)	Contact No.	:	+91 9732023093, +91 3252 - 284499 +91 3252 - 284333
(4)	Mobile	:	09732023093
(5)	E-mail	:	manik.dasgupta@gmail.com
(6)	Website	:	http://www.majhihira-ashram.org/
(7)	Address	:	P.O. – Majhihira, District- Purulia West Bengal, India, Pin- 732128.

About the Organisation: MNBEI was established in 1940 by a group of Gandhian freedom fighters with the main objective of spreading Gandhian philosophy of education and rural reconstruction. Although most of these founder members have passed away during the last 10 yrs. but the main founder Shri Chitta Bhusan Dasgupta in his nineties is still fully fit and active with his spinning wheel (Charkha). He still, dreams to establish a Rural University at this place. The members of MNBEI Governing Body now vary from reputed doctor to rural artisans but the similarity amongst them is their devotion and dedication for the cause. The well wishers and patrons of this Institute are spread throughout the country and they always tender their support and guidance for us. Be it a minister or a mere govt. peon, all these patrons are equally important to us.

(a)	Year of establishment	:	1940
(b)	Registration No	:	25 of 1952-53 under societies registration, 1860
(c)	Location	:	At – Majhihira Village in Purulia Distt. W.B. state
(d)	Coverage area	:	Purulia District of West Bengal
(e)	Staff strength	:	83
(f)	Source of funding	:	(1) Govt. of W.B. (2) Govt. of India (3) Sightsavers (4) NABARD (5) Self finance
(g)	Approximate population served	:	2 Lacs
(h)	Target groups	:	Socially and economically deprived population including PWD.
(i)	Objectives	:	To establish Sarvoday through Basic Education (Nai Talim) as enunciated by Mahatma Gandhi.

Details of Activities

(j)	Research	:	Alternative source of earning in the drought prone area
(k)	Vocational training	:	1. Charkha & Loom, 2. Carpentry, 3. Vericulture, 4. Rainwater harvesting, 5. Electrical & Electronics, 6. Computer (Basic), 7. House keeping etc.
(l)	Skill development	:	1. Carpentry, 2. Electrical, 3. Charkha

♦ ♦ ♦

Mass Education

(1)	Contact Person	:	Mr. Sukumar Singh
(2)	Designation	:	Secretary
(3)	Contact No.	:	+ 91 33 2435 2444/2445
(4)	Mob	:	0983160324
(5)	E-Mail	:	Sukumar.Sing54@Gmail.Com
(6)	Website	:	www.Mass-Education.Com
(7)	Address	:	Mahamayatala, P.O. Garia, Kolkata, West Bengal, India - 700 084.

About the Organisation: Mass Education is a development player trying to bring about changes at the structural policy level and advocating for sustainable development of the most vulnerable and marginalized people. Mass Education launched the activities in the field of education, health, water, sanitation, child protection, skill training and micro-credit for livelihoods of women and youths and emergency assistance at the time of disaster.

(a)	Year of establishment	:	1978
(b)	Registration No	:	Registered Under Society Act In 1978
(c)	Location	:	Mahamayatala, Bodia, Kolkata - 84
(d)	Coverage area	:	300 Villages
(e)	Staff strength	:	500
(f)	Source of funding	:	Local, International and Self
(g)	Approximate population served	:	10 Lakhs
(h)	Targert Groups	:	BPL Population with Special Concentration on Children
(i)	Objectives	:	To Formulate Integrated Programmes for Effective Mobilisation of Human and Natural Resources for Empowering of The Poor of Urban and Rural Areas Towards Sustainable Development.

Details of Activities

(j)	Research	:	Conducted Studies on Child Labour, Social Issues and Rain Water Harvesting in the Project Area.
(k)	Vocational training	:	Youth Camps, Education Tour and Youth Leadership and Teacher Training.
(l)	Skill development	:	Mass Education and Technical Training Institute' at Mathurapur and Primary Teachers Training Institute at Patharpratima to Provide Training to Leaders, Students, Youth Groups, Community Based Rganizations, Ngos, Health Workers and Teachers for Improving Skills and Promotion of Livelihood Opportunities

• • •

Nanritam

(1) Contact person : Ranjana Sengupta

(2) Designation : Secretary

(3) Contact No. : 09477123797

(4) Mobile : 09830044003 /

(5) E-Mail : nanritam@gmail.com/rsen.bh@gmail.com

(6) Website : www.nanritam.org

(7) Address : Flat – 6, 28/1/2 Selimpur Road, Kolkata-31

About the Organisation: NANRITAM, a non-profit earning organization (Regd no. s/11/8102 of 2001-2002) started In 2001 with a few like-minded professionals coming together with a dream to serve humanity irrespective of caste, creed, religion or profession. They had one common inspiration behind them—SWAMI LOKESWARANANDAJI MAHARAJ of Ramakrishna Mission and his ideal of service to mankind.

The work at Nanritam began in the slum of North Kolkata with a Health unit, Swami Lokeswarananda Smarak Seva Kendra, to deliver free health care service and low-cost diagnostic facility to the under-privileged slum-dwellers of Baranagar and Kamarhati Municipality. The service was later expanded to include extended health care facilities and a non-formal pre-primary school with back-up coaching classes for the children of the locality.

Later, since 2004, an Integrated Rural Development Project has been taken up in the Para Block of Purulia district, West Bengal.

(a) Year of establishment : 2001

(b) Registration No : s/11/8102 of 2001 – ' 02

(c) Location : Urban Slum of North Calcutta and Purulia District and adjoining districts. Some of our projects are covering other districts of West Bengal like Bankura, Midnapur, Birbhum, Burdwan, North and South 24 pgs.

(d) Coverage area : West Bengal

(e) Staff strength : Paid Employee : 25 , Volunteer : 35

(f) Source of funding : Mainly Donation

(g) Approximate population served : Nearly two lacs

(h) Target groups : Underprivileged youth, specially women and other backward people.

(i) Objectives :

Our objective is to bring a holistic improvement in the life of the tribal and backward community of Purulia district.

Details of activities: Primary focus will be given on Employment Generation utilizing the existing natural resources for more production, improving efficiency in life-stock management and better water management for suitable livelihood and agriculture. Side by side, we have also to work with them for improving market linkages and developing agro-based and other rural enterprises for generating employment.

(j) Vocational training : Seasonal activities like making cowdung cakes, paddy cutting, animal husbandry, collecting wood chips, daily labour etc in order to make a living, embroidery with special focus on Kantha & Fabric Printing, Eco-friendly projects, Solar energy utilisation, Rain-water harvesting, Bamboo plantation and Electrification by gasifier.

(j) Skill development : Knitting, Tailoring, Carpentry, Embroidery, Fabric painting, Puoltry farming, Health Worker training, Incense-Making etc. Comprehensive Agriculture development programme in Rural Purulia (including Livestock, Water Management, Pisciculture, Animal Husbandry, Horticulture and Organic Farming etc) in collaboration with Syngenta Foundation India.

(k) Organisations under establishment :

1. Swami Lokeswarananda Smarak Seva Kendra
2. Swami Lokeswarananda Memorial Eye Hospital, Ananda Niketan Campus,Para, Anandniketan, Para, Purulia.
3. Saradamoni Nivedita Sikhsha Niketan, Para

• • •

Siksha Niketan

(1)	Contact person	:	Ganendra Biswas
(2)	Designation	:	Secretary
(3)	Contact No.	:	0342 2586110/ 2586431
(4)	Mobile	:	9474635774/09474603238
(5)	E-mail	:	siksaniketan@ yahoo.co.in
(6)	Website	:	N.A.
(7)	Address	:	PO Kalanaba gram, Dist: Burdwan, West Bengal-713124.

About the Organisation: Siksha Niketan works for education, rural development, agriculture and health in Burwan and Purulia Blocks. The institute provides Gandhian Basic education to the children in the Burwan Block which was established in the memory of Acharya Pramathanath Mukhopadhyay.The institute continues to serve with active support and encouragement of former students who remain convinced of the need for and efficacy of Gandhiji's vision of rural India even today.

(a)	Year of establishment	:	1953
(b)	Registration No	:	20810/466 (1952-53) under Regd.Act XXI-1860.
(c)	Location	:	Burdwan Distt. West Bengal
(d)	Coverage area	:	West Bengal
(e)	Staff strength	:	74
(f)	Source of funding	:	Donation, Govt. Grant & Cultivation
(g)	Approximate population served	:	20,000 from Burdwan dist(memory1) and Purulia block (memory 2)
(h)	Target groups	:	Aadiwasis, people who are below poverty line.
(i)	Objectives	:	Promotion of Gandhian Basic education and rural development and realise Gandhian vision for rural India.

Details of Activities

(j)	Research	:	On Human Development
(k)	Vocational training	:	Music, dance, clay modeling
(l)	Skill development	:	Computer training.
(m)	Organisations under establishment	:	1) Shishu Laloni (for children of age 1 to 3 yrs) 2) Shishu Bhavan (for children from 3 to 6 yrs) 3) Acharya Pramothnath Buniyadi vidyalay (6 to 12 yrs)

4) Aurobindo Prakash vidyatan (12 to 14 yrs)
5) Open school named Rabindra Mukto vidyalaya (14 to 20 yrs)
6) Resource centre for women of age 15 to 35 yrs.
7) Health care centre which provides free medical checkups for local children and gives all types of Medicines of Homeopathy, and allopathy.
8) Eye clinic.

♦ ♦ ♦

Swanirvar

(1)	Contact person	:	Sujit Sinha
(2)	Designation	:	Founder Director
(3)	Contact No.	:	033-2465-6783, Ph. 03217- 237446
(4)	Mobile	:	09874922146
(5)	E-Mail	:	sujit568@gmail.com
(6)	Website	:	www.swanirvarbengal.org
(7)	Address	:	Vill. Andharmanik, Via. Baduria, Dist. 24 Parganas (North), West Bengal - 743 337

About the Organisation: A Non Governmental organization (NGO) working in rural West Bengal, near Calcutta, India to build a model of holistic development in villages working towards developing into a state level resource agency in the area of education and agriculture. Swanirvar is a CRY-supported resource organisation working in the areas of pre-primary and primary education, health and sustainable agriculture. The operational area of this organisation covers 10 under-developed villages in Baduria in West Bengal. The youth group Kishore Kishori Bahini is a unique programme in this initiative.Swanirvar is working towards developing into a state level resource agency in the area of education, agriculture and children in rural communities. Swanirvar has also participated in the National Alliance on Education through village based campaigning and through the Education Network in West Bengal. This has had major implications in raising awareness of the villagers as the community has come forward to address the cause and seek remedies. The strength of this organization and programme lies in the fact that it is developing into a resource organization in the area of education and agriculture.

(a)	Year of Establishment	:	1990
(b)	Registration No	:	5/64352
(c)	Location	:	West Bengal
(d)	Coverage Area	:	Baduria, Deganga , Swarupnagar, Basirhat-I, Hasnabad, Hingalganj, Habra-I blocks of North 24 Parganas district; some Arsenic work in Nadia district; school project in Kolkata.
(e)	Staff Strength	:	100
(f)	Source of Funding	:	IH, FoS, LA Friends, S&C, CIVA, Wipro, IFA, AID, Vibha, NHFDC, PRIA –CSSP, Chautary / Kolkata Seeds, Small donations, CARE, FoS, CRY, ASHA, AIIH&PH, DRDC, S&C, LA Friends, SARIQ, Swagata Deb, Pond Lease, Sakhya, Wipro, N.Sukumar, CAPART, Sahay, Small donations.
(g)	Approximate population Served	:	20000
(h)	Target Groups	:	children, farmers

(i) Objectives

- To lead to increased self reliance amongst the people
- To be sustainable-i.e. environmentally sound.

Details of Activities

The health activities were primarily conducted in 11 villages concerning maternal and child health and referral services. The nutrition status of children was also assessed. Community health activities like preventive measures of disinfecting tube wells and blood donation camps and cataract operations were carried out in association with the Kishore-kishori bahini (KKB) - the youth group, which comprises of 100 members.

(k) Research : Kishore-kishori bahini (KKB) - the youth group, which comprises of 100 members. The youth group undertook various development activities and conducted surveys, tabulated the results, conducted village mapping, etc,. They also participated in various cultural activities and the campaign on the right to education.

(l) Vocational Training : Community awareness, Democratic and decentralized decision making

(n) Organisations under Establishment : SHIKSHAMITRA -An Alternative Secondary School and Education Resource Centre.

♦ ♦ ♦

INDEX